Crises of Social Transformation in India

Crises of Social Transformation in India

Edited by

S. R. Ahlawat
Neerja Ahlawat

RAWAT PUBLICATIONS
Jaipur • New Delhi • Bangalore • Hyderabad • Guwahati • Kolkata

ISBN 978-81-316-0710-7

Published by
Prem Rawat for **Rawat Publications**
Satyam Apts, Sector 3, Jawahar Nagar, Jaipur 302 004 (India)
Phone: 0141 265 1748 / 7006 Fax: 0141 265 1748
E-mail: info@rawatbooks.com
Website: www.rawatbooks.com

New Delhi Office
4858/24, Ansari Road, Daryaganj, New Delhi 110 002
Phone: 011 2326 3290

Also at *Bangalore, Hyderabad, Guwahati* and *Kolkata*

Printed at Chaman Enterprises, New Delhi

Contents

Preface

The social transformation in contemporary Indian society as the result of economic reforms demands greater sensitivity on the part of social scientists. Social transformation is sterile without an understanding of the accompanying developmental politics, which involves the role of state with major actors. Social transformation is not a utopia of social activists. It calls for analysing social forces in historical and cultural context. There is no unilinear direction for change. It is a complex and multi-dimensional process. A number of questions can be raised for understanding social transformation. How and in which direction society is transforming? What is the role of state in bringing transformation in society? What role culture and economy play in accelerating or retarding the process of transformation? Which are the dominant forces that set direction for social transformation? Who are gainers and losers in the process of social transformation? What stresses and strains the process created in the society? We have decided to focus the book on these major themes.

Social development theory has assumed a positive linkage between social advancement and economic development, on the one hand, and economic growth and social transformation, on the other. It is assumed that 'economic development as social transformation' has an automatic link between the two. The rise of the concept of human development as distinct from economic development carries the view point that there is no necessary automatic link between the two. A theoretical trend has appeared to explain the ecological unsustainability of the prevailing paradigm of economic growth, leading to the concept of sustainable development. Yet, another conceptual advance is in terms of the category of social development which focuses on social security, justice, and harmony. The process of the economic reforms is pre-occupied with issues of fiscal and trade policy, financial and capital account convertibility, etc. To become people-friendly, its rapid growth path is expected to contribute towards employment generation and poverty eradication. Reformation in appalling governance structure engaged in the delivery of basic social services for the poor is simultaneously required in order to provide an enabling environment for social inclusion.

We wish to thank several friends and research committee members of the Indian Sociological Society, Research Committee-03 'Economy, Polity and Society', who have throughout showed deep interest in this work and encouraged us to undertake it. Majority of the papers were presented in the 37th and 38th All India Sociological Conferences held at New Delhi and Udaipur, respectively. We thank the young scholars, who throughout showed deep interest in this work and encouraged us time and again to publish their papers. The present volume is the result of their efforts.

It would be unwise if one does not acknowledge his friends. Special thanks to Prof. Paramjit Singh Judge and Prof. S. K. Sharma for their unstinting help and support. Lastly, we would like to record our profound thanks to research students in the Department of Sociology, M.D. University, Rohtak, for their comments and criticism as well as extensive discussions which have been invaluable in the editing of this volume.

S. R. Ahlawat
Neerja Ahlawat

Contributors

Ajai Kumar is Associate Professor, Department of Sociology, Government College, Mandi, Himachal Pradesh.

Aijaz Ashraf Wani is Assistant Professor, Department of Political Science, University of Kashmir, Srinagar.

Bhupendra Yadav is Professor of History, Azim Premji University, Bangalore.

Jagrup S. Sekhon is Professor, Department of Political Science, Guru Nanak Dev University, Amritsar, Punjab.

K. Gopal Iyer is former Professor and Chairman, Department of Sociology, Punjab University, Chandigarh.

Ketaki Dwivedi is Assistant Professor, Department of Sociology, University of Delhi.

Km Sohini is research scholar, Department of Humanities and Social Sciences, Indian Institute of Technology, Roorkee, Uttarakhand.

Nupurnima Yadav is research scholar, Centre for the Study of Social Systems, School of Social Sciences, Jawaharlal Nehru University, New Delhi.

Neerja Ahlawat is teaching in the Department of Sociology. Currently, she is Deputy Director, Women's Studies Centre, Maharshi Dayanand University, Rohtak, Haryana.

Pradeep Kumar Parida is Assistant Professor, Department of Sociology, Pondicherry University, Puducherry.

Paramjit S. Judge is Professor, Department of Sociology and Dean Faculty of Social Sciences, Guru Nanak Dev University, Amritsar, Punjab.

Rambabu A. is Assistant Professor, Centre for the Studies of Social Exclusion and Inclusive Policies, Tata Institute of Social Sciences, Mumbai.

Reshmi Chakraborty is Assistant Professor, Zakir Husain Centre for Educational Studies, School of Social Sciences, Jawaharlal Nehru University, New Delhi.

Satish K. Sharma is Professor, Department of Sociology, H.P. University, Shimla. Currently, he is a Fellow at the Indian Institute of Advanced Studies, Shimla.

Seema Chauhan is Assistant Professor, Department of Sociology, Government College for Women, Chandigarh.

S. R. Ahlawat served as Professor, Department of Sociology, Maharshi Dayanand University, Rohtak, Haryana.

Swati Singh is research scholar, Centre for the Study of Social Systems, School of Social Sciences, Jawaharlal Nehru University, New Delhi.

CHAPTER 1

CRISES OF SOCIAL TRANSFORMATION: AN OVERVIEW

S. R. Ahlawat and Neerja Ahlawat

Sociological literature in India has a complex but rich history, presenting curious events, exciting ideas, arguments and counterarguments at every stage of enquiry. In the 1950s and 1960s, the major themes of research in Indian sociology were by and large confined to those areas widely acknowledged to be unique – the joint family, the village community, the caste system, and Hinduism. Indian sociology witnessed a decisive break in 1970s in terms of the themes studied. Gender, social movements, science and society, education, occupations and professions, social change and development, cooperatives, population, and society were prominent areas of research, which reflected the issues and problems to be grappled with all modernising societies. This marked a shift from the inward-looking orientation of the initial phase that gradually gave way to more cosmopolitan orientation. However, the latter did not displace the former, rather a process of accretion was in play.

Indian sociology experienced the third phase of thematic evolution with the study of areas such as migration and diaspora, national identity and ethnicity, protests by marginal groups, and environment and society, which reflect the consequences of the ongoing process of globalisation. The conventional dichotomies, such as tradition and modernity, developed and developing societies as well as the trichotomy of the three worlds – the First, the Second, and the Third World, a conceptualisation that emerged during the Cold War period, is gradually receding into the background. In its place, the notion of 'One World' gained ground, especially during the 1990s, which is more in the realm of imagination than rooted in empirical reality. Yet again, it must be noted that what is happening in Indian sociology is not a process of displacement of old themes but one of accretion of the new themes to the old ones. Thus understood, sociology in India provides mirror image of the Indian society, in which tradition, modernity, and globalism coexist and constitute a continuum.

Further, one finds that Indian sociology was grounded not on a single foundation but on multiple foundations. As such, one can clearly see the political slogan of 'unity and diversity' finding a practical resonance in the way in which Indian sociology came to develop itself around varying personalities and differing ideas. One of the striking features of the early Indian sociology, however, is that be it in Bombay school or in Lucknow school, there was a common recognition that the Indian social reality was quite different from that of the Western world. For the proper understanding of the Indian social reality, Indian sociology should evolve altogether different, if not contrary, conceptual tools of research. Further, there is a need that the social scientists should not merely theorise in abstraction but should strive through their analysis for transforming the society for a better social order.

INDIA'S UNFINISHED JOURNEY OF SOCIAL DEVELOPMENT/ SOCIAL TRANSFORMATION

Social development discourse in India pledged poverty eradication at the time of 'tryst with destiny' back in 1947. Different solutions had been tried, institutional solutions in the 1950s, land reforms, community development, Panchayati Raj, and cooperatives, with the intention of improving access of the poor to productive resources. In the next two decades, target group and area-based programmes were tried to generate productive wage and self-employment opportunities for the poor. However, so long as the economy remained trapped for three decades till 1980, in the Hindu rate of growth (less than 2 per cent per annum in per capita terms), the proportion of the population below the poverty line sharply fluctuated without any declining trend. It went up in drought years and came down during bumper harvests. It seemed like the weather Gods rather than government actions made the fate of the poor!

The 1980s saw the economy come out of the Hindu growth syndrome – per capita real income growth exceeded 3 per cent annually. Although the target group-oriented wage and self-employment generation programmes expanded quantitatively, the spread of the Green Revolution initiated in the mid-1960s and a renewed spurt in industrial growth forced a declining trend in the persistent fluctuating poverty ratio till the early 1980s.

However, the fiscal profligacy of the proceeding decade made the stepped-up growth rate unsustainable and triggered the wide-ranging economic policy reforms. The economic crisis comprising of a steep fall in foreign exchange reserve, galloping inflation, huge public, and current account deficits forced the adoption of economic reforms.

The blueprint for the economic reforms was provided by the combination of macroeconomic stabilisation and structural adjustment programme of the International Monetary Fund (IMF) and the World Bank, respectively. The underlying economic philosophy of these programmes was to rely more on market forces, dismantle controls, reduce the role of state, liberalise prices, and replace the public with private sector. It is based on the presumption that the public sector leads to inefficient allocation and utilisation of economic resources.

Economic reforms initiated in India during 1991 have put the Indian economy on a higher growth trajectory. Annual growth rate in total gross domestic product (GDP) has accelerated from less than 6 per cent during the initial years of reforms to greater than 8 per cent during 2001–2006. Even during the recession period, India's growth rate did not provide a dismal picture. Indeed, it was much better than in most countries. The real task before India is to transform the rapid growth in poverty reduction. The process of economic reforms must set the agenda for social transformation in India where the state must provide all its citizens with capabilities, opportunities, and rights that they need to exercise their own choice for a decent life. In the pursuit of these objective economic reforms, accelerating economic growth must provide employment, provide distributive justice, eliminate poverty, and bring about rapid and cumulative improvements in social development. Economic growth must take care of social development indicators of health, education, inequalities, steady wages, and other forms of social security and protection.

India's unfinished journey in the development process would not be complete so long as the poverty deprivation and exclusion persist. Despite the pledge of poverty eradication, on the threshold of the new millennium, one-third of our population has been estimated to be below the poverty line. India carries the dubious distinction of hosting the largest number of the world's poor as well as illiterate persons. Despite having had the positive annual growth rates over the last 66 years, it has performed so badly comparatively and absolutely when it comes to social development or the question of growth with justice, in other words 'inclusive growth' (Nagaraj 2012).

For long, the development theory has assumed a positive linkage between social advancement and economic development on the one hand and economic growth and social transformation on the other. Stiglitz (2002) projected the 'economic development as social transformation' implying an automatic link between the two. The rise of the concept of human development as distinct from economic development carries the view point that there is no necessary automatic link between the two (Sharma 2005). A theoretical trend has appeared to explain the ecological unsustainability of the prevailing paradigm of economic growth, leading to the concept of sustainable development. Yet, another conceptual advance, is in terms of the category of social development which focuses on social security, justice, and harmony. The process of the economic reforms is preoccupied with issues of fiscal and trade policy, financial and capital account convertibility, etc. To become people friendly, its rapid growth path is expected to contribute towards poverty eradication. Reformation in appalling governance structure engaged in the delivery of basic social services for the poor is simultaneously required in order to provide an enabling environment (Bardhan 2005).

The question is, whether rapid growth due to economic reforms makes a lasting dent on poverty. It is based on the premise that rapid growth generates gainful employment opportunities at progressively higher levels of productivity and facilitates faster integration of the poor into the mainstream of the development process. It provides them with gainful employment, not temporary doles. Clearly, agriculture and rural non-farm growth has immediate impact on poverty. Industrial growth operates with a lag. In other words, rapid growth is the most powerful instrument for poverty reduction.

What triggers rapid growth? India's experience in the last two decades and of that of the other rapidly growing economies in the past clearly brings out the critical instrumental role of the international trade as a trigger for rapid growth. However, international trade is a demanding instrument. It confers benefits in terms of a rapid rise in gainful employment opportunities. But it demands in return a strict discipline on the part of society and polity, namely, sound and responsible macroeconomic management, smooth mobility of labour and capital into faster growing sunrise industries and away from slower-growing sunset industries, and finally, maintaining international competitiveness in sunrise industries (Ahluwalia 2002; Nayyar 2006). The societies that have accepted this discipline have not only reaped benefits in terms of faster growth and rapid decline in poverty but also developed in-built resilience to cope up with fluctuations in economic activity to which international economy has been prone (Stiglitz 2002).

Another important question is what sustains rapid growth? Maintenance of the above-mentioned discipline is the only necessary condition. To make it a sufficient condition requires a progressively better-skilled and healthy work force. It requires rapid eradication of educational and health poverty and continuing investment in human capital formation (Beteille 2003). Rapid growth process is known to involve costs, conflicts, and adjustments which inevitably accompany the discipline of international competitiveness.

The mainstream economists have produced a large column of literature justifying India's policy shift (Ahluwalia and Little 1998; Joshi and Little 1994, 1996; Srinivasan 2000). There is also some well-reasoned critique of this policy that tries to explain the underlying processes and to bringing out the consequences for the people (Bhaduri and Nayyar 1996; Bhalla, 1994; Nayyar 1995; Nayyar and Sen 1994; Patnaik and Rawal 2005). The discussion by scholars of different views brings out that the role of the state has diminished over the reforms period. The effort to give priority to fiscal management of the economy and withdrawal of the state from any areas has affected the capability of the Indian state and dismissed its role in economic affairs. Its role has also changed from provider to facilitator in economic development.

The agriculture sector has gone through different phases of growth, embracing a wide variety of institutional interventions and technology and policy regimes. Beginning in the late 1960s, the Green Revolution helped the sector maintain a steady pace of growth for more than two decades. But the challenges that swept through the economy in the 1990s, after the initiation of economic reforms, arrested this growth. The dominant discourse about the rural economy in recent years has been one of the 'crisis'. The agrarian structure in India experienced mushrooming growth of marginal and small farmers on the one hand, and significant rise in the number of agricultural labourers, on the other. The decline in employment opportunities for the agricultural labour has been simultaneous 'casualisation' with concomitant ills of low wages and declining job security. Apart from the relatively large proportion of households suffering from low incomes, rural households also suffer from deprivation in terms of education and health. The discrepancy is much wider when it comes to the girl child. The indicators such as life expectancy, infant and child morality, and child malnutrition are appallingly high. The incidence of all such deprivations is more severe among the rural poor. In rural India, more worrisome feature is the addition of the poor among agricultural households. The World Bank, however, estimates that India is the home to one-third of the world's poor, with nearly 460 million people or 42 per cent under the global definition of poverty. Forty-six per cent of the world's malnourished children are Indian. In 1991, India ranked 121 out of 160 countries in the Human Development Index. Two decades later in 2011, India is ranked at 134, among 182 countries. A vast majority of people in India continue to aspire to just get the next meal.

To check the malnourishment and infant mortality, the Government of India launched the 'National Rural Health Mission' in 2005. The reformation in rural health sector under this programme relied on the introduction of village health activities, improved management, and decentralisation through Panchayati Raj Institutions. National Rural Health Mission (NRHM) goal was to create solid ground in the rural health sector, but the studies mention that it could not be implemented successfully and the programme failed to improve the rural health scenario. The study was conducted in 18 states by the Institute of Social Sciences, New Delhi, during the first half of 2012 on the nature of health care services; functioning of standing committee on health, sanitation, and nutrition; Accredited Social Health Activities (ASHAs); role of women Panchayat leaders; and the dimensions of corruption prevalent in NRHM. It made the startling revelation 'There are no Primary Health Centres or Community Health Centres in most of the Gram Panchayats in our country. In a few panchayats where they exist, doctors seldom visit these Primary Health Centres/Community Health Centres. There is near absence of para-medical staff and the most anguishing fact is that even medicines are mostly not available at these centres. Since the scheme is executed through Panchayati Raj Institutions and is meant primarily for women in the reproductive age groups, it was shocking that fifty per cent panchayat women leaders are not even aware of NRHM' (Panchayati Raj Update 2012).

North Indian states' record of economic development provides a cheerful picture which is not reflected in the social sphere, and consequently, its vibrant people are subjected to traditional institutions and their barbaric injustice. This paradox in North-West India reminds us that if it does not change its culture and thought, development can sometimes be a misnomer. Over the last decade and particularly during 2010–2012, there is phenomenal increase in violence on women in Punjab, Haryana, and Uttar Pradesh. Despite constitutional provisions and safeguards to protect the rights of the women by ensuring equality of opportunity and building gender-just society, the state has the dubious distinction of growing incidence of rapes/gang rapes, eve-teasing, molestation, abduction, rampant foeticide, child marriages, honour killings, diktats by Khaps, violence against girls in natal families on the choice of their marriage partners, property issues, etc. Home Ministry's National Crime Records Bureau shows that from 1991 to 2011, the incidence of rapes in India has increased three times faster than all cognisable crimes put together, or three-and-a-half times faster than murder.

The assertion of Khap Panchayats in rural North-West India during the last two decades is playing the role of moral policing of the couples who aspire for choice marriages particularly in rural setup. The Khaps reinforce traditions and norms especially in marriage practices; the sanctions imposed by these against individuals, families, and often caste groups or sections of its own community show that caste dynamics, even in the 21st century, is taking an ugly turn. The Khaps enjoy not merely the political support but also play dominant role in local politics so as to ensure that the authority of rural elites continues to be upheld. The ruling elites always give them patronage. The patronisation of Khaps by the political parties seems to be the result of the hegemonisation of caste relations over the polity, where the political actors themselves firmly believe and support institution and their action (Ahlawat 2012; Chowdhry 2010; Kaur 2010).

The pressure of the global market forces has been felt in the spheres of social relations. There is a perceptible trend of change in inter-caste relations which is evident from the rise in Dalit consciousness and assertion marked by explosion of a new caste movement, giving birth to organisations of the other 'backward castes' or 'bahujans'. The earlier hierarchical dimension of caste system has now begun to give way to polarisation along the scheduled castes versus non-scheduled castes lines. The caste riots which were common in Uttar Pradesh and Bihar have shown their ugly teeth in Punjab and Haryana during the last two decades. The caste tensions in Tallan and Gohana are indicative of rise of mobility, both state-sponsored and market-led among the Dalits. The new social movements which were fighting for reservations or against atrocities, for the symbol of human dignity during their 'golden decade' of 1970s, started splitting on the issues of economic reforms. The leading activists from environmental and women's movement and a major section of the farmers movement started articulating or actively supporting the open market mechanism of the economic reform policy (Omvedt 2000).

Economic reforms in India, have also exasperated some social vices and problems mainly in the agricultural rich states. Prominent among the prevailing vices are mindless consumerism, lavish spending on ceremonies, alcoholism, and drug addiction. The emerging problems include unemployment, indebtedness, dowry, violence against women, female foeticide, and peasant suicides. Disappointed and disillusioned, the middle peasantry in some pockets of India, has taken to the militant ways in the form of Naxalite movements. In fact, an insidious lumpenism is growing in both our politics and our economy. Lumpenism is described as a closing down of the avenues of upward mobility; lumpenism survives on money power rather than on talent. Some of the gigantic development projects are creating a class of neo-Zamindars. Often the crony capitalism between government and corporates results in parcelling out land between themselves without first engaging, in respectful negotiations, with those who are its original owners. The raising class of lumpens has plagued the spirit of Indian democracy; the 'inclusive growth' has remained an administrative formula that breeds extreme forms of discontent in the form of Naxalism.

The pressure of the global market forces mounted manyfold for liberalisation of economy. The internal contradictions between the nation–state and the centre–periphery, sons of the soil and the outsiders, etc. have sharpened considerably, giving rise to new and complex phenomenon. This is not to say that such problems were never a part of the Indian society but their intensity and magnitude have attained sharpness after the economic reforms. There are many questions and issues of macro and micro nature that arise due to the changing scenario and emerging challenges in Indian society. The collection of papers in this volume take up all these and many other issues of economic reforms and social transformation that underscore the need for a location appropriate strategy. It is an attempt to correlate the unevenness of economic reforms and its impact on transforming the Indian society with diversity of socio-cultural dimensions.

The first two papers are theoretical-analytical pieces seeking to explain some more fundamental issues like nation-building and the spreading roots of democracy in India. Paramjit Singh Judge, in his paper 'Indian Idea of Nation and Project of Nation Building', questions the idea of nation-state and has tried to scan the Indian efforts of building the nation. The story of nation-building in practice, in the post-colonial India, is a sad saga of the efforts of the self-righteous political elite, which employed the strategy of treating difference as a threat to the existence of Indian nation. In many respects, the idea of nation-building is unique to Indian experience, because it has not been used elsewhere with such a rigour as we have witnessed in India. In answering the 'why' and 'how' of India's nation-building exercise, three crucial features and processes are interwoven and inherently linked with the post-colonial experience: diversity, development, and identity formations. The challenge to nation-building that emerged in the postcolonial India was a consequence of and reaction to these features and processes. This challenge signified the paradox in the way the nation-building process was initiated or carried out by the political elite. This paper is an attempt to situate the paradox in its proper historical and political context.

The paradoxical consequences of nation-building process are entrenched in the dilemma implicated in the notion of nation. Nation is not a concrete reality like state, which is understood as comprised by population, territory, government, and sovereignty. Nation is regarded as something subjective, a sense of belonging, and an imagined political community. Whereas community could be operationally defined and understood, imagined community belongs to the realm of unknown, as it exists in the imagination of somebody who is imagining. Paramjit Singh Judge ably argued that the trajectory of development in nation building has created two types of India: one that has access to the trinity of the modern state, modern technology, etc. and the other kept out of and way beyond any access to this trinity.

Nupurnima Yadav pleaded that the 'secular state' should not legitimise the caste system by accepting it as the basis of backwardness. In her paper, the primary objective was to examine the dynamism of capitalism through the process of 'creative destruction' and its effects on the democracy and how democracy sustains itself in the transition phase of capitalist system and how the notion of creative destruction permeates the political structure.

Many chapters that follow are empirically rich descriptive-analytical pieces about the Indian situation, which tend to rebut rather than confirm the neoliberal claim that high growth rates in GDP are the most vital elements for bringing about rapid social advancement and social development. The latest version of this mantra is not so much 'trickle-down theory', as the view that high growth rates greatly enhance state coffers, thereby enabling greater social welfare spending. The process of economic reforms experienced during the last two decades eluded the humane, social-democratic transformation of Indian society.

S. R. Ahlawat's paper on 'Inclusion of Excluded Communities: A Study of Local Governance' is lucid and persuasive. The question of empowerment of the scheduled castes and women has been addressed not through quantitative methods but by the qualitative methods of intensive interviews and participant observations. It is expected that the new 73rd Amendment will usher in an era of egalitarian society in place of the present unequal, stratified, and hierarchical society. The main focus of this study is to address the question of empowerment of scheduled castes and women. Have they been empowered? If yes, then in what sense, and to what extent? If not, why? Second, these questions have been explored not by using a quantitative or questionnaire method but by using intensive interviewing and observation, also called participant observation. This method is enabled to understand the phenomenon as clearly as possible with valuable insights in the context of Haryana state.

S. K. Sharma's paper on right to education points out that the recent researches have revealed that economic reasons coupled with family atmosphere are the important enabling factors. The enrolment of children into schools to a considerably great extent is determined by 'household atmosphere, infrastructural problems, human resources and physical facilities, alternative sources of supplementation of household income, which to some extent depends upon the child going for work and earning, financial constraints, and other issues related with the quality of education. The other factors that have always been significant and have become highly contentious in the recent past relate to the political economy of social and economic development, which has been anti-poor and aggravated poverty and resulted in displacement and marginalisation of the poor, farmers, tribal, and other vulnerable sections of the society. There is not only a contradiction between what the Right of Children to Free and Compulsory Education Act, 2009, envisages and what in reality is happening in the field of education, but the paradoxical situation also raises a question: Will the poor despite the provisions of the Act be in position to send their children to school? The already existing situation reveals that even if the students are enrolled, almost 50 per cent of such children drop out from the schools, noted by Ambrose in the concept note of this colloquium. How to sustain the continuation of children likely to dropout, particularly in the absence of measures to make compensation for the income loss due to such children's shift from work to school or alternatives available to the families for the household works, such as taking care of the younger siblings, performed by these children.

K. Gopal Iyer's paper on the analysis of Mahatma Gandhi National Rural Employment Guarantee Act (MGNREGA) is very comprehensive based on the primary data collected through detailed field work which provides exceptionally insightful account of the neoliberal policies of the state. The study on 'Planning & Implementation of MGNREGA' was undertaken to examine the process of social transformation among the workers in Ambala and Mewat districts of Haryana state. The main objective of the study was to analyse the effective implementation of MGNREGA programme during 2007–2008 with respect to the employment generation; the extent of percolation of benefits to scheduled castes, women, and other marginalised sections; the transparency in the functioning of the programme; the awareness of provisions of MGNREGA among the weaker sections; the involvement of Gram Sabha, PRI representatives, and officials in the programme; and the measures suggested for better implementation of the programme.

Two papers in the sequence examined the role of the Khap Panchayats in North-West India in the local governance. Bhupendra Yadav and Neerja

Ahlawat's papers have addressed the question of how the Khaps reinforce traditions and norms especially in marriage practices, the sanctions imposed by these against individuals, families, and often caste groups or sections of its own community. The Khaps enjoy not merely political support but also play dominant role in local politics so as to ensure that the authority of rural elites continues to be upheld. The ruling elites always give them patronage. The patronisation of Khaps by the political parties seems to be the result of the hegemonisation of caste relations over the polity, whereby the political actors themselves firmly believe and support institution and their action.

Jagrup S. Sekhon highlights the plight of the farmers living in the border belt of Punjab particularly of those unfortunate ones who have their agriculture land across the fencing on the border and who live in abject conditions. The neoliberal policies remained confined to the urban Punjab and how it eluded the rural population, has been examined keeping in view the process of social transformation to the core while examining the conditions of the people in the border areas of Punjab. The resilience of Punjab peasants, though the vicissitudes of history, especially the small farmers has been exemplary. The poor people are the 'dangling farmers' who can neither own nor disown their own land. Caught between the devil and the deep sea, they lead a cursed existence. Added to their sad state of affairs is their illiteracy. They have no voice to express their grievances; it seems there is a communication gap between these farmers and those who matter in the state of Punjab.

Rambabu A. examined the role of Dalit Christian social movement in social transformation in Tamil Nadu. One such way is conversion to other religions as a mark of protest to the discriminatory practice of caste system. For Dalits, religious conversion especially in the 19th century was often perceived as one of the ways of escaping from caste oppression. However, they also admit that such conversions have not guaranteed any assurance that their expectations were fulfilled. Rambabu studied the complex and uneven interaction between Christianity and Dalit activism in Tamil Nadu. Many Dalits in Tamil Nadu have converted to Christianity in mass movements. Through conversion, they sought to overcome the oppression of caste and their position as so-called untouchables.

Aijaz Ashraf Wani studied the sub-regional assertions in the state of Jammu and Kashmir (J&K) with particular reference to the process of social transformation. It has been established that good governance means the involvement of different ethno-cultural and linguistic groups in various societies in the process of decision-making. Further, it is considered as the only way through which we can ensure unity in diversity and eliminate real/perceived threats of hegemony and exploitation by dominant identity/identities.

The plurality of politics is the hallmark of J&K state, and this plurality is essentially the result of cultural diversities that criss-cross the geographical and cultural landscape of J&K. The J&K state is a conglomerate of three distinct regions – Jammu, Kashmir, and Ladakh. The regional and cultural diversities produce a very complex situation where the sub-regional assertion discourse has assumed tremendous significance. The issues related to the development, power balance, and ideological divide have made the situation all the more complex.

Reshmi Chakraborty studied the choice of middle class for elementary education in the era of neoliberal policies adopted in Assam. There are debates on school choice, competition, and factors affecting the ability of parents to choose a particular school. Most advocates of choice and school autonomy support the claims that competition will enhance the efficiency and responsiveness of schools and thus increase their effectiveness. Therefore, different factions of choice proponents among educators, economists, policymakers, and government did not majorly differ on the proposal to improve the public school education system even if the chosen means and goal was either equity or privatisation, diversification of school, or competition. India has made relative progress towards education policy reforms after the early 90s with the advent of policies of liberalisation, privatisation, and globalisation. Right to education, as a fundamental right, is one such step towards strengthening of the efforts towards universalising education in India. However, the clauses which govern the right have been contested by the stakeholders. No policy has been clearly made to foster choice-making in particular, in India. This paper has been divided into four sections with each explaining the key factors with regard to choice in elementary education in an urban space.

Seema Chauhan examined the role of the changing health infrastructure in Himachal Pradesh and how it has transformed the position of women. There has been considerable development and growth of health infrastructure; the number of health institutions and facilities has increased over the years to 89 hospitals, 441 primary health centres, 66 community health centres or referral hospitals and 39 dispensaries, all based on the modern allopathic medicine system. In addition, the state now has 23 ayurvedic hospitals and 1,112 health centres or dispensaries. This has resulted in making Himachal Pradesh one of the leading states in social development.

Ketaki Dwivedi's paper on social transformation in corporate social responsibility in the context of social reforms provides critique of the social welfare policies being pursued by the state. Further, she has tried to examine these very social issues that have been deliberately and successfully masked or omitted so far by the definitional boundary in favour of corporate strategies.

Km Sohini studied the plight of the child labour. She concluded that the child is a 'national asset' for nation and capital building. It is a matter of grave concern that children are not receiving the education and leisure which is important for their growing years, because they are absorbed into commercial and laborious activities which are meant for adults.

Swati Singh examined the role of the state in social transformation from human rights perspective. Her paper seeks to foreground a grassroots' perspective of certain issues which had been central to sociological enquiry (like caste and tribe) and which itself have been transformed under the hegemonic discourses of human rights and become contested issues in international debates.

Pradeep Kumar Parida has studied the gender relations and the issue of social transformation. The paper identifies several questions such as how gendered vulnerability is socially produced and maintained? How do gender relations shape disaster practice in organisations and households? How is gender relations affected, if at all, through the social experience of disaster?

Ajai Kumar's paper has examined the role of civil society in social transformation. He opined that the strength of civil society in India would rest in its commitment to the just cause of the common man and its adherence to the Gandhian values of truth, honesty, and non-violence. There is need for an unceasing struggle to constitute a society free from corruption and exploitation, which ensures individual freedom, equality and justice, and pluralism and tolerance.

Thus, the essays in this volume examine various aspects of social transformation in India. Although the contributors followed different theoretical perspectives, they provide a comprehensive overview of the transformation of socio-economic aspects of Indian society. The analytical insights at the local level, with regard to the current unequal socio-economic dimensions, employed by the contributors of this volume, examined various aspects of social transformation in India.

Through empirical case studies of different socio-economic dimensions and varied cultures that describe situations of intertwining of local socio-economic practices and global economic modernity, this volume assesses the overall situation in India. This exceptional book will appeal not only to sociologists, social and cultural anthropologists, and economists interested in development studies, but to lay public and the intelligentsia as well.

REFERENCES

Ahlawat, N. (2012). 'Political Economy of Haryana's Khaps'. *Economic and Political Weekly*, Vol. XLVII, No. 47 & 48, pp. 27–32.

Ahluwalia, I. J. and Little, I. M. D. (1998). *India's Economic Reforms and Development: Essays for Manmohan Singh.* New Delhi: Oxford University Press.

Ahluwalia, M. S. (2002). 'Economic Reforms Since 1991: Has Gradualism Worked?' *Journal of Economic Perspectives*, 16(7): 67–68.

Bardhan, P. (2005). 'Nature of Opposition to Economic Reforms in India.' *Economic and Political Weekly*, Vol. XL, No. 48.

Beteille, A. (2003). 'Poverty and Inequality.' *Economic and Political Weekly*, Vol. 38, No. 42.

Bhaduri, A. and Nayyar, D. (1996). *The Intelligent Person's Guide to Liberalization.* New Delhi: Penguin Books.

Bhalla, G. S. (ed.) (1994). *Economic Liberalization and Indian Agriculture.* New Delhi: ISID-FAO.

Chowdhry, P. (2010). *Contentious Marriages, Eloping Couples: Gender, Caste and Patriarchy in Northern India.* New Delhi: Oxford University Press.

Joshi, V. and Little, I. M. D. (1994). *India: Macroeconomics and Political Economy.* Washington, DC: The World Bank.

——. (1996). *India's Economic Reforms 1991–2001.* Oxford: Clarendon Press.

Kaur, R. (2010). 'Khap Panchayats, Sex-Ratio and Female Agency.' *Economic and Political Weekly*, Vol. 65, No. 23.

Nagaraj, R. (ed.) (2012). *Growth, Inequality and Social Development in India: Is Inclusive Growth Possible?* Geneva, Switzerland: United Nations Research Institute for Social Development.

Nayyar, D. (1995). *Economic Liberalization in India: Analytics Experiences and Lessons.* Calcutta: Orient Longman.

——. (2006). Economic Growth in Independent India: Lumbering Elephant or Running Tiger? *Economic and Political Weekly*, Vol. XLI, No. 15.

Nayyar, D. and Sen, A. (1994). 'International Trade and Agricultural Sector in India', in G. S. Bhalla (ed.), *Economic Liberalization and Indian Agriculture.* New Delhi: ISID-FAO.

Omvedt, G. (2000). 'At the Cross Roads: A Future Past the Present.' Special Issue. *The Hindustan Times*, 1st January.

Panchayati Raj Update. (2012). National Rural Health Mission Fails to Improve Rural Health Scenario, Vol. XIX, No. 9.

Patnaik, P. and Rawal, V. (2005). 'The Liberalization, Foreign Direct Investment Flows and Development: Indian Experience in 1990s.' *Economic and Political Weekly*, Vol. XL, No. 14.

Sharma, S. L. (2005). 'Economic Development and Social Transformation in North-West India: Some Theoretical Insights', in S. L. Sharma, et al. (eds.). *Ethnic Rural and Gender Issues in Contemporary North-West*. New Delhi: Anamika Publishers.

Srinivasan, T. N. (2000). *Eight Lectures on India's Economic Reforms*. New Delhi: Oxford University Press.

Stiglitz, J. (2002). *Globalization and Its Discontents*. W.W. Norton and Company, New York.

CHAPTER 2

INDIAN IDEAS OF NATION AND THE PROJECT OF NATION-BUILDING: DEMOCRACY AND CHALLENGES

Paramjit S. Judge

The story of nation-building in practice, in the post-colonial India, is a sad saga of the efforts of the self-righteous political elite, which employed the strategy of treating difference as a threat to the existence of Indian nation. In many respects, the idea of nation-building is unique to Indian experience, because it has not been used elsewhere with such a rigour as we have witnessed in India. In answering the why and how of India's nation-building exercise, three crucial features and processes are interwoven and inherently linked with the post-colonial experience. These are diversity, development and identity formations; and the challenge to nation-building that emerged in the postcolonial India, was a consequence of and reaction to, these features and processes. This challenge signified the paradox in the way the nation-building process was initiated or carried out by the political elite. This paper is an attempt to situate the paradox in its proper historical and political context.

The paradoxical consequences of nation-building process are entrenched in the dilemma implicated in the notion of nation. Nation is not a concrete reality like state, which is understood as comprised by population, territory, government, and sovereignty. Nation is regarded as something subjective, a sense of belonging and an imagined political community. Whereas community could be operationally defined and understood, imagined community belongs to the realm of unknown as it exists in the imagination of somebody who is imagining. Anderson (1983), emphasises two aspects of nationalism that are crucial to our understanding the concept. Firstly, the emergence of nationalism is linked with the development of print-capitalism. Secondly, he is of the view that nationalism creates horizontal solidarity. It overrides class and other heterogeneities/inequalities. Gellner (1983: 7) opines that 'Nations are the artefacts of men's convictions and loyalties and solidarities'. It is therefore important that nationalist dispensation is narrow and subjective in which it can be used as an ideological tool against radical ideologies by marginalising or eliminating the exploitative and discriminatory heterogeneities from the discourse. In certain respects, nationalism is a counterstructure of class struggle. It is in this context that national sentiments, national assertion, national commitment, and national-building could be used to demonstrate the underlying unity of people within a state. Whereas it is the duty of the citizen of the state to abide by its constitution and laws, there are certain core areas in which violation of laws would amount to be an anti-national act. At what stage of development of a country, a violation of law would be called anti-national by creating perfect correspondence between nation and state, is something which requires an in-depth understanding of the way the ruling elite creates the framework for the citizens of the country in which it excludes itself by virtue of its role in identifying national interests.

The entire world witnessed nothing short of revolution, as pointed out by Geertz (1973), that within two decades after the end of the Second World War, most of the colonial countries became free from the Western rule. We know that India was one of such countries. Unlike many independent countries, India was big – both in terms of population and territory even after partition – and diverse in virtually all kinds of ways. The experiment in nationhood had already caused the death and displacement of large population, and a new 'nation' had emerged, which could claim religion as the horizontal principle of imagined political community.[1] On the other hand, partition did not make any difference to the diversity of what was left as India. Despite the fact that leaders of independent India had developed the notion as well as slogan of 'unity in diversity', the partition of the country remained the major cause for jitters and some political paranoia with regard to political dissent as is exemplified by the way Nehru's cabinet dissolved two assemblies, namely, the Left government in Kerala in 1957 and Rarewala's ministry in Patiala and East Punjab States Union (PEPSU[2]) in 1953. Both were non-Congress governments – a digression in Nehru's project of nation-building.

It is clear from the above discussion that India faced a serious challenge to its project of nation-building at the time of independence, but at the same time its leaders were concerned with handling diversity to forge unity. There were multiple trajectories of Indian diversity and any could pose a challenge. India treaded upon the path of parliamentary democracy and planned development with the underlying practice of mixed economy to attain its constitutional objective of achieving socialism. This paper is an attempt at examining how the postcolonial development, both political and economic, interacted with diversity to create a challenge to the project of nation-building. The paper has been divided into five parts. The first part deals with the concept of nation-building the way it has been understood in various historical and contemporary contexts of the Western world. In the second part, the focus of discussion is the construction of Indian nation in colonial context through nationalism. The third part deals with the Indian idea of nation-building in the context of underlying diversity of the Indian society and the complex nature of the development of Indian polity and economy in the postcolonial phase. The fourth part deals with separatism, Hindutva, and long-distance nationalism as a challenge to nation-building. The fifth part concludes the discussion by way of offering certain theoretical conclusions.

UNDERSTANDING NATION-BUILDING

Literally speaking, the idea of nation-building seems to suggest as if it is a project of bringing people to a defined unity with which they feel subjectively affiliated and integrated. It also implies that before the beginning of the nation-building process the people in a particular geographical space were aggregation of otherwise segregated population due to persistent and powerful heterogeneities among them. Laughlin (2001: 2) has lucidly captured the essence of nation-building when he comments, '....nations are socio-cultural and geographical constructs which literally have to be built from the ground up... Before nations can be built from the ground up, they have to be lodged in the hearts and minds of people'. It is clear that nation-building is a conscious activity involving intentions, purposes, and ideologies. Norman (2006) clearly identifies two dimensions of nationalism, which are self-determination and nation-building. In a way, the concept of nation-building also subsumes the fact that the entity that sometimes struggled for self-determination may not necessarily remain homogenous and united owing to differences of cultures, regions, religions, and so on. In such situation, the nation-building becomes a project to 'deliberately create or reinforce a unified nation' (*ibid.*: 24). We are thus reminded of four phases of nationalism identified by Geertz (1973: 238): 'that in which the nationalist movements formed and crystallized; that in which they triumphed; that in which they organized themselves into states; and that (the present one) in which, organized into states, they find themselves obliged to define and stabilize their relationships both to other states and to the irregular societies out of which they arose'. Obviously, the fourth phase of nationalism is what we are discussing about as nation-building process.

There are certain underlying principles of all the above-mentioned notions of nation-building. Firstly, there is an agency which is involved in the process of nation-building. Secondly, the nation-building process is carried out by constantly referring to a territory which is governed under one government. Thirdly, the diversity as such or a particular element of the totality is considered a threat to the cohesiveness among the people. Fourthly, nation-building is regarded as functional for the hegemonic control of the ruling elite, because it is in the interest of the ruling classes to maintain a united population in one state territory. Finally, in the nation-building process the ruling elite are not part of it. They are involved in defining the process of nation-building and guiding the state towards that goal.

However, as is evident from Fukuyama (2006), the hegemonic content in the nation-building exercise becomes visible when it turns into the project of the major power, such as the United States, of the world. Fukuyama's effort is to show the painful effort being made by the United States to spearhead the process of nation-building in Afghanistan and Iraq. History is witness to the fact the Afghans have been committed to their sense of pride in their being, autonomy, and sovereignty. They fought relentless battles even in the nineteenth century to maintain their sovereignty. Till the invasion by the United States, the world saw no problems with the nation-building in Iraq. As a matter of fact, it was during the attacks on Afghanistan and, later on, Iraq that the knowledge of diversity in these countries could be known as problems. In both the cases, the rulers were accused of being oppressive against certain communities rather than arguing for the state that was facing the challenge of nation-building. In this hegemonic content of nation-building, the role of the Unites States is considered crucial. Ultimately, the introduction and establishment of liberal democracy and capitalism (free market) becomes the basis of the assessment of whether nation-building has been accomplished. Fukuyama (*ibid.*) goes to the extent of delineating 'guidelines for future nation-builders'. Let us look into the same to understand how a superpower can be helped by its intellectuals to hide its empire-building ambitions and acts under the garb of nation-building that is helping the post-conflict state to develop and grow into a liberal democracy and capitalist system. Here are the four components of nation-building in the context of Afghanistan and

Iraq prescribed by Fukuyama (*ibid.*: 233): 'Peacekeeping; Peace enforcement; Postconflict reconstruction; and Long-term economic and political development'.

The first and second components identified by Fukuyama are concerned with policing and security, whereas the third is specific to the situation in which the United States has militarily intervened. The fourth component is general and concerns all countries that are aspiring to attain certain high development levels. Such an understanding of nation-building is not accidental and has not emerged only after the US-led intervention in Afghanistan and Iraq. Ekbladh (2006) and Sutton (2006) have clearly demonstrated that the efforts of the United States began after Second World War in this direction. Ekbladh (2006: 19) writes, 'Nation-building in the years after World War II, was understood by a spectrum of U.S. policymakers and international actors to be collective activity. The nation-building energy expended during the Cold War was not solely that of state agencies. Nongovernmental, international, and particularly, private business organisations were involved in the complex task of reconstructing and developing nations'. Sutton (2006) has examined the role of Ford Foundation in this involvement, particularly when Paul Hoffman was the 'Ford's first president'. Sutton (*ibid.*: 45) makes it quite clear that in the context of Cold War, development was an ideological agenda. In the light of these facts, nationalism, in the sense of nation-building, was not simply a process of defining and stabilising the relationships of people within a state, as Geertz (1973) has mentioned, but implicating national and international state and non-state actors.

It is erroneous to assume that the project of nation-building began only after the United States started intervening in international affairs in a decisive manner after the Second World War. It seems, as Laughlin's (2001) work suggests, that the British Empire also actively engaged itself in this process much earlier. The case of Ireland was classical in this context when different actors began to imagine nationhood differently and the English hegemonic intervention remained overwhelmingly present during the last three centuries. It is thus clear that nation-building is not an end in itself, but a means to an end. The end belongs to the motives, intentions, purposes, and ideologies of different actors, which may either be competing and confronting or collaborating with each other. To understand the underlying principle and logic of pursuing the end, it is first important to bring in the Marxist theory and its ambivalence towards nationalism, but of crucial significance and relevance in understanding the logic of nation-building as an end/goal.

The position of Marxist theory with regard to nationalism is quite clear. Marx propagated internationalisation of working class struggle. He wrote,

> National differences and antagonisms between peoples are daily more and more vanishing, owing to the development of the bourgeoisie, to the freedom of commerce, to the world market, to uniformity in the mode of production and in condition of life corresponding thereto.
>
> The supremacy of the proletariat will cause them to vanish still faster. *(c.f. Connor 1984: 8)*

Obviously, the internationalism of Marxism discouraged any attempt at making serious investigation into various issues relating to nationalism. However, as Connor (*ibid.*) has rightly suggested, nationalism was effectively used by Marxists for achieving their objectives. When Stalin made a speech 10 days after the Nazi invasion in 1941, he invoked Russian nationalist symbols. Ironically, as Laughlin (2001) has commented, postmodernist theory also undermines the significance of nation and nationalism. Globalisation is being defined as breaking the barriers of nation-state in the movement of people, goods, and capital. Thus a paradox emerges in understanding the nation-building as a concept as well as a process. The symbolic representative of globalisation and postmodernity, whose main thrust is against nations and states and have begun to question citizenship, is the Western world that has rallied behind the US leadership, whereas the same set of actors is making an attempt at nation-building in Afghanistan and Iraq.

The above paradox opens the way for the understanding of nation-building as an ideological and hegemonic project. It is in this context that Gramsci becomes important for having an adequate understanding of nation-building. Laughlin (*ibid.*: 242) has elaborated how Gramscian concept of hegemony is useful in understanding and situating nation-building in a proper context. Thus,

> The category of hegemony occupies a central position in his [Gramsci's] analysis of capitalist and pre-capitalist societies. It referred to the cultural as well as the economic modes of incorporation adopted by dominant sectors of class-structured, including nation-building, societies. The latter used this dominance to establish control over their social subordinates and to legitimise their monopoly of state apparatuses of local government and education.... As used by Gramsci the concept 'hegemony' is not simply synonymous with ideological domination or manipulation. It constitutes instead the very substance and outer limits of 'common sense' for most people.

The contextualisation of Gramsci's concept of hegemony by Laughlin is important in relation to the nature of query with regard to the need for nation-building. It identifies actors and agents for whom the continuity of the hegemony is crucial. These actors could be classes or political elites that make no difference. We can further introduce the Gramscian idea of myth which becomes a categorical imperative as an instrument of creating consent among the ruled masses so that the particularistic differences creating hurdles in the state-building could be overcome. In other words, there is hardly any distinction between state-building and nation-building. Marxian idea that the dominant ideas of the epoch are the ideas of the ruling class, situates the concept of hegemony and creation of myths in a proper context.

IMAGINING INDIA AS A NATION: COLONIALISM AND NATIONALISM

The imagining of India as a nation has some distinct historical features, which remained points of contestations during colonial period and interestingly, still continue to be so. Oommen (1999: 1) identifies 'seven ways in which nation has been defined in the Indian subcontinent. These are; (1) ancient civilisational entity, (2) composite culture, (3) political entity, (4) religious entity, (5) geographical/territorial entity, with a specific cultural ethos, (6) a collection of linguistic entities, and (7) unity of great and little nations'. With the exception of the last category, all others could also be the categorisation of Indian society in six ways. There is a fundamental distinction between society and nation and the starting point of it is that the latter is political concept. As a matter of fact, Oommen is trying to identify how India could be one entity, which makes the nature of inquiry teleological.

There has been a widely asked question during the last century and even now: is India a nation? An honest answer was invariably negative, but certain observations, such as diversity, disparity, and linguistic and regional variations having given birth to chauvinism, were always added. In other words, the question relating to India as a nation was always understood whether the people of India felt a sense of belonging as the basis of imagining as an imagined political community. There are historical reasons for such an understanding. The pre-colonial India was a fragmented and segmented polity and society. In the words of Desai (1948:26), 'The objective and subjective prerequisites (such as common economic, social and state existence, and the consciousness of such existence) for the emergence of a national culture did not exist'. It is also argued that the British colonial rule laid the foundation of the emergence of India as a nation. Fukuyama (2006: 3), while referring to Sunil Khilnani, comments that 'the notion of

India as a nation-state was something that was invented under British rule. Prior to Britain's arrival, the subcontinent was a hodgepodge of princely states, languages, ethnic groups, and religions, with the Mogul Empire's writ limited only to parts of India. Under the British, India got a sense of itself as a single, unified political space (even if that space was carved into Muslim and Hindu areas at Partition) and acquired a common language, a civil service and bureaucratic tradition, an army, and other institutions that would be critical to the emergence of democratic India in 1947'. The most important component that has been missed in the above quote is that even the Congress party, that began to symbolise the national liberation movement under the leadership of Gandhi, was also the contribution of the British rule.

However, it is quite clear that the second half of the nineteenth century witnessed the emergence of nationalism among the middle classes in India. Chatterjee (1993), identifies the character of nationalism in the sense of Gramscian passive revolution that the Bengali middle class resisted the onslaught of Western modernity. Therefore, it becomes clear that the encounter with the colonialists' culture compelled the Indian educated middle classes and intellectuals to imagine India as national entity. It is interesting to note that since the colonialism was decentralising the local culture and was becoming hegemonic, role of English being crucial in this regard, there was a great degree of ambivalence in the India of their imagination. As Fanon (1968), illustrates the responses of the intellectuals in the colonial country, it was a situation of appreciation, a sense of awe for the master's culture as well as a great sense of danger to the identity of the self-rooted in its traditions and civilisation. A reaction to the dominant political power in colonial context, in general, and in India, in particular, took refuge in the selective acceptance of modernity and reinterpreting the rich heritage that the educated middle class considered India had possessed. Obviously, the net direction of such a stream of consciousness flowed backwards, towards the past rather than the present. Indian nation, in its inception, essentially founded upon the construction of India in a particular manner and existed as an imagined political community for the middle class Indians, who swung like pendulum between two extremes of supporting the British colonialism and looking back at the past glory of India. The third dimension that entered into this imagining was the fact that it went as back as the pre-Mogul and pre-Sultanate periods.

As lucidly illustrated by Chandra (1992), the nineteenth-century literature showed this ambivalence in different parts of India being written in different languages. The emergence of imagining India as a nation towards the end of nineteenth century, before the arrival of Gandhi on the national scene, was a confluence and divergence of various tendencies and perceptions. In his discussion of how India was defined as the nation in late nineteenth century, Chandra (*ibid.*) mentions hosts of writers, prominent among them are Harishchandra and R. C. Dutt. Dutt, known for his work *The Economic History of India*, has been widely regarded as one of the finest examples of economic nationalism. Chandra (*ibid.*: 59) informs,

> The neglected dimension of Dutt's nationalism pertains to what he called his 'literary patriotism'. It prompted him to translate Rig Veda, the Ramayana, and the Mahabharata, and to write the *History of Civilization in Ancient India* as well as four historical and two social novels. His 'literary patriotism' reveals why this anglicized civilian viewed himself as a progressive conservative. The translations and *Civilization in Ancient India* recall a glorious past. Elegiac in tone, the historical novels, in particular, lament the loss of this past. This lament is also implicitly an attempt to recover the past in order to make bearable the oppressive present.

Chandra's emphasis on the ambivalence in defining the Indian nation is to be understood the way the religious nationalism began to *define* the imagined community. This ambivalence was built into the paradox that Shakespeare depicts in his play *Hamlet*, 'To be or not to be'. The success of Indian nationalism predicated upon the unity of Hindus and Muslims, but at the same time, the imagining of India tended to be exclusionary with regard to the Muslims.

The arrival of Gandhi on the Indian scene and his taking over the leadership of the Congress signified major changes in the nationalist movement. Much before he took over the leadership of the Congress party, he had already authored *Hind Swaraj*. Combination of the Hindu *Sanatana* tradition and his inclusive approach to nationalist struggle, stood apart from what Tilak was doing at that time. Gandhi's Hinduism was to differ radically from Hindutva of Savarkar (Heradia 2009). It is but natural that the kind of India he imagined was distinct, unique, and marked by *dharma*. We shall return to Gandhi little later, as it is important to make a comment on the religious nationalism that, in certain respects, paved the way for the partition of the country in 1947.

When secularism and communalism entered into the nationalist movement, the division between the two, which was blurred in the beginning, began to get demarcated into rigid stances. In this regard, Ramananda Chatterjee's conception of India could be taken as one of the best illustrations of the way India was imagined as a Hindu nation. 'Hinduism was inseparable from his [Ramananda Chatterjee] concept of India, and he was convinced that a strong, reformed and united Hinduism was essential to the achievement of national political health and unity. As a young convert to Brahmo Samaj, he committed himself to a view of India's problems centred on the need of a revitalized Hindu India, to be accepted and appreciated by Christian Europe on terms of equality. This ideal was intrinsic to his identity as nationalist' (Israel 1983: 3). Ramananda Chatterjee was not the lone figure who was imagining India in terms of Hindu identity. Scores of other preceded as well as followed him. The Hindu nationalist imagining radically changed with Savarkar followed by Golwalker who set the project of converting India into a Hindu state and re-occupy lands 'which once belonged to Hindu nation' (Dixit 1986).[3]

We may now turn to Gandhi–Nehru dialogue on the future of independent India.[4] At the end of the Second World War in 1945, independence was imminent and it was the time when, as Chandra (1994) informs, Gandhi wrote a letter to Nehru, which reiterated his position with regard to his conception of independent India. Gandhi believed that in order to attain true freedom we would have to live in villages. He wrote to Nehru,

> 'You will not understand me if you think that I am talking about the villages of today'. 'My villages today exist in my imagination', he wrote, and added by way of a generalised justification: 'After all, every person lives in the world of his own imagination'. He then outlines the village of his imagination:
>
> 'The villager in this imagined village will not be apathetic – he will embody pure consciousness. He will not lead his life like an animal in a squalid dark room. Men and women will live freely and be prepared to face the whole world. The village will not know cholera, plague or smallpox. No one will live indolently, nor luxuriously'. (Chandra 1994: 45–46)

It is clear from the above that Gandhi was building a utopia, but in the process, at the same time, he was constructing the Indian nation and showing the way for nation-building. Chandra (*ibid.*) informs us that Nehru received the letter and 'sent off a provisional answer on October 9'. His answer implicated an altogether different notion of India – a notion representing European modernity. He wrote, 'Briefly put, my view is that the question before us is not one of truth versus untruth or non-violence versus violence .... I do not understand why a village should necessarily embody truth and non-violence. A village, normally speaking, is backward intellectually and culturally and no progress can be made from a backward environment. Narrow-minded people are much likely to be untruthful and violent' (c.f. *ibid*.: 46).

Within a couple of years of this exchange of ideas between Gandhi and Nehru, the country got independence and was also partitioned on religious basis – the event that gave legitimacy to the religious basis of nationhood, the ghost of which was destined to weigh like nightmares on the minds of ruling elites. The dawn of freedom necessitated the effort towards nation-building, which was conceptualised and understood, with the help of experts and foreign aid. The next part of the paper takes cognizance of how diversity of India was understood as a factor to be handled in building a nation rather than as an asset.

INDIAN PROJECT OF NATION-BUILDING: DEVELOPMENT AND DIVERSITY

Immediately after getting independence, the political elite under the leadership of Nehru initiated the twin process of nation-building and state-building. Although the two were fundamentally different, the latter could be realised by recognising the presence of various nationalities within the territory, but were inseparable, because the former could be realised through the latter. However, the task before the leaders posed numerous challenges. Diversity, diversity within diversity, poverty, traditional and backward economy in agriculture and industry, communalism etc. were to be handled. Development, both political and social, was to be required in such a way that every citizen of the country would feel a sense of belonging with India. Some work had already been done by the British in the form of well-established bureaucracy, judiciary, army, rail and road transport services, and so on. What was required was expansion and strengthening of the already available network. This is what the Government of India did in these areas, and in the process of doing so created new problems, the reasons for which could be located in the process which was adopted in strengthening state organisation.

The four major steps that were undertaken immediately after independence were – writing and adoption of constitution, introduction of political democracy, enactment and implementation of land reform laws, and reconstruction of rural life through community development programmes.[5] All these four steps were expected to be steps towards state-building and in the process nation-building. It was expected that the Constitution would recognise diversity and would provide for federal system in which the states should have greater autonomy. However, as Yamaguchi (2004) has pointed out that the Constitution provided for a strong Centre. With the sole exception of linguistic reorganisation of the states – that too half-heartedly leaving certain states untouched – the centralising tendencies have been rather more visible than any other aspect. It seems that the drafters of the Constitution thought that the federal system with greater autonomy to the states could leave certain social groups in the perpetual state of discrimination and dehumanisation. In other words, in a situation of greater autonomy to the states, certain social groups would not be able to improve their conditions. This is another paradox of nation-building process that was an outcome of the multi-polarity of diversity in the country. If region and language could be two axes along which diversity was handled, then religion, caste, tribe, and culture were ignored in handling this diversity. Caste discrimination and untouchability were abolished, and social equality was the objective of the new republic.

Political democracy could be considered to be the most significant and desirable achievement of India. Despite the fact that experts predicted its doom, it, in all its deviations and weaknesses, is still the cornerstone of Indian polity and state-building. The level of liberal democracy, achieved so far in the country, is still short of characterising it as 'end of history'. Rather if we go by Marx who once said that India did not have history, but past, it is now quite possible that India's short period of history that began with colonialism, for Marx, is going to end with the rise of liberal democracy if we go by Fukuyama's (1992) assertion that liberal democracy is the end of the road for history as nothing would be changing after that. However, the problems with the democracy in the country are marked by twin threats: firstly, the emergence of identity politics, and secondly, the centralising tendencies among political elites. An extreme example of the latter is the imposition of Emergency in 1975, by the then Prime Minister Indira Gandhi.

We may now turn to the economic development of the country that was affected through the efforts of ruling class, which consisted of political elites and bureaucracy. There is a widely held view that India adopted economic planning in pursuance of its mixed economy model and socialism. It is one of the greatest myths that has been nurtured and widely articulated even now to justify the present free market economy. It should be reminded that neither the mixed economy with public sector domination in enterprises was socialistic, nor is the present free market economy practice as free as it is understood. The state remains relevant in determining the amount of freedom that is required in every set of activities.

To make it clear what the above assertion means, we may go back to the post-Second World War times when the United States took upon itself to contribute to the nation-building process in the newly liberated countries.

The US government invited the non-state actors to participate in the process of nation-building in the Third World. One of the first non-state actors was the Ford Foundation whose first president, Paul Hoffman, got involved with India among other countries in this pursuit. Sutton (2006: 50) informs, 'Hoffman's initial engagement in India with Nehru centred on the Planning Commission that Nehru chaired. This encounter led to Ford's largest initial development project, the India community development'. Interestingly, Hoffman was able to convince the Pakistani leaders too, to abandon their project of Islamic economics and constitute planning board along the 'modernist' lines. Let us return to India and see how Ford Foundation was a party to nation-building. Thus,

> The Ford Foundation's first major overseas development program was its support of Indian community development, a program that was planned and worked out in 1951 and subsequent years, in conjunction with the Indian Planning Commission chaired by Prime Minister Nehru. It was a program of rural development and nation-building that was initially much admired and imitated, with help from Ford, in other countries. (Sutton 2006: 53)

Despite the fact that Moore (1967) failed to situate the community development in the context of Ford Foundation and traced its genealogy to Gandhi's notion of Village Swaraj, he, however, was able to assess correctly that it had nothing to do with socialistic goal of altering the village social structure and property relations. The result was that it failed to touch the core of Indian rural and agrarian structure of exploitation, discrimination, and exclusion.

Frank (1969), stated that land reform is a political action, the purpose of which is to bring the large mass of people in direct contact with the state. The motivation and ideology behind land reform legislations in India were no different from this purpose. Since land reform was the state issue, all land reform legislations were enacted at the state level. Among various kinds of legislations, the three most prominent were abolition of intermediaries, tenancy reforms, and ceiling on landholding and redistribution of surplus land to the landless. The success and failure of land reforms in India should be understood in the light of the political motivation of the ruling classes in the country. There is consensus among most of the scholars that the most successful component of the implementation of these laws is the abolition of intermediary tenures. The abolition of zamindari system created by the British in 1792, by Lord Cornwallis, was the major target as the new ruling class shifted its base from the rural elites to large mass of peasants.

Land reform as a nation-building process constitutes a landmark in the history of India both as a success and a terrible failure. The presence of the Ford Foundation was unmistakably visible in the form of an international expert, Ladejinsky (1977), who in the Cold War period apprised the non-state actors of the possibility and probability of red revolution, feared most by the United States and its allies at that time, in India and other countries.[6] Subsequently, the ruling class lost its political will to implement the land reform laws, only to be woken up in late 1960s, when the Naxalite movement emerged and the land question became the burning issue. The then prime minister instructed all the states to enact land reforms laws (Judge 1999).

Various trajectories of success of development programmes were awfully short of expectations. Luce (2006) has made a pertinent remark that the Indian society is like a gigantic structure with diversity, and building consensus on various issues takes a long time. However, the failure of nation-building process could be seen in terms of emergence of regional diversity, unabated perpetuation of caste atrocities, discrimination against minorities, and exploitation of tribal communities. There was only one united force during the first 25 years after independence – the ruling class which also transformed itself into a nation. Kothari (1976: 220) captured this reality in a very perceptive manner. Thus,

> Imperceptibly, the class that started as the vanguard of national awakening and reconstruction becomes an exclusive elite, commanding the nerve centres of decision-making, enjoying special rights and perquisites, and utilizing all these for self-aggrandizement and self-perpetuation. … this elite makes gestures towards distributive justice and even concedes some of it, but it has now become a vested interest itself. It appropriates the nation's resources for maintaining a life style and a pattern of consumption that are the distinguishing features of all ruling classes in societies characterized by massive inequality and underdevelopment of overall human resources.

Kothari's generalisation of explanation about why the ruling class begins to defeat the project that it had initiated is interesting, but it does not satisfy our curiosity with regard to Indian situation, particularly in the light of the fact that the people at the helm of affairs were well-intentioned, committed, and honest leaders. What did go wrong? The answer lies somewhere else. Fanon (1968: 103) brings out the issue of liberation in a lucid manner by pinpointing the problems thus, 'The liberation of the individual does not follow national liberation. An authentic national liberation exists only to the precise degree to which the individual has irreversibly begun his own liberation. It is not possible to maintain one's distance with respect to colonialism without at the same time taking it with respect to the idea that the colonized holds of himself through the filter of colonialist culture'. Most of the leaders of free India were not educated in the Indian universities supposed to be producing the *babus*, but had got education form the West. After 60 years of independence, the rulers have not changed in terms of their education, as is evident from the cattle class taunt of Shashi Tharoor. Obviously, the change is that the cattle class has now access to a section of the ruled. The transfer of power in 1947, was not liberation the way Indian people would have imagined. Despite the fact that India achieved sovereignty, the partition left a permanent scar. If we grant that Jinnah was modern secular leader, it becomes clear that how potent and deadly the virus of religious nationalism had proved to be.

Where India failed was that the very colonial mindset of its leaders did not allow them to change the regulatory rules in free India. By adopting new Constitution, the constitutive principles of the new republic were set in place, but it also required the change in the regulatory principle, which never happened. The British colonial rulers always regarded themselves as angels, who had come to enlighten the heathens and pagans with their philosophy, culture, and traditions. They regarded the natives as savages, backward, and resistant to change owing to which they framed regulatory rules in terms of legal enactments, service rules, and penal code. The postcolonial rulers let the same unchanged. Just to give one example, the act governing the land acquisition was framed by the British in 1880s and it continued to be the same till recently. Even now it has only been amended. The paradox between the new constitutive rules and old regulatory rules separated the ruling class from the nation-building process. Like *sutradhar* the ruling elite became the executor of a process of which it did not consider to be a part. The consequences of this paradox were multi-directional and the underlying commonality among them was that the masses began to further drift away from the nation-building process and began to question the legitimacy of the state. The next part of the paper discusses some of these issues succinctly.

CHALLENGE TO NATION-BUILDING: SEPARATISM, HINDUTVA, AND IDENTITY FORMATIONS

Huntington (1968), by taking into consideration the parameters of institutional development, tried to examine the reasons for political instability in the developing societies. His basic thesis was interesting and was widely accepted as a plausible explanation. He argued that the political instability in these societies was not due to their backwardness, but because of the fact that they were trying to modernise. Various groups and communities begin to aspire for better bargain in the political system. Such an understanding is quite close to the theory of revolution of rising expectations. Many aspects of India's political instability could be explained by virtue of such a thesis. However, there was much that was the result of either its colonial past or its economic policies. The processes that threatened national integration after 1947 could be covered under three major headings: separatism, Hindutva, and identity formation. Jayaprakash Narayan (1982) – the major political leader who influenced a generation of social activists till 1970s – remained obsessed with the problems of nation-building in India. For him, nation-building was another name for national integration and the major threats to it surfaced from Kashmir and Nagaland – both these states had (and still have) unique status with regard to the Indian government. Unfortunately, like the story of Junagarh, the history of Manipur has never figured in the discourse of nation-building.[7] Still more states were to join these above states which questioned the Indian path of nation-building process. Mizoram, Meghalaya, Tripura, and Punjab became volatile and some of them began to demand separation from the Indian union. All these states witnessed separatism of a kind claiming to be different from the dominant claims of nationhood in the country. Punjab witnessed the Khalistan movement – a movement that articulated the religious identity. Kashmir issue is generally seen in terms of religious identity, whereas the north-eastern states claim autonomy and sovereignty on the basis of their history and anthropological past.[8]

The most distinctive feature of postcolonial India is the emergence of Hindutva as the ideology of nationhood which caused atrophy to the nation-building process in a big way. Whereas nation-building was inclusive in content and practice, Hindutva nationhood is exclusionary in which other religious communities could be accommodated, but may not necessarily be made equal partners. Despite the fact that the Bharatiya Janata Party (BJP) did not do something like what it was constructing, except for coining the term *pseudo-secularism* to attack Left parties and others. The rise of Hindutva in India occurs at a particular historical time when the age of religion emerged as a lethal force in 1980s with Sikh separatism. Communal riots gave the kind of push which militant violence gave to religious identities. The BJP, supported by various religious organisations that were patronised by the Rashtriya Swayamsevak Sangh (RSS), put the then Congress government under Rajiv Gandhi on the defensive. The issue of Babri Masjid ultimately culminated into its demolition. Despite the fact that the temple at 'Ram Janma Bhoomi' in Ayodhya could be a distant dream, the BJP was not worried about it. The attacks on Christians by the Hindu fundamentalists add to the apprehension that the ideology of Hindutva aims at marginalising other religious communities.

Separatism of any sort and Hindutva, both are fundamentally related to the construction of exclusive identities. The mode of separation from the defined other is articulated within the group to build homogeneity among the class divided groups. Both religious and national identities are not hierarchical but horizontal unities. The Naga or the Mizo identity shares certain commonality with the Sikh identity created by the separatists. There was a construction of separation and creation of a sense of belonging in contradistinction to the 'dominant/hegemonic other'.

Identity formation and articulation did not remain confined to religion and region, but rather extended to other diversities like tribe, language, culture, and caste. The emergence of the discourse on identity was an addition to the already existing politics of separation. The identity assertion among the Dalits and OBCs has been on the rise in recent years, who are also raising and expressing doubts about the way India has been imagined as a nation. We have already talked about Gandhi's imagined village as the basis of the future Indian nation. In contradistinction to Gandhi, Ambedkar rejected the Indian village, as for him it symbolised the epitome of human oppression. He wrote, 'In this republic there is no place for democracy. There is no room for equality. There is no room for liberty and there is no room for fraternity. The Indian village is very negation of the republic' (Moon 1989: 26). Ambedkar thought of city as the place where Dalits could remove caste stigma. Mayawati's criticism of Gandhi falls in line with Ambedkar's critique of Gandhi's idea of Indian nation. In recent years, Ilaiah (2004) has built a critique of the Hindutva concept of nationalism in his populist and polemical essays. He brands the BJP's nationalism as cow nationalism, whereas the Dalit construction of nationalism is buffalo nationalism. The Dalit dissent is raising issues with regard to the nature of nation-building process in the country. The rise of OBCs and their mobilisation for a share in the educational seats and government jobs is an aggregative gain they are demanding after their successful gains in politics. The caste identities – in any form – are antithetical to the inclusive politics, which is the requisite for national integration.

However, the major threat that has emerged in the age of globalisation is the rising tide of, both positive and negative, long-distance nationalism. There is a sizable presence of Indian diaspora in various countries. Among themselves they are divided along regional, cultural, and religious lines. As such we can only think of Gujaratis, Punjabis or Sikhs, Tamilians, etc. The concept of Indian diaspora has no empirical validity. However, the Sikhs constitute the oldest among the Indian diaspora in North America. Some of the Indians abroad have been involved in separatism by articulating either their cultural/religious separation from mainstream India or the suppression of their brethren in India. Schiller (2004) is of the view that there are four types of long-distance nationalism. These are anti-colonialism, separatism, regime change, and participation. The Sikhs, the Nagas, the Kashmiris, and the Mizos, irrespective of their number among the Indians abroad, have been involved in separatism. The case of Nagas, as shown by Ranganathan and Roy-Chowdhury (2008), is interesting as they have the longest history of demand for separate state, but with the help of the Internet they have been able to combine and rally around the idea of separate state. However, the most important record of long-distance nationalism is that of the Sikhs. The Sikh diaspora created Ghadar movement to liberate India from the British colonialism through armed struggle. After independence, they participated in the nation-building process by sending help to develop the economy of Punjab. They also participated in the Khalistan movement demanding separate state for the Sikhs. It is interesting to note that if the Non-Resident Indian (NRI) money was important for coming out of the balance of payment crisis, then the same money also financed hate campaign against certain communities, as is widely talked about in the case of the Gujarati diaspora. Such developments have strongly jeopardised the sense of belonging that is the precondition for the nation-building process.

The above delineation of challenges that India has faced in the postcolonial period and which continue to haunt the body politic of India, clearly shows that something seriously went wrong with the way the ruling/governing class handled diversity. Following Huntington (1968), it could be added that certain challenges emerged as a result of the development process. We may take, in the first instance, the example of Nagaland. Just about the time when the independence was round the corner, the Nagas began to assert their distinct identity and made it clear that they did not want to be part of Indian union. Sir Akbar Hydari, the then governor of Assam, arrived at an agreement – known as the Hydari Agreement–in June 1947, with the Naga leaders. This agreement recognised the rights of the Nagas to develop according to their free will. Pou (2009: 233) informs, 'In 1949, Gopinath Bordoloi, then Chief Minister of Nagaland announced that the Government of India no longer considers the Hydari agreement valid'. The struggle that Nagas have carried across time has been brutally treated and the army actions have always been questionable. The mode of dealing with the Naga insurgency has been the major cause of their continuous struggle.

However, the most important instance of postcolonial India where the ruling class could be singularly made responsible for the entire problem is Punjab crisis. Punjab was always the part of mainstream. The present Punjab came to exist in 1966 when Punjabi Suba was formed on the linguistic basis. Punjab was the last state to be reorganised along linguistic lines – that too after prolonged struggle. This delay was largely due to the fact that the linguistic issue in Punjab had been communalised in 1951, when Punjabi was identified with the Sikhs rather than as the language of the Punjabis. What could be the reasons for this? Narang (2000: 305–306) clearly points out, 'During the war [Indo-Pak war of 1965], the role of Punjabis in general and Sikh population in particular was highly appreciated. In view of all these developments, within two days of the cease-fire, the central government appointed three-man committee consisting of Y. B. Chavan, Indira Gandhi and Mahavir Tyagi, to examine afresh the demand for Punjabi Suba'. The important aspect of this fact is that the Sikhs had to show their loyalty to the Indian nation in situation of war to have Punjabi Suba. Despite the fact that the Akalis wanted Punjabi Suba to capture legislative power in the state, which was not possible in the united Punjab, the manner in which the linguistic reorganisation of Punjab was communalised and kept in abeyance, betrayed a sense of discrimination against the Sikhs.

The Green Revolution, a phenomenon of high agricultural productivity, was initiated in Punjab with the help of the inputs from the Indian government. Within a few years, Punjab showed remarkable production of wheat. Punjab was the state that gained from the Green Revolution in terms of dramatic reduction in poverty levels, but at the same time it also suffered in various ways. The Green Revolution was one of the factors in the emergence of the issue of centre–state relations as the Punjabi leadership began to experience some degree of deprivation in the approach to the development of Punjab.

During emergency, the only party that struggled for democracy by constantly agitating and protesting was the Akali Dal. After emergency, now it is a well-known fact, when the Congress was already out of power, Giani Zail Singh propped up Jarnail Singh Bhinderanwala, who started his political career by opposing Akali Dal in the Shiromani Gurdwara Parbandhak Committee (SGPC) elections in 1979.

Interestingly, the Dal Khalsa was allegedly formed as a result of the encouragement from Giani Zail Singh in 1978. On April 26, 1982, two severed heads of cows were found hanging at two Hindu temples at Amritsar. Packets of cigarettes were also thrown in the gurdwaras around that time. Within a week of this incident, the Dal Khalsa was banned. It may be just reminded that in the second half of the nineteenth century, the Kuka Sikhs attacked and killed butchers selling beef. The issue of eating beef in the Sikh community has been settled for long. Nobody eats beef. The Indian government, instead of investigating the matter with regard to the heads of cow hanging in front of temples, banned the Dal Khalsa, which allegedly took the responsibility.

We may now return to the major incident that occurred in Orwellian year of 1984, namely, the Blue Star Operation. It has now been reasonably established that Jarnail Singh Bhinderanwala and his companion could be flushed out without using the might of the Indian army and sending the tanks within the precincts of the temple. In the month of June, the same could have been achieved by controlling the supply of power and other essential commodities, as was done four years later in the Operation Black Thunder. The reaction to the violation of the most sacred place of the Sikhs had disastrous consequences. A noticeable number of Sikh soldiers mutinied immediately after hearing the news. Some of them turned terrorists in the second half of 1980s. Mrs. Indira Gandhi was assassinated about five months after the attack, which was followed by anti-Sikh riots in Delhi, Kanpur, and other places in India. When Rajiv Gandhi came to power, he initiated dialogue with Akalis that culminated into Rajiv-Longowal Accord in 1985, which was never honoured by the Indian government during the period of Rajiv Gandhi's tenure as prime minister. For seven years, from 1986 to 1993, Punjab experienced unforeseen escalation of terrorist violence with the clear and unambiguous objective of achieving the sovereign state of Khalistan.

The Khalistan movement was suppressed with brutality, which led the elderly people to remark that British rule was better than this, killing large number of terrorists without observing any due process of law. Fake encounters of both militants and innocent Sikhs were carried out by the state police and paramilitary forces with no respect for human life. A number of killed persons were unidentified and later on, were cremated in the various cremation grounds in Amritsar and other cities. Jaswant Singh Khalra, who was investigating the human rights violation cases of missing individuals, was kidnapped from his house. His body was never traced.[9]

The story of Punjab is no different from the stories of Kashmir, Nagaland, Mizoram, Manipur, etc. Mizo society had the courage to coin the new term 'curfew sons' to remember the atrocities on their women. Other states, including Punjab, have no different experience of the atrocities of the armed forces. What has been the most tragic and dehumanising dimension of police and paramilitary actions is that these are carried out in the area/state as if that area/state does not form part of the Indian Union with equal rights of freedom and citizenship. It will be appropriate to conclude this part of the paper by quoting Gautam (2007):

> The post-colonial Indian 'nation-state' and its ruling elite demand from the people a crude political and social commitment for loyalty and obedience as if they are subjects of a colonial state and not equal citizens of an Independent democratic republic. Such a demand is asserted and enforced without any dialogical engagement with the people to convince them of its justification. During the post-independence era, the legacy of the old colonial policies of subjugation, oppression, exploitation, co-option and adjustment remains intact in the name of maintaining and safeguarding the structures and powers of authority inherited from colonial masters.

CONCLUDING REMARKS: MAKING SENSE OF NATION-BUILDING IN INDIA

In this final and concluding part of the paper, my aim is to come to terms with the issues concerning and challenges of nation-building by summarising the entire discussion and situating it in the theoretical context so as to identify the paradoxes involved in the specific Indian experience. I must begin by reiterating the opening sentence of this paper, which has been stated as a metaphor, that the Indian ruling class did not remain a participant in the project of nation-building. It acted through co-option and suppression to deal with the challenge from the emerging elite. It never followed the dictum that nation has to be built, as Laughlin would say, through heart and mind from the bottom to the top. In other words, nation-building must not be confused with state-building, though they are two sides of one coin. The former implicates consent and the latter entails coercion. The notion of hegemony in the context of the American project of nation-building, in the developing countries through the introduction of liberal democracy, becomes most relevant to unfold and uncover the underlying structures of power involved in the process.

The story of imagining India as a nation in the colonial era and the subsequent idea of national integration among the nationalist forces shows diversity of perspectives and approaches to achieve the goal. It has been argued that the dominant trends in nationalism were mainly of two kinds of approaches: exclusive/cultural/religious nationalism and inclusive/secular nationalism. Gandhian Hinduism was inclusive, whereas Savarkar's Hindutva was exclusive. At the threshold of independence, India was partitioned as religious nationalism triumphed. However, two major figures who were at the helm of affairs, namely, Gandhi and Nehru, exchanged views about the path of nation-building. What happened later on clearly demonstrated that Nehruvian vision of future India had won the day with the ruling class. The vision of future India was the capitalist development with the slogan of socialism as the objective. The American presence in community development programme and the land reforms clearly demonstrates how Nehru was trying to build the new India. Democracy is the most important achievement in the nation-building process by giving opportunity to the people to participate in electing the party to form the government. It is still to achieve the ideal of liberal democracy. However, the modernist agenda regarded diversity in Indian society as a hurdle against development, which led to the abandoning or half-hearted implementation of its earlier commitment of respecting diversity. Linguistic reorganisation of states, implementation of land reforms, effective execution of various development programmes, etc. met with partial failure largely due to the invented term 'lack of political will'.

The major paradox of the nation-building process was that the regulatory rules remained unchanged, whereas the constitutive rules were changed with the adoption of new constitution. The outcome of this paradox has proved to be disastrous for India. The ruling elite did not dismantle the colonial structure of governance; instead, it separated itself from the masses. Separatism, Hindutva, and long-distance nationalism posed major threat to the Indian nationhood. However, the only area of positive development has been the practice of democracy that has struck root in the Indian political consciousness and culture. However, the articulation and mobilisation of particularistic identities threaten the emergence of the liberal democratic culture and practice, but consolidation of democratic principles has not yet taken place. The major threat from the political mobilisation of identities along caste, religious, regional, and tribal lines requires understanding of Indian diversity and its acceptance. Nation-building process, if it has to succeed, must recognise the diversity as the basis of its strength rather than threat. The ruling elite should stop behaving like angels – as if they are above reproach. The starting point should be to overcome and remove narcissism of structural and small differences. Still there is a long way to transform society along lines in which only class differences become the major point of contention. It should be understood that both, the Khalistan movement and the Maharashtra Navnirman Sena (MNS), pose equal threat to the nation-building process in India.

NOTES

(This is the revised version of the paper presented in the symposium 'Development, Diversity and Identity: Contemporary Challenges to Nation-Building' in XXXV All India Sociological Conference held at University of Kashmir, Srinagar, on October 9–11, 2009.)

1. Ironically, the religious basis of nationhood crumbled within two and half decades when Bangladesh was born as a new nation.
2. Gian Singh Rarewala became the chief minister of the PEPSU (Patiala and Eastern Punjab States Union).
3. The construction of two-nation theory and the formation of Pakistan are well-known though controversy still raises its head on whether Jinnah or Congress leaders were responsible for the partition.
4. The entire discussion in this paragraph is based on an article by Sudhir Chandra (1994).
5. Kothari (1976: 195) identifies four major tasks of the independent India: national integration, economic growth, social justice, and political democracy.
6. Reading Ladejinsky (1977) makes it clear that when he presented his report apprehensions were expressed. Ideologically loaded queries and his responses have been expunged from the book.
7. Recently, *Eastern Quarterly*, a publication of Manipur Research Forum, has been bringing out the unique history of Manipur in relation to state-building process in India.
8. The popular expression nowadays is ethnic differences. Incidentally, Manipur has Hindu population with Kuki and Naga tribes living in hilly areas around Imphal valley.
9. The political leaders of different shades still defend the brutality of police and armed forces. Sometimes in the beginning of 2009, Arun Shourie defended these killings in a show anchored by Bikram Chandra of New Delhi Television Limited (NDTV) and criticised those who were demanding actions against the guilty police officers including K.P.S. Gill.

REFERENCES

Anderson, B. (1983). *Imagined Communities: Reflections on the Origin and Spread of Nationalism*. London: Verso.

——. (1994). 'Exodus', *Critical Inquiry*, 20(2): 314–327.

Chandra, S. (1992). *The Oppressive Present: Literature and Social Consciousness in India*. New Delhi: Oxford University Press.

Chatterjee, P. (1993). *Nation and Its Fragments: Colonial and Postcolonial Histories*. New Delhi: Oxford University Press.

Connor, W. (1984). *The National Question in Marxist-Leninist Theory and Strategy*. Princeton: Princeton University Press.

Desai, A. R. (1948). *Social Background of Indian Nationalism*. Bombay: Popular Prakashan.

Dixit, P. (1986). 'The Ideology of Hindu Nationalism', in T. Pantham and K. L. Deutsch (eds.), *Political Thought in Modern India*. New Delhi: Sage Publications, pp. 122–141.

Ekbladh, D. (2006). 'From Consensus to Crisis: The Postwar Career of Nation-Building in U.S. Foreign Relations', in F. Fukuyama (ed.), *Nation-Building: Beyond Afghanistan and Iraq*. Baltimore: The Johns Hopkins University Press, pp. 19–41.

Fanon, F. (1968). *The Wretched of the Earth*. Harmondsworth: Penguin.

Frank, A. G. (1969). *Latin America: Underdevelopment or Revolution*. New York: Monthly Review Press.

Fukuyama, F. (1992). *The End of History and the Last Man*. New York: Avon Books.

——. (2006). 'Introduction: Nation-Building and the Failure of Institutional Memory', in F. Fukuyama (ed.), *Nation-Building: Beyond Afghanistan and Iraq*. Baltimore: The Johns Hopkins University Press, pp. 1–18.

Geertz, C. (1973). *The Interpretation of Cultures*. New York: Basic Books.

Gellner, E. (1983). *Nations and Nationalism*. Ithaca: Cornell University.

Gautam, S. P. (2007). 'Reflections on National Question'. (Originally published in *Eastern Quarterly*). http:/www.manipurresearchforum.org/reflecting_national.htm.

Heradia, R. C. (2009). 'Gandhi's Hinduism and Savarkar's Hindutva', *Economic and Political Weekly*, XLIV(29): 62–67.

Huntington, S. P. (1968). *Political Order in Changing Societies: An Adaptation*. New York: Feffer and Simons Inc.

Ilaiah, K. (2004). *Buffalo Nationalism: A Critique of Spiritual Fascism*. Kolkata: Samya.

Israel, M. (1983). 'Ramananda Chatterjee and the Modern Review: The Image of Nationality in the National Press', in M. Israel (ed.), *National Unity: The South Asian Experience*. New Delhi: Promilla & Co., pp. 1–46.

Judge, P. S. (1999). *Social Change through Land Reforms*. Jaipur: Rawat Publications.

Kothari, R. (1976). 'Integration and Performance: Two Pivots of India's Model of Nation Building', in R. Kothari (ed.), *State and Nation Building*. Bombay: Allied Publishers, pp. 193–228.

Laughlin, J. M. (2001). *Reimagining the Nation-State: The Contested Terrains of Nation-Building*. London: Pluto Press.

Ladejinsky, W. (1977). *Agrarian Reforms as Unfinished Business: The Selected Paper of Wolf Ladejensky*. L. J. Walinsky (ed.). New York: Oxford University Press.

Luce, E. (2006). *In Spite of the Gods: The Strange Rise of Modern India*. London: Little, Brown.

Moon, V. (1989), *Dr. Babasaheb Ambedkar: Writings and Speeches*. Vol. 5. Bombay: Government of Maharashtra.

Moore Jr., B. (1967). *Social Origins of Dictatorship and Democracy: Lord and Peasant in the Making of the Modern World*. Harmondsworth: Penguin.

Narang, A. S. (2000). 'The Punjabi Suba Movement', H. K. Puri and P. S. Judge (eds.), *Social and Political Movements: Readings on Punjab*. Jaipur: Rawat Publications, pp. 291–307.

Narayan, J. (1982). *Nation Building in India*. Brahmanand (ed.). Varanasi: Navchetna Prakashan.

Norman, W. (2006). *Negotiating Nationalism: Nation-Building, Federalism, and Secession in the Multinational State*. Oxford: Oxford University Press.

Oommen, T. K. (1999). 'Conceptualising Nation and Nationality in South Asia', *Sociological Bulletin*, 48(1 & 2): 1–18.

Pou, S. (2009). 'Quebec and Nagaland: Towards Inclusive Nationalism?' in C. S. Raj and M. Mc. Andrew (eds.), *Multiculturalism: Public Policy and Problem Areas in Canada and India*. New Delhi: Manak, pp. 222–244.

Ranganathan, M. and Roy-Chowdhury, S. (2008). 'The Naga Nation on the Net'. *Economic and Political Weekly*, July 19, 61–68.

Schiller, N. G. (2004). 'Long-Distance Nationalism', in M. Ember, et al. (eds.), *Encyclopaedia of Diasporas: Immigrant and Refugee Cultures around the World*. New York: Kluwer Academic/Plenum Publishers, pp. 570–579.

Sutton, F. X. (2006). 'Nation-Building in the Heyday of the Classic Development Ideology: Ford Foundation Experience in the 1950s and 1960s', in F. Fukuyama (ed.), *Nation-Building: Beyond Afghanistan and Iraq*. Baltimore: The Johns Hopkins University Press, pp. 42–63.

Yamaguchi, H. (2004). 'National-Building and Fragmentation in India – Implications of the General Elections'. *Paper Presented in the 18th European Conference on Modern South Asian Studies*, Lund University, Sweden, July 6. Available online http://www.sasnet.lu.se/ESSAS papers/30Hiroichiyamaguchi.pdf

CHAPTER 3

CREATIVE DESTRUCTION AND SURVIVAL OF ENTERPRISING DEMOCRACY

Nupurnima Yadav

> The fundamental impulse that sets and keeps the capitalist engine in motion comes from new consumers' goods, the new methods of production and transportation, the new markets, the new forms of industrial organization that capitalist enterprise creates [...] the same process of industrial mutation. If I may use that biological term – that incessantly revolutionizes the economic structure from within, incessantly destroying the old one, incessantly creating a new one. This process of Creative Destruction is the essential fact about capitalism.
>
> Joseph Schumpeter (1942)

INTRODUCTION

In this paper, the primary objective is to reflect upon the dynamism of capitalism through the process of *creative destruction* and its effects on the democracy. We know that democracy sustains itself in the transition phase of capitalist system and the notion of creative destruction permeates the political structure.

Capitalism, by nature, is a form or method of economic change, which can never be stationary. And this evolutionary character of the capitalist process is not merely due to the fact that economic life goes on in a social and natural environment which changes and by its change alters the data of economic action; this fact is important and these changes (wars, revolutions, and so on) often condition industrial change, but they are not its prime movers. Nor is this evolutionary character due to a quasi-automatic increase in population and capital or due to the vagaries of monetary systems, of which exactly the same thing holds true. The fundamental impulse that sets and keeps the capitalist engine in motion comes from the new consumers' goods, the new methods of production or transportation, the new markets, and the new forms of industrial organisation that capitalist enterprise creates. The essential point to grasp is that in dealing with capitalism we are dealing with an evolutionary process. It may seem strange that anyone can fail to see so obvious a fact which moreover was long ago emphasised by Karl Marx. Yet that fragmentary analysis, which yields the bulk of our propositions about the functioning of modern capitalism, persistently neglects it.

> Modern bourgeois society, with its relations of production, of exchange and of property, a society that has conjured up such gigantic means of production and of exchange, is like the sorcerer who is no longer able to control the powers of the nether world whom he has called up by his spells. [...] It is enough to mention the commercial crises that by their periodical return put the existence of the whole of bourgeois society on trial, each time more threateningly. In these crises, a great part not only of existing production, but also of previously created productive forces, are periodically destroyed. In these crises, there breaks out an epidemic that, in all earlier epochs, would have seemed an absurdity – the epidemic of over-production. Society suddenly finds itself put back into a state of momentary barbarism; it appears as if a famine, a universal war of devastation, had cut off the supply of every means of subsistence; industry and commerce seem to be destroyed. The utilitarian fathers of democratic doctrine failed to see the full importance of this, simply because none of them seriously considered any substantial change in the economic framework and the habits of bourgeois society. They saw little beyond the world of an eighteenth-century ironmonger. (Schumpeter 1942)

CONCEPT OF CREATIVE DESTRUCTION

The entire economic structure did not simply expand along any fixed framework but it underwent a process of qualitative change. Similarly, in order to quote, Schumpeter (1942), 'the history of means of production, from small-scale factories to large-scale industries is categorized as history of revolutions'. So is the history of the productive apparatus of the iron and steel industry from the charcoal furnace to our own type of furnace, or the history of the apparatus of power production from the overshot water wheel to the modern power plant, or the history of transportation from the mail-coach to the airplane. The opening up of new markets, foreign or domestic, and the organisational development from the craft shop and factory to colossal industries, illustrates the same process of "industrial mutation". However, Schumpeter christened this process as "Creative Destruction", that incessantly revolutionizes the economic structure from within, incessantly destroying the old one, incessantly creating a new one. This process of "Creative Destruction" is the essential fact about capitalism (Schumpeter 1942). This concept of capitalism, encompasses all the possible concerns with which a capitalist struggles in a dynamic economy. This enables us to formulate the distinct characteristics about this process.

- Creative destruction is an oxymoron that combines two contradictory ideas – creation and destruction – that are fused together in a way that makes the concept both quite striking and quite confusing. It is a contradictory and tension-filled concept that seems to fit well with a contemporary social, especially global, world that is also contradictory and laden with tension.
- Schumpeter was primarily concerned with social processes and social change (rejecting dominant stable and equilibrium models in economics). Creative destruction can be seen as both a social process and a social change and, as such, fits well in a world that is in continual process and undergoing constant change. Such a world needs to be analysed dynamically and a dynamic concept like creative destruction is perfect for such a world.
- Creative destruction was designed to analyse economic developments, especially those that are business-related. Clearly, the economic and business worlds are increasingly paramount in the contemporary world and creative destruction is well-suited to examining it.
- Specifically, creative destruction was created to be of particular use in thinking about new economic- and business-related developments. As Schumpeter (1942: 83–84) puts it, 'Every piece of business strategy acquires its true significance only against the background of that process and within the situation created by it. It must be seen in its role in the perennial gale of creative destruction.' New economic and business developments are abound, as do many other types of developments, and creative destruction is well-equipped to deal with them.

- While creative destruction was developed in an economic context and was used by Schumpeter to think about that domain, he had a broader multidisciplinary perspective that encompassed not only the economic, but also the social and the cultural (among others). We will see that creative destruction applies not only to just economic phenomenon, but also to a wide range of social and cultural phenomena in latter part of the paper.

According to Schumpeter, the problem that is usually being visualised is how capitalism administers the existing structures, whereas the relevant problem is how it creates and destroys them. As long as this is not recognised, the investigator does a meaningless job. As soon as it is recognised, his/her outlook on capitalist practice and its social results changes considerably.

The primary task is to understand the traditional conception of the motive and functioning of competition. Economists, though late, are overcoming the obsession with price in competition. As soon as quality competition and sales efforts are included in the sacred confines of theory, the price variable is ousted from its dominant position. To this, Schumpeter annexes that it is still competition within a rigid pattern of invariant conditions, methods of production, and forms of industrial organisation, in particular, that practically monopolises attention. But in capitalist reality, as distinguished from its textbook picture, it is not that kind of competition which counts but the competition from the new commodity, the new technology, the new source of supply, and the new type of organisation (the largest-scale unit of control, for instance) – competition which commands a decisive cost or quality advantage and which strikes not at the margins of the profits and the outputs of the existing firms but at their foundations and their very lives.

To illustrate the above-mentioned lines of how the process of capitalism leads to change in economic structure through novelty and advancement via new technologies, I would like to employ the pattern and development of the mobile technologies market. Communication is essential for society to function on both macro- and micro-levels of interaction, and developments in communication technology have played an integral part in the rise of modern societies. Giddens (1999) believes that there is no single driving force behind globalisation, although instantaneous communication has had the most profound effects on society today. Giddens' work is supported by Habermas (1984, 1987) who asserts that communicative action stimulates, organises, and facilitates social transformation. The process of understanding and agreeing with other social actors, through rational discourse, allows communal plans to develop and revolutionary processes to occur.

The emergence of mobile communication has influenced the information technology and telecom industry at all levels. Licensing and frequency management have been the main regulatory issues for the introduction of mobile services. Furthermore, the regulatory design related to interconnection and tariff regulation, pricing, numbering, etc. has been important in making a competitive and innovative mobile market to develop. Due to its 'time to market' and flexibility, mobile communication has been important in offering telephone to developing countries. In the developed world, the connectivity options available have multiplied enormously. Once there was only the fixed-line telephone and people had to wait for more than six months for the telephone company to install the phone. Then, from 1990, the mobile phone changed people's way of living and communication. In the developing world, mobile has, for the first time, brought communications to many people living in remote and rural locations. Particularly, in those countries where the subscriber does not have to commit to a long-term contract, the availability of prepaid services has helped fuel the take-up of mobile. In India, the process of liberalisation began in the right earnest with the announcement of the New Economic Policy in July 1991. Telecom equipment manufacturing was de-licensed in 1991 and value-added services were declared open to the private sector in 1992, following which radio paging, cellular mobile, and other value-added services were opened gradually to the private sector. This has resulted in a large number of manufacturing units being set up in the country. As a result, most of the equipment used in telecom area are being manufactured within the country. A major breakthrough was the clear enunciation of the government intention of liberalising the telecom sector in the National Telecom Policy resolution of May 13, 1994. The entry of private service providers brought with it the inevitable need for independent regulation. The Telecom Regulatory Authority of India (TRAI) was thus established with effect from February 20, 1997, by an Act of the Parliament called the Telecom Regulatory Authority of India Act (1997), to regulate telecom services, including fixation/revision of tariffs for telecom services which were earlier vested on the Central Government. TRAI's mission is to create and nurture conditions for the growth of telecommunications in the country in a manner and at a pace, which will enable India to play a leading role in emerging global information society. One of the main objectives of TRAI is to provide a fair and transparent policy environment, which promotes a level playing field and facilitates fair competition. In pursuance of the above objective, TRAI has issued from time to time a large number of regulations, orders, and directives to deal with issues coming before it and provided required directions to the evolution of Indian telecom market from a government-owned monopoly to a multioperator, multiservice open competitive market. The directives, orders, and regulations issued cover a wide range of subjects including tariff, interconnection, and quality of service as well as governance of the authority.

Today, the mobile phone can play MP3 files and handle MPEG4 tasks. This represents a total shift in the communications paradigm. However, another striking shift or rather promising innovation has been the shift of 1G technology to 2G to 3G to 4G and further on. The first-generation mobile standards were based on analogue technology. The mobile market in this era was fragmented, where a variety of standards were developed and used in different countries. Today the analogue mobile systems are not in use any more and many countries are reallocating the frequency resources to be used by 2G, 3G and other mobile/wireless systems/standards. The second-generation or 2G mobile standards are based on digital technology.

Digital technology utilises the transmission of resources in an efficient way, both due to advances in audio compression standards and also due to advances in digital modulation technologies. Another important characteristic of the 2G mobile is the less fragmented mobile market. In the transition from 2G to 3G, a number of standards have been developed, which are categorised as 2.5G. The digital mobile phone has become ubiquitous because of the interoperability of mobile phones and low establishment costs, rapid deployment and cheap terminals across different networks and countries. Technology change poses major challenges to existing companies. It also provides opportunities for new entrants into the industry. These dynamics of change and adaptation are most visible in the telecom industry. The opening up of the market and the changes in the regulatory framework in India has created a very competitive telecom industry in India. There is always pressure on the service providers to increase average revenue per user (ARPU). The transformational nature of the mobile technology in the world makes analysis of this space very interesting. The mobile set is undergoing a sea change. From a device meant for voice communication, it is being transformed into a device that carries out multiple functions. It is precisely because of these reasons that the emerging new technologies have shaped themselves to serve both voice and data capabilities. This has implied an explosion in connectivity. However, this has also led to overthrowing of old mobile handsets in optimism and anticipation of new ones. The rapidly changing technology has reduced the expectancy and expiry date of many products as they fail to be in sync with the new technological innovations, which results in escalating consumerism. Changing mobile markets propel short-term calculations and make way for dumping waste on others, to avoid costs by an easy and unavoidable road to profit. As a result, money grabbers accumulate and accumulate, ignoring or wilfully obscuring the impact not only on workers and consumers, but also on environment and resources. They exploit the notion of 'reaching out' and 'dissolving spaces' between people through continuous shifting inventions.

As technology advances and different forms of wireless communication unify into a single piece of equipment, the blending of public work and personal privacy also occurs. Nowadays cell phones and personal digital assistants (PDA) are merging with web browsing and digital managerial software. This increases tensions in the workplace and at home when those two lifestyles reach into each other's realm. The technology of new cell phones seemingly increases personal freedom and mobility, but actually tends to take away some of those suggested freedoms. People are so committed to keeping in touch with e-mail correspondence and being up-to-date in the fast-paced commerce that they may become more plugged in and less thoughtful (Ghose 1984).

SURVIVAL OF ENTERPRISING DEMOCRACY

Thus, from the above-mentioned instance of the establishment and thriving of mobile technology, we arrive at a conjecture that capitalism sustains itself on two grand pillars which are market economy and democratic polity. But the swift market, propelled by capitalism, has sweeping outcomes on evolving democracies.

When we use the word 'enterprising' for democracy, we intend to highlight the assistance provided by the democratic system to promote and enable individuals and businesses to create, produce, transform, develop, innovate, and compete in the market place. They produce goods and services for profit in the backdrop of advancement.

Establishment of democracy was an invitation by the Indian elite to the ordinary Indians to join them in playing a new game. It is true that the invitation must not have come as a surprise to keen observers of nationalist politics in the decades prior to independence. In opposing the British rule, the nationalist leaders drew upon the most progressive strands of modern European thinking. No wonder, democracy was an article of faith for them. Besides, the last two decades before independence were marked by intensification of popular movements that gave rise to expectations of self-rule among the lower orders of society (Kohli 2001).

Democracy was not just one of the goals, it was also the principle instrument of realising various goals simultaneously. The power of a modern state, the mobilising capacity of universal adult franchise, the dynamics of competitive politics, the firm grip of a system of political institutions, and the vision of enlightened elite were the main elements in the politics-centred approach to modernisation adopted by India (Singh 1973). The colonial state had expanded considerably the boundaries of the political and had annexed for politics the crucial self-reflexive privilege of deciding what the boundaries of the political were going to be. The nationalist movement expanded it further by including within the political domain various social and economic issues that the colonial power had steered clear off. The modern Indian state was to exercise power over this wide arena and bring about a social transformation. In the realm of the economy, the Indian elite opted for Western-style development in the hope that the path to development was open to anyone who cared to step in. They may not have hoped for a miraculous entry to the world of consumer goods for everyone, but they did expect a substantial and speedy economic growth in aggregate terms. The economic goals included, a reduction in the historical gap that distinguished India from the developed world and a substantial trickle down of the gains of economic growth to the worst off. Finally, they aimed at bringing about fundamental changes in the structure of the society they inherited (Chatterjee 2008).

However, it may be useful to specify here that such a direct involvement of the state in economic sphere was not guided merely by the lofty ideals of socialism. The native bourgeoisie (the local industrial class) was also keen that the state mobilises its resources and invests in vital sectors, such as infrastructure and basic industries. The so-called Indian bourgeoisie at that time was too 'weak' to be able to mobilise such resources privately (Moore 1966). The famous Bombay Plan (originally titled 'The Economic Development of India') was drawn up by a few native industrialists under the leadership of J.R.D. Tata in 1944, in which they had called upon the independent Indian state to play an active role in laying the ground work for future industrialisation of India (Sen 1982: 91–92).

India has reasons to feel proud of its ability to work with democratic institutions. Not only have the democratic institutions worked, more or less undisturbed, over the last more than six decades, but have also played a role in shaping socio-economic and cultural life of the Indian people. Democracy is valuable not merely as a political system, it also plays a crucial role in shaping economic structures and social institutions.

In 1947, when the native elites took the reins of power from the British colonial rulers, India was not only a country torn with communal strife that followed partition, but was also a poor country. India's choice to pursue democratic system of governance was seen by the global community with scepticism and doubt. Democracies had generally been a feature of developed nations. The political elite of India were acutely aware of this fact. It was for this reason that democracy in India, at least during the early decades after independence, was always seen to be dependent on its ability to economically develop fast and improve the well-being of its citizens. Developing infrastructure for rapid industrialisation, expanding sphere of economic opportunities, providing basic services – education, health, food security – all became part and parcel of India's agenda for development. At the time of its independence from the colonial rule, India was primarily an agrarian society with more than 80 per cent of its population living in over half a million villages. Agrarian economy was largely stagnant and caste ties still played a crucial role in the everyday social and economic life.

However, the future of India and its democratic institutions cannot be understood by looking at its villages alone. Although in simple demographic terms more than 70 per cent of the Indian population continues to live in rural India, the centre of activity has increasingly moved towards the city. The contribution of agriculture to the gross national income of India has come down to below a quarter of the total.

Although the Indian economy over the last two decades has been growing at a much faster rate than in the first 40 years after independence, the momentum of growth in the agrarian economy has slowed down. With growing mechanisation, the capacity of Indian agriculture to absorb additional population has also been declining. The urban industry and service sectors have indeed been growing, but nature of their growth may not be what one would desire for the working of healthy democracy. The Indian middle class has expanded in every sense of the term, particularly after the introduction of economic reforms during the early 1990s.

While the rate of economic growth has been quite satisfactory, and some sections of the Indian society, particularly the middle classes and the rich, have experienced upward mobility, globalisation and liberalisation have not been good for everyone. The effect of stagnant agriculture and its inability to provide additional employment has produced tremendous amount of distress for those dependent directly on agriculture. The sudden spurt in cases of suicides by small and marginal farmers in different parts of India over the last couple of years has created a sense of unprecedented crisis in Indian agriculture. The fact that this has happened simultaneously in different regions of India – from Karnataka and Andhra Pradesh to Maharashtra and Punjab – has understandably made social scientists, activists, and policy makers wonder about its causes and the connection that such a phenomenon could have with the wider processes of change operating at the national/global levels. Growing obsession with the so-called new economy, information technology, media, and the urban consumers led to a complete marginalisation of the 'rural' and agrarian sector. This neglect of agriculture and rural economy has affected not only the farming communities but also the landless labourers, who because of the crisis of agriculture are finding it much more difficult to find employment on viable wage (Ghosh 2004).

Moreover in India the innovation brought about in the telecom industry (change from 1G/first generation to 2G/second generation) has blatantly affected the functioning of democracy which can be mapped through the incidence or rather the scam involving 2G spectrum. While introducing the 2G technology in Indian Telecom Network huge money laundering was revealed. In the process of 2G spectrum allocation, there was violation of rules, misuse of power, and as a result an unbelievable amount of public money was lost by the Government of India. In the allotment of license for telecom companies for 2G spectrum, massive manipulation of rules and regulations happened. According to Comptroller and Auditor General (CAG) of India, the loss for government in 2G spectrum allocation is a whooping 1,76,379 crores. The technology of 2G and 3G may still be Hebrew to most of the Indians, but the figures of scam is mind boggling for the entire nation, where for millions hunger is routine, malnutrition rife, employment insecure, social security non-existent, health care expensive and livelihoods are under threat. Capitalism and its innovative abilities to improve economies are not in doubt. It has always been argued that what is good for large corporations, is good for national economies furthering development. Gross domestic product figures inflated by phenomenal successes of the rich are often impressive. However, they conceal the poverty and suffering at the bottom of the economic pyramid.

This projected that the capitalism has both the ability to exploit labour and to impose the dictates of its class interest upon the management of the political affairs of the community; the political power of the capitalist class thus appears to be but a particular form of its economic power. The inferences are, on the one hand, that there cannot be democracy so long as that power exists – that mere political democracy is of necessity, a facade – and, on the other hand, that the elimination of that power will at the same time end the 'exploitation of man by man' and bring about the 'rule of the people'. This argument is essentially Marxian of course.

Corruption and the economic enterprising of the state necessarily challenge a value-free, purposeless definition of democracy. Although the market economy assists the transition and consolidation processes by strengthening the economic self-sufficiency of the society, the corruption in the market economy may be exploited by elites. Funds supplied by corrupt elements allow corrupt elites to become independent of legitimate financial interests and to defeat the candidates those legitimate interests support. In these circumstances, democratic procedures disguise their unaccountability to the public. This unaccountability is furthered by the globalisation of the financial capitalist economy. With the rise of corrupt political regimes, the transnational capitalist economy has become increasingly excluded from the control of legitimately elected officials.

Schumpeter in his book, expounded a theory of democracy which sought to challenge what he called the 'classical doctrine'. He disputed the idea that democracy was a process by which the electorate identified the common good, and politicians carried out this for them. He argued this was unrealistic, and that people's ignorance and superficiality meant that in fact they were largely manipulated by politicians, who set the agenda. This made a 'rule by the people' concept both unlikely and undesirable. Instead he advocated a minimalist model, much influenced by Max Weber (2002), whereby democracy is the mechanism for competition between leaders, much like a market structure. Although periodic votes by the general public legitimise governments and keep them accountable, the policy programme is very much seen as their own and not that of the people and the participatory role for individuals is usually severely limited. The democracy is frequently affected by the technological changes and innovation in the market place creating an ever altering democracy. The government which is a face of democracy is often entangled between the development by capitalism and welfare through socialism. In democracy free enterprising is allowed, which means that people or groups can have their own businesses. This can lead to rich and poor in society. Inequity in the transforming capitalistic system is given. Hence, controlling the excesses of capitalism, while showing off economic progress, is a serious consideration before mature democracies and governments. However, others argue that such controls are only possible in theory and do not work in practice. Capitalism, driven as much by individual greed and aspiration as by individual capital, will always strive to break free of controls and would seldom have consideration for the democracy. The rich, who control capital, contend that minimal controls are required for free markets to flourish. They support minimal taxation policies, reject increased levies to meet public expenditure, and oppose enhanced duties for social justice initiatives. Nevertheless, these viewpoints actually cover libertarian beliefs that governments have no right to tax people because taxation is nothing but stealing personal property obtained by merit, history, and inheritance.

Capitalists also control governments, even hold them hostage. The funding of elections by private capital mandates moderation in the election rhetoric of politicians, during their tenure in government. Consequently, most governments take up right-of-centre positions, which do not allow for taxation policies required for social justice in our grossly iniquitous world. Nevertheless, the recent collapse of many international banks, the massive bailouts required by many reputed pillars of finance for survival, and the global economic recession exposed the limitations with thriving and changing capitalist system. They documented the excesses of unregulated capitalism and laid bare the greed and intellectual dishonesty undergirding the system. Surely, a more honest conceptualisation of the conflicts of interest and biases among the rich and powerful players, who have benefited from the system is needed; the focus on the wealth created should also highlight the resultant gross inequity.

Free market arguments are always used by rich and developed nations to force open poor economies to their advantage. The conditions imposed by their banks (The International Monetary Fund and the World Bank) in exchange for credit have crippled many developing economy by removing trade barriers and reducing subsidies, which are required to protect local and fledging markets against international competition. The obvious double standards on protectionism by rich nations are never mentioned.

Economic structures should combine the efficiency of capitalism with socialistic ideals of equity and justice and the government should regulate this conception as it is the representative of the population. China has reworked capitalism on its own terms. It has showed the way in using direct government control to protect its economy, create wealth, and improve its indices of health and human development. It leads India on the indices, arguing that investing in social justice projects for the majority will provide the demographic dividend needed for economic prosperity.

CONCLUSION

Creative destruction is an inevitable process of the capitalist regime whereby the technology paves the way for new innovation and annihilation of the old existing one. However, the process does not only restrict its effects to economic structure but permeates the nucleus of democracy. As a consequence it would foster inequality in the distribution of economic and political resources in the country and generate social differences. Democracy in the long run may become a victim of this 'impending' socio-economic inequality.

The vision for better societies as contested by several national constitutions is to accomplish the collective aspiration of the masses. But in the absence of judicious regulation of the capitalist regime, the state solitarily provides to classes. Capitalism and its dynamism often disregard the hopes of the average citizen. Democratic system should seek solutions which are sensitive to the aspirations of majority, like it does in formulating and altering its policies in order to match up to the incessant innovations induced by the capitalist system.

Market economy, if properly steered and controlled may help to reduce social problems, as the first generation of Indian reforms demonstrated. The role of the state is very crucial here. The state must guide the market towards the benefit of the people. That should precisely be the role of the 'limited' state in an era of free market economy. Democracy essentially means power of the people. While civil rights and political freedoms equip people to raise their voice against governmental authoritarianism, economic freedom empowers them to protect and nurture institutions of civil society, besides contributing to the economic growth of the nation. Market economy has the potential to raise the economic standard of the people. In a country like India, where people enjoy civil rights and political freedoms, economic empowerment of the people would certainly strengthen the democratic values. Economic development of the people is meaningless without political freedom – that only strengthens the market and ignores democracy. But in the case of India, where political freedom of the people has been in existence for nearly six decades, economic empowerment of the people would further boost democracy. Market economy is all set to play a crucial role in this context in India in the foreseeable future.

REFERENCES

Chatterjee, P. (2008). 'Democracy and Economic Transformation in India'. *Economic & Political Weekly*, April 19, pp. 53–63.

Ghose, A. K. (ed.) (1984). *Agrarian Reforms in Contemporary Developing Countries.* New Delhi: Select Books.

Ghosh, J. (2004). 'The Rural Gloom'. *Frontline* 21(24), November 20–December 3.

Giddens, A. (1999). *Runaway World: How Globalization is Reshaping Our Lives*. London: Profile.

Habermas, J. (1984). *Reason and the Rationalization of Society*, Volume 1 of *The Theory of Communicative Action*, English translation by Thomas McCarthy. Boston: Beacon Press (originally published in German in 1981).

——. (1987). *Lifeworld and System: A Critique of Functionalist Reason*, Volume 2 of *The Theory of Communicative Action*, English translation by Thomas McCarthy. Boston: Beacon Press (originally published in German in 1981).

Kohli, A. (2001). *The Sucess of India's Democracy*. New York: Cambridge University Press.

Moore, B. Jr. (1966). *Social Origins of Dictatorship and Democracy: Lord and Peasant in the Making of the Modern World*. Middlesex: Penguin Books.

Schumpeter, J. (1942). *Capitalism, Socialism and Democracy*. London: Routledge.

Sen, A. (1982). *The State, Industrialization and Class Formation in India*. London: Routledge and Kegan Paul.

Singh, Y. (1973). *Modernization of Indian Tradition*. New Delhi: Thompson Press.

Weber, M. (2002). *The Protestant Ethic and the Spirit of Capitalism*. New York: Penguin Books.

CHAPTER 4

INCLUSION OF EXCLUDED COMMUNITIES: A STUDY OF LOCAL GOVERNANCE

S. R. Ahlawat

Panchayati Raj Institutions (PRIs) are vital for self-governance at the grassroots level. It provides an ideal forum for decentralised planning and implementation for development work in accordance with people's needs and aspirations. With this assumption, the Government of India made 73rd Constitutional Amendment in December, 1992. It was a landmark event in which lakhs-elected representatives in India made efforts in planning, monitoring, and implementing the development programmes through Gram Sabhas, thus making India as the world's largest functioning democracy. An important radical measure underlying this legislation is regarding the reservation for women, scheduled castes (SCs), and scheduled tribes (STs) not only in membership but also in positions of office such as Sarpanches. It has opened doors for participation and share, in power at the local level for the hitherto marginalised and excluded communities.

It is expected that the new 73rd Amendment will usher in an era of egalitarian society in place of the present unequal, stratified, and hierarchical society. The main focus of this study is to first address the question of empowerment of SCs and women. Have they been empowered? If yes, then in what sense, and to what extent? If not, why? Second, these questions have been explored not by using a quantitative or questionnaire method but by using intensive interviewing and observation, also called participant observation. This method has enabled to understand the phenomenon as clearly as possible with valuable insights in the context of Haryana state.

Haryana is known to be a less progressive state in the field of Panchayati Raj. It had introduced the three-tier Panchayati Raj system (soon after the passing of 73rd Amendment) in 1994 with great deal of enthusiasm by reserving 33 per cent seats for women. The Haryana government also committed to appoint statutory financial bodies. This statutory mechanism is yet to be put into place. The state authorities have not delegated requisite powers to the Gram Panchayats, block samitis and zila parishads.

First election to PRIs was held in 1994 with the introduction of four categories of seats: General or open, and SCs separately for males and females. Since there is no tribe in Haryana, this special category was not included for the Panchayat elections. In the Panchayat elections of 2010, 1,978 women were elected as Sarpanches of which 397 were SCs. Out of the 17,918 women elected as members of the Panchayats, 3,851 belonged to the SCs. Thirty-seven women were elected as chairpersons of Panchayat samitis, out of them seven belonged to SCs. Out of 806 Panchayat samiti women members, 161 belonged to the SCs. Currently, there are only five women zila parishad chairpersons, out of them one belongs to SC. During the elections the main political parties, Indian National Lok Dal (INLD), Congress (I), and Bharatiya Janata Party (BJP) were active. So far, four elections of PRIs in 1994, 2000, 2006, and 2010 have been held (Panchayat Bulletin 2010).

Keeping in mind the main objectives of the study, we examined the extent to which the new provisions have enabled the hitherto excluded underprivileged groups or categories, such as SCs and women, to be included in the rural power structure. To what extent and in what way they have been empowered? And if not, what are the socio-economic factors leading to their exclusion? What is the response of the dominant communities to the inclusion and participation of excluded groups? Lastly, we propose to examine and explain the impact of these changes on the social structure and ethos of the rural society at various levels.

THE SETTING

We decided to study three Panchayats in the Meham block of Rohtak District, which in our view is a fair representation of rural Haryana. The three Gram Panchayats studied were (1) Farmana, with an SC Sarpanch; (2) Samain, with a woman as the Sarpanch; and (3) Madina, with a male Sarpanch from the general category.

Village Farmana

Farmana is located at a distance of 40 km from Rohtak, towards the north, and lies on the NH 10, connecting Delhi with Ferozpur in Punjab. It is a multi-caste village having population of 19,760 people as per the 2001 Census. Village is divided into four divisions (*pannas*). Each panna represents a village within the village (Lewis 1958); Farmana Khas is the second largest village of Meham block and is divided into four Panchayats. All four Panchayats are reserved since 2010, with two having SC male Sarpanches and two having female Sarpanches from the general category. We studied Farmana Khas Panchayat headed by a male SC Sarpanch. During the household survey, we noticed that a majority of the respondents did not know how many voters were there in their house. We obtained the voters list from the block development office for analysing the caste composition and the number of households (Table 1).

Table 1 Caste-wise Distribution of Voters in Farmana Khas Village

Caste Hierarchy	Traditional Occupation	No. of Voters	No. of Households
Higher castes			
Jats	Agriculture	1,667 (66.68)	504 (72.31)
Brahmins	Agriculture/priesthood	59 (2.36)	12 (1.72)
Banias/Khatris (Aroras)	Traders	48 (1.92)	8 (1.15)
Backward castes			
Khatis	Agriculture/carpenter	263 (10.52)	47 (6.74)
Kumhars	Pot-maker	21 (0.84)	4 (0.57)
Lohars	Blacksmith	26 (1.04)	4 (0.57)
Chhipis	Tailor	14 (0.56)	2 (0.29)
Nai	Barber	28 (1.12)	5 (0.72)
Scheduled castes			
Chamar	Agricultural labour/ Shoemaking	189 (7.56)	60 (8.61)
Balmiki	Agricultural labour	103 (4.12)	32(4.59)
Sansi	Sheep rearing labour	82 (3.28)	19 (2.73)
Total		**2,500 (100.00)**	**697 (100.00)**

Note: Figures in parentheses represent percentage.

Around 87 per cent of the land is owned by the higher castes, mainly the Jats and the Brahmins. Among the backward castes in the village, only Khatis own land and a majority (around 96 per cent) of them are working as small farmers having less than 2.5 acres of land. All SC households are landless. Their main occupation is agricultural labour. The Chamars among the SCs are no more dependent on the landowners. During the fieldwork, it was observed that they had been able to achieve social mobility through education. Literacy, which among them was only 17 per cent in 1971, has risen to 43 per cent according to the 2001 Census. The significant achievement has enabled them to shift from agricultural labour to government jobs, or other non-agricultural occupations (Census 1991, 2001).

The other two communities among the SCs, namely, the Balmikis and the Sansis, having 103 and 82 voters respectively, did not achieve impressive occupational mobility. Literacy among them is less than 24 per cent.

A survey of the household revealed that 66.68 per cent voters were from the dominant Jat caste. Among the backward caste, the Khatis (carpenters) dominated with 263 voters from 47 households. One backward caste *panch* was elected unopposed from the Khati caste in 2010 Panchayat elections, due to their numerical strength. The Chamars have 60 households with 189 voters. They are the dominant SCs. We tried to examine the relationship between various castes, the notion of untouchability, the political process of mobilisation on caste lines, and the emergence of caste identity or the Dalit identity in all the three villages.

Farmana experienced economic prosperity due to Green Revolution. With the consolidation of the landholdings, use of high yielding variety (HYV) of seeds, and other inputs, the village as a whole experienced the economic gains. It was not only landowners who gained in the phase of the agricultural development of 1970s but also the landless communities such as the traders (Banias) and the SCs. The trickle-down effect was felt among all the sections of the village society (Bhalla 1974, Ahlawat 1988). It was only after the changes in the rural political economy that the Dalits could acquire certain autonomy and began to assert themselves in village politics (D'souza 1983, Jodhka 2000).

The Gram Panchayat in Farmana

The Gram Panchayat elections in 2006 gave rise to factional politics of intense rivalry between the two *pannas* (divisions). Two candidates were put up, one by Badashpur *panna* and the other by Mandian *panna*. The Sarpanch post was reserved for a woman. Badashpur *panna* was dominated by the Jats, Chamars, and the Sansis, whereas Mandian *panna* had a concentration of Jats, Brahmins, Balmikis, and Khatis. The elections created tremendous bitterness between the two *pannas*, and the old distrust and caste rivalry between Jats and Brahmins, between Jats and Khatis, and within the SCs between Chamars and Balmikis turned into *panna* hostility. Both the *pannas* had Jats as the dominant caste, and the contesting candidates were also from the same caste. Therefore, it was not caste prestige but the honour of the *panna* which became the main issue during the elections.

Rajo, an illiterate woman from Mandian *panna* was elected Sarpanch, defeating her rival from Badashpur *panna* by a margin of 89 votes, Badashpur *panna* succeeded in getting 10 members elected as *panches* in the 14-member Panchayat. This gave Badashpur *panna* the confidence of getting Panchayat decisions in their favour.

The atmosphere of hostility and distrust on a *panna* basis had an adverse impact on the functioning of the Panchayat. Lewis (1958) has discussed *panna* factions as the basis for Jat-dominated village politics. The *panna* factional Gram Panchayat politics created crisis of legitimacy for the Panchayat. The government officials took advantage of the situation and manipulated most of the decisions by taking the traditional Panchayat into confidence.

During the field work, it was observed that the traditional/customary Panchayat known as 'local Panchayat' is constituted by the elite Jat (the dominant caste) patriarchs (no women), and it has no legal standing but draws its legitimacy from tradition.

Ram Narayan, an 80-year-old Dalit and a member of the Gram Panchayat said that the new legislation has created some space for the SCs and women in the Gram Panchayat, but the parallel centre of power, that is, the local Panchayat and the government functionaries do not allow their participation in the development programmes. 'The higher caste members do not allow us to sit on the same cot in the Gram Sabha meetings', says Renwa, a Dalit member of the Panchayat. The SC Panchayat members supported the woman Sarpanch and, unitedly, voted against a no-confidence motion against her. For their support to the woman Sarpanch, Mandian *panna* gave one acre of land for the Harijan *chaupal*. This donation of one acre of land by the landowners of Mandian *panna* was a big gesture towards the Dalits for their support in the Gram Panchayat functioning.

The *panna* faction politics of the Gram Panchayat during 2005 to 2010 had far-reaching consequences for the village as a whole. During the June 2010 elections, it was not the *panna* politics but the SCs versus the higher castes. The post of Sarpanch was reserved for the male SC member. Forgetting, the *panna* factions, the Jats of both the *pannas* had a meeting to decide on a strategy. Each *panna* wanted its SC candidate be elected unopposed. Five meetings of the local Panchayat were held during April 2010 to decide a consensus candidate for the post of Sarpanch. But, consensus could not be reached among the customary Panchayat members, and it was agreed not to project any candidate on either caste lines, or on *panna* basis. Ram Krishan, an active member of the local Panchayat, commented on the decision saying, 'the local Panchayat members consisting of Jats and Brahmins realised their mistake of *panna* factional politics during the last five years of Panchayat's tenure. The fight between the two *pannas* deprived us of any share in power. This time, let there be a fight between the SCs. Why should we *savarna* Jatis (higher castes) fight? In any case, the power will go to the Dalits.' The traditional Panchayat decided to give a free hand to the SCs regarding the choice of their candidate for Sarpanch. The Farmana Gram Panchayat is composed of 14 *panches* (members) elected from various wards. Four women Panchayat members were elected from Jat caste and two from the Chamar scheduled caste (Table 2).

Table 2 Caste-wise Distribution of the Elected Panchayat Members (2010)

Caste	Farmana	Samain	Nadina	Total
Jat	8 (4F)	5 (3F)	8 (3F)	21(10F)
Brahmin	1	1	2 (1F)	4 (1F)
Bania	–	1	–	1
Khati	1	2	1 (1F)	4 (1F)
Kumhar	–	–	1	1
Lohar	–	1	–	1
Chamar	2 (2F)	3 (2F)	3 (2F)	8 (6F)
Balmiki	1	1 (1F)	2	4 (1F)
Sansi	1	–	–	1
Total	**14 (6F)**	**14 (6F)**	**17 (7F)**	**45 (19F)**

Note: F – female.

Source: Panchayat records.

For the Sarpanch elections, the fight was reported to be very tough between Dharma (Sansi) and Dayanand (Chamar). The villagers reported that each candidate spent around Rs 2 lakh for the prestigious post. The moneylenders, mainly the Jat landowners, gave money to the contesting candidates and charged a very high interest rate, to the tune of 48 per cent per annum, four times higher than the market rate of interest. Both the candidates spent money on liquor and for around 15 days both turned their houses into village bars. Free liquor offerings by the candidates eroded the notion of untouchability persisting between the higher castes and the SCs. Rajbir Singh, a 50-year-old villager reported that the higher castes and the SCs drank from the same glasses during the elections, whereas they do not take water even from the same earthen pot in their day-to-day life.

During the Panchayat elections, an atmosphere of festivity can be seen in almost the entire state. The villagers reported that the inflow of liquor assumed greater significance. The higher caste voters said, 'Before the new Panchayati Raj reservation policy, we used to lure the SCs voters by offering liquor. Now, with the reservation for them, it will be their turn to repay us.' There is common saying in the entire Jat-dominated areas,

> *Jo pilaye Desi, Uski vote kaisi*
>
> *Jo pilaye Rum, Uski vote kum*
>
> *Jo pilaye Whiskey, Sabhi vote uski*
>
> (He, who offers country liquor, no vote for him
>
> He, who offers rum, less votes for him
>
> He, who offers whiskey, all votes for him)

Political networking, during the Panchayat elections, was confined to liquor offering. It played a major role for capturing the votes. Dayanand, a 45 year old from the SCs (Chamar) won the Sarpanch election by a margin of 107 votes. He is an ex-serviceman, who had served in the army for 23 years. The SCs and the backward caste villagers had many expectations from him regarding developmental work in their settlements. At the very first meeting of the Gram Sabha, which he called after 15 days of his election, he constituted three committees. Committee one constituted of three women Panchayat members from the Jat caste, headed by an SC woman Panchayat member. Their task was to look after the welfare of women in the village. The second committee constituted of five members of whom two were Jats, one from Bania and one from Sansi caste. The committee was headed by village Sarpanch to look after the village school and village health centre. The third committee had five members led by a Khati caste Gram Panchayat member, three members from SCs and one from the Jat caste. Its main responsibility was to look after the construction work of the school building, village *chaupal*, etc. The formation of committees was perceived as the domination of the SC Sarpanch over the claim to power by the dominant Jat caste.

The eroding hereditary claim to power of the Jat-dominant caste played a major role in bringing the two rival Jat *panna* factions together. The Jat leaders of the two *panna* factions joined hands against the SC Sarpanch. The Jat Gram Panchayat members wrote a letter to the Block Development Officer (BDO). They also asked the *Bhola Nambardar* to call the local Panchayat meeting to discuss their poor representation in the three committees constituted by the Sarpanch. The local Panchayat members along with the BDO met the local Member of Parliament (MP) at Meham rest house. The MP directed the BDO to constitute the Village Development Samiti (VDS), a parallel body, to subvert the Panchayat power for all developmental works and, till then, no grant was to be released to the Gram Panchayat. The Jats (the dominant caste), who have traditionally been affluent and had monopoly over political power, could not digest the formation of the committees by the Dalit Sarpanch, whose caste people still work in their fields for wages. This created hostility and distrust between the Sarpanch and the Jat Panchayat members. The relations between Dalit Panchayat members and Jats came to a flash point when the Dalits objected to the interference of VDS members in the day-to-day functioning of the elected Panchayat.

Annoyed by their protest, Jag Ram, a Jat member of the Panchayat, called a meeting of the higher caste Panchayat members, and it was decided to 'socially boycott' the Dalit Panchayat members. The Dalits Panchayat members complained to the Deputy Commissioner (DC)-cum-Collector of Rohtak against the higher caste Panchayat members decision of 'social boycott' and directed the Deputy Superintendent of Police (DSP), Meham, to register a criminal case against the violators of the order. The district administration, the BDO, and the DSP succeeded in bringing the two parities, that is, the higher caste Panchayat members and the Dalit Panchayat members, to the negotiation table, and a deal was worked out that all the Panchayat committees would be headed by the Jat Panchayat member. The Jat Panchayat members agreed to lift their 'social boycott' of the Dalit members.

During the fieldwork, we observed that the VDS has been purposely created by the state to bypass the statutory Panchayat and also to rehabilitate the ruling party workers. The authority of the elected Gram Panchayat members has been marginalised by constituting the parallel centre of power in the name of VDS. In Farmana, VDS was constituted by the local Panchayat, consisting of Jat patriarchs, and state officials at the block level. It was formed to sideline the statutory Panchayat headed by SCs. The formation of VDS was never discussed in the Gram Sabha meetings. Signatures of the higher caste Gram Panchayat members, regarding their consent, were taken and the seven-member VDS was constituted on February 24, 2010. The SC Gram Panchayat members along with the Sarpanch reported the matter to the DC at his office in Rohtak on February 26, 2010. But, due to pressure from the VDS members, who are active members of the ruling party, the DC did not take any action, and the VDS was shown to be a Non-Governmental Organisation (NGO). The Jats combined with the state bureaucracy (BDO and others) to sideline the SC-headed Panchayat.

The Gram Sabha is visualised as the main instrument in promoting the principle of people's participation in planning and development. We observed that this has been negated in its actual functioning. The act stipulated that Gram Sabha should meet four times in a year. Dayanand, the village Sarpanch, and Ram Rati, the Gram Panchayat member, reported that due to infighting in the Gram Sabha meetings twice, over the allotment of a pond for fishing and distribution of grains among the weaker sections, under the 'food for work programme', the Jat Gram Panchayat members, in connivance with the fish contractor and the BDO, insisted that these matters should be decided by the local Panchayat or the VDS. On this issue, the Sarpanch pleaded that it cannot be entrusted to the local Panchayat, and he postponed the meeting twice during 2010. In any stand-off between the local (traditional) and the statutory Gram Panchayat, the Jats want to assert their power through the local Panchayat. Facing strong opposition from the dominant Jat caste and the government officials, the Sarpanch, now, prefers not to call Gram Sabha meetings. He said that he was fed-up with the upper caste politics domination through the parallel institutions like the local Panchayat and the VDS. On further inquiry, he elaborated that now he follows whatever directions come from the BDO or the VDS. The SC Sarpanch is reconciled to compromise with Jats, VDS, and government officers. Jats and the BDO are pocketing development funds. To survive in the village political structure dominated by the Jats, the Sarpanch has compromised with the existing system and says that in the name of developmental work the VDS members and the BDO are pocketing the money. We took the list of developmental works undertaken by the VDS during the 2009–2011 (Table 3).

On our checking the development works undertaken by the VDS, it was very surprising that only two construction works out of the 12 undertaken by them are completed because they are entrusted to the District Rural Development Agency (DRDA), said Prakash, the 29-year-old junior engineer, working in BDO office at Meham. He was vocal in stating that 70 per cent of the development works allotted for 2010 have been

Table 3 Developmental Works Undertaken by the Farmana VDS/Gram Panchayat during 2009–2011

Developmental Work	Estimated Cost (in Rs)	Remarks, If Any
Brick lining of the streets	1,50,000	
Construction of wall around the cremation ground	20,000	
Construction of cow shed	25,000	
Construction of two rooms in the school	90,000	
Earth filling work at the girls school	3,50,000	
Provision for dry latrines for SCs	1,30,000	
Provision for drinking water in the school	40,000	
Potable drinking water	70,000	
Cleaning and digging of the village pond	200,000	
Repair of cattle ghat	10,000	
Construction of water tank	25,00,000	chief minister's grant through DRDA
Construction of primary health centre	27,00,000	chief minister's grant through DRDA

Note: DRDA – District Rural Development Agency.

Source: Panchayat Records

completed. We ascertained the facts regarding the developmental works from the villagers themselves. Sewa Singh, a 35-year-old school teacher, showed us two rooms without a roof, and the VDS members claimed that they were complete. Potable water is not available in the village. It was a shocking experience that in the name of rural development, VDS members along with the officials from the BDO office are looting public funds.

Village Samain

Samain, about 5 km from Meham block, is a relatively small village, having 374 households consisting of 1,558 voters and according to 2011 Census, its population is 9,380 people. The land is mainly owned by the Jats, Brahmins and the Khatis. Around 80 per cent of the land is owned by the Jats. Among the landowners, about 76.3 per cent own less than 7 acres of land and around

23 per cent are having less than 2.5 acres (Patwari Records, 2010). During fieldwork it was realised that the non-availability of jobs, apart from the agriculture sector, is the major factor for the agrarian crisis. Ram Phal Singh, an elderly man of eighty years, commented, 'Land is not rubber which can be stretched, that is, it can't be asked to produce more and more and feed more and more people. Limited production and the dependence of people on land, the increasing population pressure,' he said, 'is the cause of all rural ills'. Like Farmana village, Samain also experienced, the green revolution. All section of the village community gained substantially through the trickle-down effect in the 1970s. 'Two castes were the main beneficiaries, the Jats among the landowners and the Chamars among the SCs', said Ram Parshad, a trained agricultural scientist from this village. Traditionally, the Chamars were working in agriculture as permanent labourers or attached labour in the form of *Siris* whose term of contract was one-fifth of the agricultural produce. The sheer hard labour by the Jat peasants and the Chamar agricultural labourers improved their economic conditions. With economic prosperity, they were able to get education. Literacy was as low as 18 per cent during 1971 Census, which rose to 59 per cent in 2011 Census. Literacy among the SCs was only 5 per cent in 1971 Census, which rose to 51 per cent in the 2011 Census (Table 4).

According to the 2011 Census, 38.7 per cent of the SCs have attained education up to matriculation. Unlike in the past, 93 per cent of the Chamar households are not working in agriculture, or as agricultural labour. As has been the case with much of Rohtak district, the Dalits of Samain too have dissociated themselves from their traditional caste-related occupations and they even avoid working for Jat farmers on the land. Their diversification into non-farm activities has also brought some prosperity and economic independence. They have been able to construct *pucca* houses with hand-pumps and modern toilets – an undreamt luxury in earlier time. Earlier, the Dalits lived in almost ghetto-like conditions outside the main village.

There used to be no drainage facilities and dirty water and other effluents would just collect on the lanes along their houses. The Dalit consciousness does not arise in a vacuum. It is only when they achieve some upward mobility that they feel that they must also get an equal share in the resources provided by the state. This fact is amply demonstrated by Jodhka (2000) in the state of Punjab and Pai (2003) in the case of Uttar Pradesh. A household survey among the Jats revealed that on an average at least one family member is engaged as a school teacher. Godhu Ram, 70 years old, ex-block *samiti* chairman, said, 'A working woman is most preferred as a bride.' He further said that the employment of woman in government jobs takes care of the

Table 4 Caste-wise distribution of voters in Samain village

Caste Hierarchy	Traditional Occupation	No. of Voters	No. of Households
Higher castes			
Jats	Agriculture/Govt. jobs	903 (57.96)	261 (69.79)
Brahmins	Agriculture	174 (11.17)	27 (7.22)
Banias/Khatris (Aroras)	Traders, petty shop keepers	33 (2.11)	7 (1.87)
Backward castes			
Khatis	Agriculture/carpenter	99 (6.35)	18 (4.81)
Kumhars	Pot-maker, Agricultural Labour	19 (1.22)	3 (0.80)
Lohars	Blacksmith	23 (1.48)	3 (0.80)
Nai	Blacksmith	23 (1.48)	3 (0.80)
Chhipis	Tailor	16 (1.03)	4 (1.07)
Scheduled castes			
Chamar	Shoemaking and non-agricultural occupation	168 (10.78)	28 (7.49)
Balmiki	Agricultural Labour and sweeping	104 (6.67)	19 (5.08)
Total		**1,558 (99.99)**	**374 (100.00)**

Source: Field notes.

Note: Figures in brackets represent percentage.

entire generation. On the contrary, we observed that woman's engagement in government jobs is only 1.5 per cent; a majority of them, that is 56.3 per cent, are engaged in agricultural and its allied tasks. It would not be wrong if one may suggest that Haryana's agricultural development and prosperity is due to hard labour of women. They are the ones who take care of major agricultural operations, besides dairying and household chores (Bhalla 1981 and Ahlawat 2003).

Samain Panchayat

The relationship between the Jats and Brahmins alongwith Khatis (a backward caste) in Samain is marked by a subtle distrust and rivalry, and sometimes open hostility. Though the Jats dominate by virtue of ownership of land and numerical strength in the village, ritually Brahmins consider themselves as upper caste and for the Khatis, Brahmins are the reference group in the process of sanskritisation. The Khatis prefer to be identified as Jangra pandits in Haryana. The Gram Panchayat elections of 2005 gave the indication of intense rivalry between the Jats and the Brahmins-Khati combine. Traditionally, majority of the Jats voted for the Indian National Lok Dal (INLD) and the Brahmins and Khati voted for the Congress. At the *Panchayat* level, the Chamars used to support the Brahmins-Khati combine faction and the Balmikis used to support the Jats. Jai Bhagwan Singh, a thirty-five year old Jat, won the election for the post of Sarpanch and as many as eight Gram Panchayat members got elected from the Brahmin caste panel consisting of two Khatis, followed by three scheduled castes of which two were women candidates. Three Gram Panchayat members who got elected were from the Brahmin caste.

Jai Bhagwan never called the mandatory Gram Sabha meetings, for the required paperwork was taken care of by the BDO on the instructions of the local MLA. An investigation into the functioning of the *panchayati raj* revealed that the people of the village regarded the *panchayat* as the private 'corporation' of the local Congress MLA. The events during the previous Gram Panchayat had far-reaching consequences for the village as a whole; no development work was undertaken on participatory basis. On paper, we found that around Rs 35 lakh was spent on village development work, but in reality nothing happened. This was reported by an enquiry team constituted by the Deputy Commissioner regarding the use of grants given to the Gram Panchayat. The Sarpanch and the Gram Panchayat members were so corrupt that the entire village lost confidence in them. The Samain panchayat's Sarpanch post was reserved for a woman in the 2010 *panchayat* elections. There was no hostility or resentment against the reservation of seats for the Sarpanch or for the Gram Panchayat members. The two dominating political faction, therefore, followed the strategy of manipulating the situation to safeguard their own interests. The Brahmins decided to support the Jat woman candidate. This decision of the Brahmins alienated the Khatis who were traditionally supporting the Brahmins in the village power structure. The Khati faction along with a few Dalit voters was still with the ex-Sarpanch, whose wife Krishna Devi was accepted as their faction's candidate for the post of Sarpanch. The atmosphere of hostility and distrust created during 2005 elections between the two dominant factions turned into bitterness towards the ex-Sarpanch. The Brahmins faction joined the Jat faction with the firm determination of teaching the ex-Sarpanch a lesson. Raj Kaur, a thirty-seven year old Jat woman, won the election by a huge margin of 730 votes. The coming of Jat and Brahmin factions together paved the way for friendship between the two caste groups who were traditionally hostile towards each other.

Samain Gram Panchayat has fourteen elected members, of which six were women, three from the SCs and three from Jats. Contesting the election in the general category three backward caste candidates were elected as members, of whom one was a Lohar and the other two belong to the Khati caste (Table 2). Raj Kaur, the elected Sarpanch of Samain, is a matriculate. She said, 'Due to my educational background, the local *panchayat* in its meeting, decided to field me for the post of Sarpanch'. Regarding the village politics, she elaborated that at the very first meeting of the Gram Sabha, the village elders who matter in the village politics, expected her not to intervene in the meeting and sit in one corner and leave everything for them to decide. She said that presiding over the Gram Sabha by a woman was the first of its kind experience in the village. She further stressed that though she was an elected Sarpanch, she still behaved as a *bahu* (daughter-in-law) of the village. She never hesitated to tackle and solve issues of women's interest. On being asked, how he felt being a woman Sarpanch of the village, she replied that she had got the power and official status, which was very important and provided a platform to solve various problems related to development at the village level. The government had done a great service by giving 33 per cent reservation to women. She, being from the dominant Jat caste, had found herself in an advantageous position. No man could defy her. Lower caste men never questioned or raised voice in her presence. She considered herself fortunate that she belonged to the Jat caste and had overall control on the affairs of *panchayat.* As regard the conduct and schedule of the Gram Sabha meeting, it was observed that though most of the time meetings were held on time, sometimes, if some government official did not keep up the date, they were cancelled at the last minute. The lack of communication between Gram Panchayat office and other officials at the block level and zila parishad has been the main hindrance, as reported by the Sarpanch.

In the Gram Sabha meeting held in November 2010, Raj Kaur put forward three proposals. She proposed to consider free school uniforms for the poor girls, a payment of Rs 1,000 to expecting mothers for meeting their delivery expenses and that the commitment on behalf of the village to honour its players, who won the medals in the international games, by presenting a cheque of Rs 2 lakh, from the fund. It was adopted by the Gram Sabha and Rs 3 lakh were sanctioned for them (Table 5). This proposal was welcomed by the majority of womenfolk. Seema Devi, a forty-five year old agricultural labourer from the Balmiki caste, received Rs 1,000 from the Sarpanch for meeting her delivery expenses. Paying tribute to the village *panchayat*, she equated the woman Sarpanch with goddess (*devi*) and said that for the first time in her life she had got the monetary help from the *Panchayat*.

Other developmental works were entrusted to the VDS, of which Raj Kaur's husband was a member. There was a long list of developmental works undertaken by the VDS during the years 2009-11. When specific questions were raised regarding the priorities of the tasks, the Sarpanch stressed the need for improving infrastructure in the school. Even if there were buildings, there were no chairs, benches or blackboards and chalk.

The condition of health centres were similar. Pregnant women do not have access to adequate health care in the village. Although Rs 1,000 is being given to the them from *panchayat's* resources in times of distress, they are shifted to nearby private hospitals, often run by quacks, where the quality of services is deplorable and there is no surety of survival. 'Everything is left to God' (*sab ram bharose hai*), one villager commented. General health services, hygienic surroundings, clean drinking water, electricity supply, *pucca* roads are some of the other important necessities, which were stressed by the Sarpanch.

Table 5 Developmental Works Undertaken by the Samain VDS/Gram Panchayat 2009–2011

Developmental Work	Estimated Cost (in Rs)	Remarks, If Any
Repair of the *chaupals*	20,000	
Construction of school wall	60,000	
Earth filling work	2,00,000	
Drainage paving	60,000	
Digging of village pond	1,05,000	
Development of war heroes park	1,05,000	
Free school dress to poor girls	50,000	G.P. Fund
Provision for smokeless *chulhas*	20,000	
Sports fund for players	2,00,000	G.P. Fund
Ring dam	1,10,000	
Water tank repair	30,000	
Construction of houses for scheduled castes	6,00,000	
Aid to expected mothers	50,000	G.P. Fund
Cleaning of street	40,000	

Source: Panchayat office records; 2011.

No doubt, the Sarpanch being a woman was more sensitive to the needs of people, especially women and small children. Her confidence, articulation and straightforwardness were visible and commendable. She was able to communicate with other officials and present the problems faced by the village in an efficient and constructive manner. Being optimistic in outlook she pointed out, 'I have got the chance to set the things right and it is a very good opportunity. I do have difficulties in solving many of the problems due to lack of understanding, communication and information, but even then I always feel I am doing better than many of my male counterparts. At least, I am spending every government penny on the development of my village and not on myself or my family.' Such revelations are relevant, especially in a situation where we do not have a history of women's empowerment.

Apart from interacting with the Sarpanch, a Dalit woman Gram Panchayat member was also interviewed. Ruldi Rani is 31 years old and an illiterate. Both husband and wife work as farm labourers and have two sons and one daughter ranging between six and thirteen years. She was asked how she felt on becoming a member of the *panchayat*. She stated, 'I am very proud to be a *panchayat* member. I could never think of it before. But since I was asked to contest and people voted for me, I am here as member'. At the same time, she was also aware of her social handicap. She is illiterate and belongs to the SCs. All this make her vulnerable and she cannot air her opinions and feelings strongly. She further stated that when one is not from the dominant caste, the task is not easy. Rather, one has to face a lot of hardships. Higher caste groups never accept a low-caste *panchayat* member or Sarpanch. What agonised Ruldi Rani the most was the fact that though constitutionally they are supposed to be at par with other caste and no discrimination is supposed to take place against SCs, but in social living untouchability is practised at all levels. Dalit Gram Panchayat members are asked to sit on the floor, away from other higher-caste members. They are not allowed to drink water from the same pot. Not only this, when some serious discussions are taking place regarding some village issues, their opinion, consent and feelings are ignored.

It was observed that the prevalence of veil (*purdah*) is there among the elected women Sarpanch or *panchayat* members in the same spirit and intensity as it is observed among the other women of the village across caste and class lines. In the Gram Sabha meetings, one could notice women *panchayat* members observing *purdah* while sitting together in a corner. We enquired about this practice from the Sarpanch of the village. She stated, 'This practice is not a matter of preference or non-preference. This has been practised over the ages. Though, we want to get rid of this, yet we are unable to do it, because whenever there is any violation of *purdah*, the negative sanctions are used by the village elders'.

Some significant observations were also made during group discussions with Gram Sabha members regarding the efficiency of *panchayats*, development tasks undertaken by *panchayat* and various problems faced by them, especially by women. In one such meeting, while issues of common interests were being discussed like price-rise, indebtedness, eve-teasing, rape, etc., certain starting remarks were made by some women. One of them pointed out that what was not openly discussed, admitted or recognised was the extent of domestic violence that every third woman in this village had been the victim. She further said, 'I know that I am not safe outside my home, but what to do when I am not safe inside my home in the presence of my own kith and kin.'

Many women who were attending the meeting narrated their own pathetic cases of beating, sexual abuse, verbal and mental torturing by their menfolk. Men resort to violence even on the smallest pretext. Wife-beating is a routine affair. One woman narrated, 'My mother-in-law provokes her son against me every time he comes home in the evening and he starts kicking me with blows till I start bleeding. This had reduced me into a mental wreck'. Several such cases of domestic violence were reported by women and this issue was discussed at length with the woman Sarpanch, who herself admitted the wide prevalence of domestic violence. She explained that, 'Domestic violence is taken as one's personal affair. I alone cannot do much about it, unless and until women themselves unite and fight against it'.

Village Madina

Madina is a large village, divided into two panchayats with a population of 20,300 inhabitants as per 2001 Census. The village *Panchayat* is headed by Sarpanch from the general category. There are 522 households comprising of 2,505 voters. Among the voters, Jats were 1,447 having 306 households followed by 230 voters and 42 households among the Brahmins from the higher castes. There are 37 households among Khatis and 181 voters, the highest number from the backward castes. There are 104 households and 493 voters among the SCs. Like the other two villages, Chamar caste voters and households outnumber the other two SCs. There are 267 voters from 53 Chamar caste households followed by 202 voters from 44 Balmiki households and 26 voters from only 5 Sansi households (Table 6).

Most of the land in Madina village is owned by the Jats, the Brahmins, and the Khatis, a backward caste group. Around 82 per cent of the land is owned by the Jats. Land ownership pattern suggests that 27 per cent peasants have

Table 6 Caste-wise Distribution of Voters in Madina Village

Caste Hierarchy	Traditional Occupation	No. of Households	No. of Voters
Higher castes			
Jats	Agriculture	306 (58.62)	1,447 (57.76)
Brahmins	Agriculture	42 (8.05)	230 (9.18)
Banias/Khatris (Aroras)	Traders	07 (1.34)	38 (1.52)
Backward castes			
Khatis	Agriculture/ carpenter	37 (7.09)	181 (7.22)
Kumhars	Potmaking	35 (7.40)	4 (0.57)
Lohars	Blacksmith	06 (1.15)	35 (1.40)
Nai	Barber	06 (1.15)	17 (0.68)
Chhipis	Tailor	05 (0.96)	21 (0.84)
Mamiyar	Banglewala	03 (0.57)	14 (0.56)
Scheduled castes			
Chamar	Agricultural labour/ Shoemaking	53 (10.15)	267 (8.06)
Balmiki	Agricultural labour and sweeping	44 (8.43)	202 (8.06)
Sansi	Sheep rearing labour	5 (0.96)	26 (1.04)
Total		**522 (100.00)**	**2,505 (100.00)**

Note: Figures in parentheses represent percentage.

less than 2.5 acres, 39 per cent have between 2.5 and 5 acres, 15 per cent owned land between 5 and 7.5 acres, 17 per cent had between 7.5 to 15 acres, and only 2 per cent owned land more than 15 acres (Village Patwari Records 2010).

Gram Panchayat in Madina

The relationship between the dominant Jat caste and the Brahmins is not marked by any subtle distrust and rivalry. Brahmins have more or less accepted the domination of the Jats due to their greater numerical strength, more landownership, and social status. The Brahmins have accepted the Jats as their 'jajmans' due to their domination in socio-economic and political sphere. Hostility arises when the dominant caste groups are more or less balanced in terms of numerical strength, land ownership, and social status (Lewis 1958). One can hear villagers of both the caste groups, i.e. the Jats and the Brahmins, talking against the SCs and particularly against the Chamars. The upward mobility of the Chamar caste is perceived as a threat against their hegemony (Ahlawat 1988). The agricultural labourers, majority of who are SCs, revealed that, 'we don't work at the will of the landlords in their fields. We freely bargain for wages as per the nature of work'. The traditional paternalistic relations no more exist between the landowners and agricultural labourers or the SCs. They have been replaced by master-servant relations. Sheila Bhalla (1981), calls it as the emergence of capitalistic relations of 'Master and Naukar' in rural Haryana.

Two factions emerged within Jat votes during the election, one supported by the local Member of Legislative Assembly (MLA) and Revenue Minister and the other faction led by Sunil Kumar, a patron of Ch. Devi Lal's Lok Dal party and also husband of Shankuntala Devi. Madan Lal, a 43-year-old blacksmith, said that 'it was not the Sarpanch election but the two big political party leaders fighting each other i.e. Anand Singh Dangi of the Congress and Sunil Kumar of the Lok Dal. Their prestige was at stake'. He further elaborated that the leaders like Bhajan Lal, Devi Lal, Hukam Singh, etc. came to the village for canvassing. Anaro Devi, a 60-year-old Dalit woman, said that for the first time in her life she was offered Rs 500 for voting in favour of a particular candidate, she refused the money but accepted one quintal wheat for her vote. Hari Chand, an 86-year-old former school teacher, was of the view that the Panchayat election of 1994, was the turning point in the village. Distrust and rivalry between the two Jat factions (the Congress Jat faction supported by the Brahmins, Khatis, and Chamars and the Lok Dal Jat faction supported by the majority of Jats, Banias, Lohars, and Balmikis) intensified to such an extent that for the first time there was a nearly complete breakdown of social intercourse between the two factions. The two factions even stopped smoking hookah together.

When the elections to Panchayat approached in March 2010, the local Panchayat called the meeting of the entire village for a consensus candidate. Not reaching a consensus among the voters in the meeting, two panels of candidates were put, one by Kartar Singh, from Anand Singh Dangi faction, and the other led by Bali himself. Since the chairpersonship of Meham Panchayat samiti was reserved for an SC candidate, Bali who was the chairman of the Block Samiti during 1994–1999 shifted from the block politics of the Panchayat Samiti to the Gram Panchayat politics of Madina village. He won the Sarpanch election by a margin of 90 votes. Of the 17 Gram Panchayat members elected, 7 members are from the dominant Jat caste, of which 3 are women. Two illiterate women of 60 to 65 years got elected from the SCs ward along with 2 male SCs members. Two women, one from Brahmin and one from Khati caste, got elected as the members of the Gram Panchayat. For the first time in the history of Madina Gram Panchayat, a Kumhar caste member got elected (Table 2). He contested the election purely on the support of the Sunil Kumar faction, and was able to get as many as 130 votes, the highest among the elected Gram Panchayat members. Discussing the Gram Panchayat functioning with Sunil Kumar, the village Sarpanch, 35 years old and educated up to matriculation, it was revealed that he became very popular among the villagers due to his guts of swimming against the current. During his Block Panchayat Samiti's chairmanship tenure and also during the current Sarpanchship, he functioned as the strong opponent of the ruling party. The ruling party created problems through the government officials like denial of government grants for development purposes or stopping the electricity supply of his *panna*, etc. He said that, 'I faced every challenge due to my voters' support'. The Customary Panchayat and the elected Gram Panchayat meet at least once a month to discuss issues like construction work, auction of the Panchayat land, fund raising for the common cause, settling the disputes, monitoring of the school, etc. He said that in the Gram Sabha meetings, the villagers discuss, negotiate, and arrive at consensus on issues of common concern. The mandatory Gram Sabha meetings, which he termed as the 'Sarkari meeting', are called by giving at least 15 days notice to the members of the Gram Panchayat where issues are discussed. We noticed, while attending the Gram Sabha meeting, that the Sarpanch in connivance with the Customary Panchayat has evolved such a mechanism that all developmental works that are government-aided are entrusted to the VDS. Whenever any issue pertaining to the government grant is announced by the Education and Panchayat Officer, the standard formulated practice is time and again repeated as 'Sarkari Kam V.D.S. Ka Naam'. All government works are entrusted to the VDS. Sarpanch nominated two women Gram Panchayat members to the VDS, which is mandatory, and he himself is its chairman. Two active workers of the ruling party Indian National Lok Dal (INLD), are nominated as the members of the VDS. Further it was observed that the Customary Panchayat along with the Gram Panchayat has evolved such a mechanism that VDS is always projected as an agency that fetches government grants. Ram Prakash, a 51-year-old active member of the Gram Sabha, said that the job of the VDS is to work independently for getting the governmental grants for the village and to keep good coordination with the Panchayati Raj technical staff who monitor the works. We observed that in one of the Gram Sabha meetings the Sarpanch invited DC of Rohtak to show the work done in Madina village. Table 7 represents the list of works undertaken by the Panchayat during 2008-2010.

Table 7 Developmental Works Undertaken by the Madina VDS Gram Panchayat during 2008–2010

Developmental Works	Estimated Cost (in Rs)	Remarks, If Any
Repairing the platform in the grain market	50,000	
Earthwork in the school	2,00,000	
Provision for drinking water in both the schools	1,50,000	
Construction of Harijan *chaupal*	2,30,000	
Playground and stadium construction	27,00,000	Half the money was collected from the village by Panchayat
Water tank construction for potable water	32,00,000	DRDA grant
Dam, earthwork around the village	–	Voluntary work done by villagers
Pond cleaning	2,00,000	Under food-for-work programme

The positive aspects of development observed are that the Gram Panchayat and the Customary Panchayat executed some developmental works on participatory basis, which was missing in the other two study villages. One worker from every household worked without wages on the ring dam around the village settlement for 15 days along with the Customary Panchayat members and the Gram Panchayat. It was a collective work which the villagers undertook despite the rivalry between the two dominant political factions in the village. All the castes participated with strong sense of collective interest which acted as a silver lining in the process of rural development. This positive aspect of voluntarism can be attributed to the good efforts of the Gram Panchayat specially the motivation aspect of the Sarpanch and the Customary Panchayat. To this aspect Sunil Kumar, the Sarpanch said, 'we have to learn how to live without government support in the shape of grants. The government aids have made the Panchayat parasites and corrupt'. Ram Singh, a 27-year-old member of the Gram Panchayat, said that their Panchayat led by the Sarpanch keeps itself away from the grant-related works, which the Gram Sabha through its resolution has entrusted to the VDS.

Another remarkable feature of the self-help concept of rural development was observed in Madina village which was initiated by the Gram Panchayat. Construction of village stadium was undertaken in 2010 with the estimated cost of Rs 27 lakhs for which Gram Panchayat collected Rs 13.5 lakhs from the village. Sarpanch Sunil Kumar organised door to door meetings with the villagers to raise funds. They were able to collect the required amount. The collected amount of Rs 13.5 lakhs was deposited with the DRDA office which directed the Panchayati Raj technical staff to get the stadium constructed. The Gram Panchayat played the role of accelerator in motivating the villagers for collective work on self-help basis.

STRUGGLE FOR IDENTITY

We conclude that the political processes which were set in motion by the 73rd and 74th Amendments are slowly beginning to make some impact on the rural power structure. It has given a sense of identity and dignity to the Dalits and the women who never visualised occupying the seats of power in the village. Their being able to get elected as Sarpanches or members of the Panchayat has forced the members of the dominant castes to renegotiate their relationship with them. We observed in the case of one Gram Panchayat elections that the dominant Jat caste and the Brahmins used all kinds of political networks to make SCs as their ally for winning the Panchayat elections. The increased influence of politics at the PRI level has led to the rise of caste-based political mobilisation among Dalits. Although caste has lost its 'moral basis' ideologically, the subjugation of the Dalits was seen to be due to their dependence on the landowners (Medha 2001).

However, despite these changes in the rural power structure, caste-related structures of domination have not disappeared in day-to-day functioning of the Panchayats. We noticed that the Dalits remain marginal in local politics, despite the fact that a Dalit became a Sarpanch in Balamba village Panchayat. The dominant castes resist the power-sharing process with the Dalits, who they consider as their clients. Further, it was observed that when a Dalit or a woman from non-dominant caste becomes Sarpanch, the dominant caste Panchayat members create the crisis of legitimacy for the Gram Panchayat. The VDS has no legal standing, but draws its legitimacy on very strong footings from the dominant caste factions. The SC women PRI leaders are sidelined by the VDS. Their opinions in the Gram Sabha meetings do not carry as much weight as those of the dominant caste Sarpanch. We also observed the domination of state-level politicians along with the bureaucrats stifling the growth of PRIs. They are the ones who helped forming the VDS to sideline the statutory Panchayats headed by the SCs. The Jats dislike visiting the house of a Dalit Sarpanch, unless they urgently need his/her favour. The SC PRI representatives are not treated at par with the higher caste Panchayat members. Despite changes in social composition due to reservation, decision making is largely in the hands of the Jats who control Panchayats with the help of government officials at the local level. Although Dalits have formal authority, they have failed to acquire control over Panchayats. The benefits of the government programmes have not been utilised by the Dalits, but the fact that the Dalits have acquired new 'opportunity and space' due to PRIs cannot be discounted. Dalit assertion does not confine itself to state-sponsored Panchayats. The traditional Panchayats use sanctions/social-boycott against SCs and women and compel the underprivileged to obey their orders in the functioning of the PRIs. The power of imposing community sanctions goes on to prove that it will take long before these parallel structures give way to modern institutions.

We observed that a few SC Panchayat members are forward looking. One Dalit member said, 'the day is not far away when we shall occupy the chairs along with the higher castes in the Panchayat meeting'. Another woman Dalit Panchayat member forcefully argued that unless they are given land in the villages, their dependence on landlords from higher casts would continue. To make the participation of women and the SCs more effective, they need to be empowered economically and educationally, so that they are not exploited by the dominant castes and government officials.

REFERENCES

Ahlawat, S. R. (1988). *Green Revolution and Agricultural Labour.* New Delhi: Deep and Deep Publication.

——. (2003). 'Sociology of Agrarian Crisis: Peasant Suicide and Emerging Challenges', *Man and Development,* 25(3): 39-43.

Bhalla, G. S. (1974). *Changing Agrarian Structure in India.* New Delhi: Meenakshi Prakashan.

Bhalla, S. (1981). 'Islands of Growth: A Note on Haryana Experience and Some Possible Implications', *Economic and Political Weekly,* June 23.

Census. (1991, 2011). Director Census, Government of Haryana, Chandigarh, Haryana.

D'Souza, V. S. (1983). 'Economic Transformation, Mobility and Social Stratification in the Rural Areas of Punjab', *PSE Economic Analyst*, IV(1).

Jodhka, S. S. (2000). 'Prejudice without Pollution? Scheduled Castes in Contemporary Punjab'. *Journal of Indian School of Political Economy*, XII(3 & 4).

Lewis, O. (1958). *Village Life in Northern India*, Urbana: University of Illinois.

Medha, K. L. (2001). 'Local Governments: Conflict of Interests and Issues of Legitimisation', *Economic and Political Weekly*, December 22.

Panchayat Bulletin. Haryana 2010, Government of Haryana, Chandigarh, Haryana.

Pai, Sudha (2003). 'Social Capital and Collective Action', *Economic and Political Weekly*, XXXVIII (14).

Village Patwari Land Records, Madina, District Rohtak, 2011.

CHAPTER 5

RIGHT TO EDUCATION ACT 2009: WILL THE LEGISLATION TRANSFORM THE SOCIETY?

Satish K. Sharma

The views expressed in this paper neither present pessimism nor tend to challenge the nature of intent and content of the Right of Children to Free and Compulsory Education Act (RTE Act) 2009. However, the way the Act agitated private-aided school organisations, the apprehensions expressed by the parents of children studying in such schools, and others making the Act contentious give rise to a need for its examination. Another reason to suspect the Act arises from the historical experience of numerous acts with deterring and punitive components enacted by the Union of India, but little is achieved as the problems continue to exist. In the light of above, two aspects of the RTE Act 2009 are scrutinised as follows:

1. What does the RTE Act 2009 envisage in legal terms, its rationale and whether certain ambiguities still remain; and
2. To place the Act in the context of social structure and culture of Indian society, the historically perpetuated social and economic inequalities and inequities, the structure of consciousness that have been institutionalised and perpetuated, further mitigated by the corporate sector through commercialisation of education, widening gap between the rich and the poor, and marginalisation of the disadvantaged and the economically weaker sections due to neo-liberal economic policies of the Indian state – a sovereign, democratic, and socialist republic.

There is no doubt that the Act under discussion is an outcome of the government's efforts since its independence and particularly two-decade-old policies, programmes, and educational campaigns. Its rationale and objectives, therefore, are welcome:

1. The directive to the government-established and government-aided private institutions of elementary education to admit 25 per cent students from the poor sections of the society reminds these institutions of their social responsibility;
2. Although it remains contentious due to the apprehensions, opposition, and even dissenting note given by one of the three judges on the Bench, the apex court without any doubt viewed it as a measure aiming at uplifting the socially and economically weaker sections of the society by extending them opportunities to study at privately owned government-aided institutions of elementary education keeping in view the tenets of the Constitution; and
3. The Act seeks to remove all those barriers including financial and psychological which a child and his/her parents belonging to weaker section and disadvantaged groups confront while seeking admission.

Given the promising rationales, it is expected that in the times to come the impact of the Act would be visible, if not in absolute terms, certainly taking enrolment of children of economically weaker sections and other disadvantaged groups to relatively higher levels. However, optimism notwithstanding, the fact remains that the Act is not only contentious with opposition from within the judicial system, but it does not address the fundamental question of political economy of elementary education, reflecting certain, intentional or unintentional, class biases, and leaves it to the state.

The recent researches have revealed that economic reasons coupled with family atmosphere are the important enabling factors. The enrolment of children into schools, to a considerably great extent, is determined by 'household atmosphere, infrastructural problems, (human resources and physical facilities) alternative sources of supplementation of household income which to some extent depends upon child going for work and earning, financial constraints, and other issues related with quality of education.'[1] The other factors that have always been significant and have become highly contentious in the recent past relate to the political economy of social and economic development, which has been anti-poor and aggravated poverty and resulted in displacement and marginalisation of the poor, farmers, tribal and other vulnerable sections of the society. There is not only a contradiction between what the Act envisages and what in reality is happening in the field of education, but the paradoxical situation also raises a question: Will the poor, despite the provisions of the Act, be in position to send his children to school? The already existing situation reveals that even if the students are enrolled almost 50 per cent of such children drop out from the schools (Raina 2012).

How to sustain the continuation of children likely to drop out, particularly in the absence of measures to make compensation for the income loss due to such children's shift from work to school or alternatives available to the families for the household works, such as taking care of the younger siblings, performed by these children?

A perusal of the Act also brings to the fore some problems. One such problem is the very use of the concept of neighbourhood schools about which neither there exist any census nor any classification in terms of their level (pre-school, primary, elementary, high and secondary, government, public, private-aided, private-unaided, infrastructural facilities, availability of qualified teachers, adequacy to admit, and other minimum facilities). In the absence of the said, to assume that there exist such schools is unrealistic foundation on which the entire structure of RTE Act 2009 stands. Most of the schools in the neighbourhoods that have mushroomed are private-unaided. Non-inclusion of the unaided private schools and the Act not providing any provisions of reimbursement of parents' claims of the expenditure incurred on the admission and fee of the child to such schools, pose further problems. In all its sincerity, the Act also enjoins upon the local authorities that wherever such schools are not in existence, the same be created so that the children are not made to go to distant places. But to talk of constructing schools and providing infrastructure, the problem confronted by the local authorities is severe financial constraints and inability to provide even the basic amenities, like potable drinking water to people. The lack of directive to the state to enter into public–private partnership in the creation of new structures with adequate infrastructure also makes one suspect the delivery of some tangible results.

There are certain technical problems raising doubts about whether the purpose of free and compulsory education is limited only to enrolment or to equip the child with modern scientific knowledge to develop scientific understanding of the society and its processes. One of the clauses stresses, 'Where a child above six years of age has not been admitted in any school, or though admitted, could not complete his or her elementary education, then he or she shall be admitted in a class appropriate to his or her age'. What about the classes and curriculum missed during the gap years? How the child would fill up the knowledge gap? Why should the child not be admitted in the class from where he left irrespective of his or her age? These questions concern with the quality and knowledge aspects of admission of a child to school and not with mere admittance. Similarly, problem arises when a child is required to move from one school to another, either within a state or outside. The Act says, for any reason whatsoever, such child shall have a right to seek transfer to any other school for completing his or her elementary education. First of all, there is problem in getting admission in other school within or outside one's state. Along with that the problem of adaptation to new environment, compatibility of curriculum, language, parents' ability to admit child, and many other such problems that are not visible at the theoretical plank but certainly arise in the practical life when children move from one school to another. In case the child is to be put in boarding school and the new place does not have those facilities, then how to manage, is one unanswered question in the Act. In other words, mere prescriptions cannot solve the practical problems or rule out problems in reality in the process of transfer. It is a considered view of scholars[2] that until the Act becomes child-centric or there exists a common school system across the nation the process will continue to be marked by numerous problems. In addition, it is a fact that the financial constraints and the psychological barriers already prevalent in the society due to the deeply imbedded structure of inequalities and inequities based on caste, class, gender, regional imbalances in development, and linguistic and cultural diversities of extreme kind are further mitigated by the limitations of the Act.

The second part of this paper places the Act in the historical context of social structure of Indian society characterised by 'extremely complex stratification system based on structured inequalities and inequities, hierarchical segmental and economic divisions based on caste, class, status and power, and above all a structure of consciousness in the education system itself and the society at large' which despite various legislations enacted as early as 1950s continues to rule the minds of the people even in 2012. With due apologies to esteemed scholars who even today look at Lord Macaulay, the very foundation of education in India under him totally disregarded India's scientific knowledge and set in a system which *produced educated class which was Indian in blood but English in tastes, in opinion, in morals and intellect.*[3] Even today, after the Act has been passed and upheld keeping in tenets of constitution, the general public expressions of the dignified people with responsible social positions react to it in adverse manner, bringing out the class biases and the nature and kind of structure of their consciousness. For instance, a Principal publically expressed, 'we are at the receiving end'. This clearly implies that their acceptance of the Act is against their will and implementation is carried out only under compulsion. Why should a Principal oppose when the school receives 95 per cent grant-in-aid from the government. The prejudices and class biases are often visible in the news media too when captions, like *Halwai Ki Beti Ne Pratham Sthan Hasil Kiya,* or *Dalit or Rikshawala or Mali Ka Beta IAS Mein,* when referring to their achievements.

Why cannot media simply mention the name of the candidate who achieves distinction? All this is indicative of the fact that the structure of consciousness that makes such distinctions and perpetuates the traditional mindset through media or many other means continues even in the schools vis-à-vis children from weaker sections or from the disadvantaged groups.

Apart from the historical follies and their legacy embedded in the present system of education, there are many questions related to the operational aspects of the Act, which have been raised and circulated in the concept note of the colloquium. These significantly pertain to the present status of primary education; existing approaches and strategies; high dropout rate; need for community involvement; quality of private schools; psychological impact on poor children in elite schools; State, its responsibility and escaping attitude; privatisation of school education; and neo-liberal education policy. The very rise of such questions suggests that despite the best efforts made during the last more than six decades, though the position of enrolment have changed in comparison to what it was in 1950s, yet there are 12.80 per cent and 7.3 per cent in rural and urban areas, respectively, who have never[4] enrolled in the elementary schools. The high dropout rate after admission is another critical issue prevalent in both rural and urban areas. Beyond elementary school, of the 90 per cent enrolled 50 per cent have dropped out which include 66.7 per cent in the rural and 33.3 per cent in the urban areas.

Such questions have also been raised, discussed, and debated by social scientists and others from time to time ever since India's independence, though with somewhat tangible results in terms of rise in the literacy rates, but certainly far from the desired. It is a truism that educating such a vast population divided culturally and linguistically, socio-economic classes ranging between extreme poverty to abundance, inequities in distribution of resources, and the dual and divisive approach to education is indeed a daunting task and could not be achieved overnight. However, the fact remains that it was way back in 1950s, the Constitution of India under the *Directive Principles of the State Policy* had made provisions for *Free and Compulsory Education for Children*. Article 45 (Part IV) clearly stated,

> The State shall endeavour to provide, within a period of ten years from the commencement of this Constitution, for free and compulsory education for all children until they complete the age of fourteen years.

Moreover, in addition to the above, Article 29 (Part III) and Articles 15 and 17 in elaborating *Fundamental Rights* clearly indicated the educational rights of minorities and the weaker sections, respectively. Given the constitutional provisions for free and compulsory education to children, the question that arises here is why did the state, after six decades, needed to formulate an Act? Has the need arisen due mainly to state's own failure to fulfil its constitutional commitments? Why does a state need an Act to implement constitutional provisions, when the Constitution and its Articles remains supreme and gives absolute power to the state? Why should the question of 25 per cent arise and why not all children, which the Constitution of India had endeavoured?

The fact that emerges from the historical analysis of the way the state went ahead with the issue of elementary education reveals the following:

1. The efforts were not focused with a clearly defined policy aiming at uniform standards of instructions and financial allocations for education. While the investments in education remained scanty, the educational curriculum remained divorced from the actualities of Indian life. Since the goal of education, right from the British times in India, remained oriented towards the strengthening political authority of the ruling class,[5] its results are visible today. Instead of academics and intellectuals in the centre stage of education planning and policy formulations, the bureaucracy and political bosses make decisions.
2. The policy assumed education was affordable and accessible to all sections of the society notwithstanding the fact that society was highly caste and class stratified, posing all kinds of social, psychological, and financial barriers to the entry of poor in general and the scheduled castes, scheduled tribe, and children belonging to the underprivileged and disadvantaged sections, especially those living in the backward, inaccessible mountains, and remote areas of the country. The Article 19, which promotes right to free economic enterprise, added commercial dimension to education, which in fact further strengthened the private education system with higher fee structures.
3. The educational efforts were characterised by dualism at the core, reflected in the two different systems of education, one meant for the elite, wealthy, rich, and the urban upper middle class, and the other for the rural masses and the urban poor. The latter, falling in the public sector with cent percent government grants-in-aid, no doubt remained a process marked by gradual and slow pace. This was, perhaps, guided by the principle *slow and steady wins the race.* No doubt, the government schools reached most parts of the Indian society but majority of these schools remained inadequate in terms of teaching staff, infrastructure, such as

> building, facilities including the minimum needed facilities – blackboard and writing chalks. The situation in the hill states spread over a vast territory in the western Himalayas and the North-East, tribal areas and the urban slums, instead of making any improvement continued to deteriorate as far as the quality of education and infrastructural facilities were concerned. In the process, the children belonging to the urban slums, marginalised sections of the society, scheduled castes and scheduled tribes, and women remained deprived; resultantly there has been uneven educational development. The increasing inequalities further added to the marginalisation of the poor and the vulnerable sections of the society. The quality of schools and the accessibility of the child to the school remain a problem due to distances, lack of public transport, and affordable private transport. Given the rising oil prices the private transport are bound to go up time and again. Although government orders that each and every bus should carry children free, how many buses stop for them when they raise their hand at the bus stands remains an unresolved question.

What the Act is likely to accomplish amidst intensification of structural inequalities and inequities due to increasing unemployment, lack of social security measures for the families in the informal and unorganised sector, the distances involved in reaching schools in the hills and the remote areas lacking effective transportation facilities for the children, and the unresolved issue *who is poor*? Whether the status poor to be determined by the Planning Commission's Rs 26 a day criteria or the declaration of Parsi Panchayat a Parsi earning less than Rs 90,000 falls in the category of poor or some other such innovative method which may be adopted suiting neo-liberal economy?

In relation to the question raised above, it is also pertinent at this juncture to view the future success of the Act in the light of end products of other legislations passed since independence of the country. The enactment of legislations, as the experience suggests, is not going to realise much until and unless other structural factors enabling education to children are adequately addressed. The fact also remains that neither there has been paucity of initiatives in the form of programmes nor the grants received from international agencies like World Bank, for universalisation of primary education or expenditure incurred in the running of various educational schemes. But achievements have been limited. When the state itself with all its might has not been able to achieve cent percent enrolment in primary schools, how can it expect that by way of directing private government-aided schools to enrol 25 per cent, the purpose of free and compulsory education will be achieved. Even projects like Operation Blackboard, headed by senior bureaucrats, have not yielded complete success. In view of which it appears that after having failed to do the needful, the Act is enacted to shift the burden to private institutions of elementary education.

It is quite admirable that the Act, according to judgment will break the financial and the psychological barriers at the time of admission. What about these barriers operating in the class room situations and the inter-personal interactions among students? Also what about the agitating parents against the entry of poor students in the class rooms of their wards and the discrimination that would flow from home? These questions remain unaddressed in the Act and even judgement on the petition filed against the Act.

Lastly, it is not wrong to point out that the much-needed will to accomplish the constitutional objective of free and compulsory education has been lacking throughout, specifically with regard to promoting quality education and educational equality. However, the implementation of Act alone is not of much significance until and unless the impediments to the implementation of the Act are adequately addressed. The solution to the problem, right to free and compulsory education in the given systemic imperfections and socio-economic and cultural biases, is a highly daunting task needing social and cultural transformation, destruction of prevailing structure of consciousness, and rebuilding civil sensibilities. The Indian state must also intensify its own efforts in this direction and enable society bringing all the children in the ambit of free and compulsory elementary education. However, given the factual realities discussed above, the question 'Will the Legislation RTE 2009 make a difference for the poor, the disadvantaged and the under-privileged?' remains unsolved.

NOTES

1. Sikdar, A. and Mukherjee, A. N. (2012). 'Enrolment and Drop-Out Rate in School Education', *Economic & Political Weekly*, January 7, XLVII(1), pp. 27–31.
2. Vinod Raina made this argument at the Colloquium on RTE 2009 held at Indian Institute of Advanced Study, Shimla, on June 13–14, 2012.
3. Desai, A. R. (1959). *Social Background of Indian Nationalism*, Bombay: Popular Prakashan, p. 145.
4. Sikdar and Mukherjee, 2012, p. 27.
5. B. C. Pal, *The New Spirit*, 1907, cited in A. R. Desai, 1959, p. 155.

CHAPTER 6

SOCIAL TRANSFORMATION AND MAHATMA GANDHI NATIONAL RURAL EMPLOYMENT GUARANTEE ACT (MGNREGA): AN EMPIRICAL STUDY

K. Gopal Iyer

INTRODUCTION

This study was undertaken to examine the process of social transformation among the workers in Ambala and Mewat districts of Haryana state. The main objective of the study is to analyse the effective implementation of MGNREGA programme during 2007–2008 with respect to employment generation; extent of percolation of benefits to scheduled castes, women, and other marginalised sections; the transparency in the functioning of the programme; the awareness of provisions of MGNREGA among the weaker sections; involvement of Gram Sabha; Panchayati Raj Institution (PRI) representatives and officials in the programme; and to suggest measures for better implementation of the programme.

Objectives of the Study and Study Areas

Given the issues identified for the study, the objectives derived are as follows:

- Study the MGNREGA-related processes adopted for generating awareness among stakeholders and for registration, issue of job cards, and employment generation.
- Assess qualitative and quantitative aspects of awareness on MGNREGA among stakeholders.
- Assess the tangible and intangible benefits of MGNREGA to the people.

Method of Study

The universe of the study includes the districts of Ambala and Mewat in Haryana. MGNREGA programme was introduced in these two districts during 2007–2008. The sampling design comprised of selection of representative blocks, villages, beneficiaries, elected PRIs, and official representatives. Mewat is one of the most backward districts, whereas Ambala is a relatively developed district in the state. The selection of blocks and village Panchayats in the two districts were based on best performance indicators of MGNREGA programme. Accordingly, two best performance blocks from each of the two districts were selected and these were the blocks of Ambala-I and Barara from Ambala District and the blocks of Nuh and Jhirka from Mewat district. A sample of two best performing villages was selected from each of the block. The actual sample cases consisted of beneficiaries (workers employed in MGNREGA programme); the PRI representatives at village Panchayat, block, and zila parishad (ZP) level; and the officials involved in the implementation of MGNREGA programme at all the three-tier Panchayat system. The actual selection of beneficiaries from each village Panchayat was based on simple random sampling method. Discussions were held with the key stakeholders of the MGNREGA at different levels of development administration, i.e., zila parishad, Panchayat samiti (PS), and Gram Panchayat level. Apart from this, the views of the local community on social audit, transparency, accountability of officials, participation of the Gram Sabha and the planning process were also ascertained. The final sample design is shown in Tables 1 to 4.

Table 1 Sample of Beneficiaries – Workers

Districts	Block	Village	No. of Workers
Ambala	Ambala-I	Sullar	**24**
		Tejan	**25**
	Barara	Kambasi	**25**
		Dadupur	**26**
Mewat	Nuh	Marora	**25**
		Namak	**25**
	Jhirka	Hirwari	**25**
		Jharpuri	**25**
Total			**200**

Table 2 Sample of PRI Representatives and Officials at Gram Panchayat Level

Villages	Sarpanch	Members	Gram Sachiv	Rozgar Sahayak	Total
Sullar	1	2	1	1	**5**
Tejan	1	2	1	–	**4**
Kambasi	1	2	1	1	**5**
Dadupur	1	2	–	1	**4**
Marora	1	2	1	1	**5**
Namak	1	2	1	1	**5**
Hirwari	1	2	1	1	**5**
Jharpuri	1	2	1	1	**5**
Total	**8**	**16**	**7**	**7**	**38**

Table 3 Sample of PRI Representatives and Officials at Block Level

Blocks	BDPO	ABPO	MGNREGA	Account Assistant	JE/SDO (PRI)	Members of PS	Total
Ambala-I	1	1	1	–	2	3	**8**
Barara	1	1	1	1	2	5	**11**
Nuh	1	1	1	1	1	5	**10**
Jhirka	1	1	1	1	2	5	**11**
Total	**4**	**4**	**4**	**3**	**7**	**18**	**40**

Note: PS - Panchayat Samiti, JE - Junior Engineer, SDO - Sub-Divisional Officer (PR), PR - Panchayati Raj, BDPO - Block Development and Panchayat Officer, ABPO - Additional Block Programme Officer.

Table 4 Sample of PRI Representatives and Officers at District Level

Districts	ADC	DDPO	MGNREGA I/ Accountant	XEN (PRI)	Members of ZP	Total
Ambala	1	–	2	1	2	**6**
Mewat	1	1	2	1	0*	**5**
Total	**2**	**1**	**4**	**2**	**2**	**11**

* Mewat was constituted on April 4, 2005, i.e. after the general elections to PRIs held in March 2005. Therefore, zila parishad for Mewat would be constituted at the time of next general elections to the PRIs. At present zila parishad, Gurgaon consists of area of Mewat District. *Note:* ZP, Zila Parishad, ADC - Additional Deputy Commissioner, DDPO - District Development and Panchayat Officer, XEN - Executive Engineer, APO - Assistant Panchayat Officer, PR - Panchayati Raj.

The final sample included 200 workers; 44 PRI representatives (including sarpanches, panches, members of PS, and ZP); and 45 officials/officers at Panchayat, block, and district level.

Data Collection and Tools

The data collection consisted of both secondary and primary sources. The secondary sources included district census, *Haryana Statistical Handbook*, and district, block, and village level records and statistics; the primary sources included structured interview schedules, case studies, focused group interviews, and observational methods.

Analytical Framework

Having elicited information on various issues and variables that play a vital role in implementation of MGNREGA and its spin-off effects, along with the implementation and facilitating issues, the analytical framework of the study is shown in Table 5.

Table 5 Variables and Issues of MGNREGA

	Variable	Issues
Impact	• Participation of poor/people in development • Responsive delivery systems	• Right to work • Right to information • Decline in intensity of incidence of poverty • Citizen-centric governance
Effect	• Actual employment vs. 100 man-days guaranteed employment • Improved working relations among local institutions • Social audit of MGNREGA	• Aspects related to migration in search of work • Sensitised institutions and delivery systems • Decline in unemployment • Transparency and accountability
Output	• Quantum of employment days; minimum wages • Suitability of plans • Interest generated among stakeholders • Field interaction by officials • Implementation mechanism (physical/administration)	• Demand for employment at family level • Information network and process of dissemination • Suitability of procedures • Adequacy of institutions and networking

	Variable	Issues
Input	• Role of institutions • Social and economic background of workers • Need assessment	• Level of awareness • Preferred medium for disseminating information • Participation of community • Link between projects and causes of poverty

SOCIAL PROFILE OF WORKERS AND THEIR AWARENESS AND EFFECTIVENESS OF MGNREGA PROGRAMME

In this section, the social profile of sampled workers ($N = 200$) from all the eight villages of Ambala and Mewat districts has been analysed. Two blocks (Ambala-I and Barara from Ambala District and Nuh and Ferozpur Jhirka from Mewat District) were selected for sample and two villages were selected from each block. From each village, 25 workers who were employed in MGNREGA programme were selected by adopting the method of systematic random sampling (every third or fifth worker was selected from the muster rolls depending on their numbers). The social profile includes their age, gender, caste, land holding, occupation, income, and other associated characteristics. Table shows the number of workers selected from different villages for the study.

Besides this, in this chapter the opinion and views of the workers on their awareness of different components of the programme, payment of wages, transparency and accountability, mandatory facilities, impact of MGNREGA on local wages, usefulness of the work undertaken, and the effectiveness of MGNREGA programme have been analysed.

SOCIAL PROFILE OF SAMPLED WORKERS IN AMBALA AND MEWAT DISTRICTS

Age of Workers

The average age of workers in the overall sample of MGNREGA beneficiaries in Ambala and Mewat districts was 37.53 years, indicative of the productive age group. The average age was marginally higher in the villages of Ambala District (39.55 years) as compared to Mewat (35.51 years) (Table 6).

Table 6 Mean and Standard Deviation of the Workers' Age

Village	Mean	SD	Block	Mean	District	Mean
Sullar	42.67	16.96	Ambala-I	40.96	Ambala	39.55
Tejan	39.32	14.29				
Kambasi	42.80	13.34	Barara	38.20		
Dadupur	33.77	12.01				
Marora	34.12	10.71	Nuh	36.60	Mewat	35.51
Namak	39.08	9.82				
Hirwari	34.84	10.13	Jhirka	34.42		
Jharpuri	34.00	8.70				
Total	**37.53**	**12.55**		**37.53**		**37.53**

Graph 1 Mean of the Workers Age

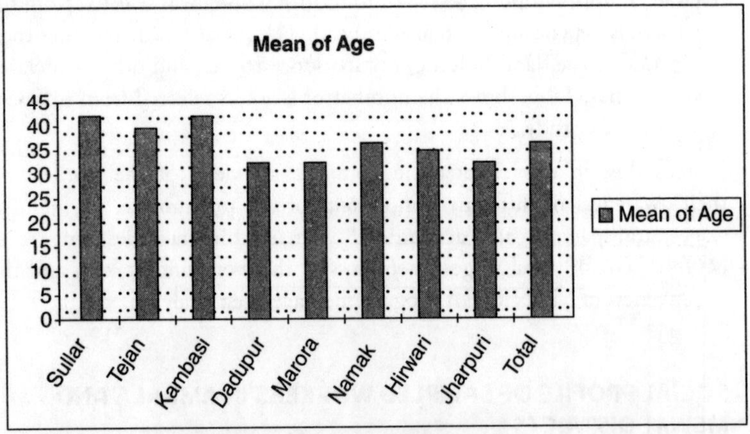

X-Axis represents age & Y-Axis represents village

The block-wise position also confirms the above observation, which shows that the average age is higher in the two blocks of Ambala District (40.96 and 38.20 years) as compared to those in the Mewat District (36.60 and 34.42 years). The average age was highest for Ambala-I block (40.96 years). The overall age range of sample is 18 to 75 years.

Gender of Workers

Of the total 200 sample workers, 68.50 per cent were males and rest 31.50 per cent were females (Table 7). The participation of women workers was higher in Ambala District (41 per cent) as compared to Mewat District (22 per cent). The highest participation of women workers was in Barara block (46 per cent) followed by Ambala-I (36 per cent). The lowest participation of female workers was in Jhirka (18 per cent) followed by Nuh (26 per cent). Village-wise highest participation was in village Kambasi (52 per cent) of Barara block and the lowest was in village Namak (16 per cent) of Nuh block.

Table 7 Gender of Workers at Panchayat Level

District	Block	Village	Male	Female	Total
Ambala	Ambala-I	Sullar	15	9	**24**
		Tejan	16	9	**25**
	Barara	Kambasi	12	13	**25**
		Dadupur	16	10	**26**
Mewat	Nuh	Marora	20	5	**25**
		Namak	17	8	**25**
	Jhirka	Hirwari	21	4	**25**
		Jharpuri	20	5	**25**
Total			**137**	**63**	**200**

Graph 2 Gender Distribution of Sample Workers – Village-wise

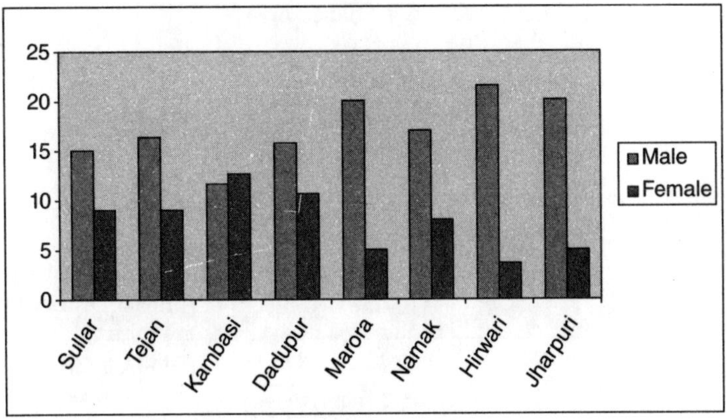

X-Axis represents gender & Y-Axis represents village

Caste Status

There is a significant difference in the caste composition of workers in the two districts. In the Ambala District, scheduled caste workers were predominant (72 per cent), and in Mewat District, other backward class (OBC) workers were overwhelming (97 per cent), who were invariably Muslims. The highest percentage of scheduled castes in sampled villages was in Dadupur (24 per cent) and Kambasi (21 per cent) of Barara block. In the overall sample, only 3 per cent were from general castes. This again substantiates the fact that the benefits of employment in MGNREGA programme were availed mainly by the marginalised and vulnerable sections (Table 8).

Table 8 Caste Status of Workers

District	Block	Village	SC	OBC	General	Total
Ambala	Ambala-I	Sullar	15	9	–	**24**
		Tejan	12	11	2	**25**
	Barara	Kambasi	21	2	2	**25**
		Dadupur	24	1	1	**26**
Mewat	Nuh	Marora	–	25	–	**25**
		Namak	–	25	–	**25**
	Jhirka	Hirwari	–	24	1	**25**
		Jharpuri	2	23	–	**25**
Total			**74**	**120**	**6**	**200**

Graph 3 Caste Status of Workers in Studied Area

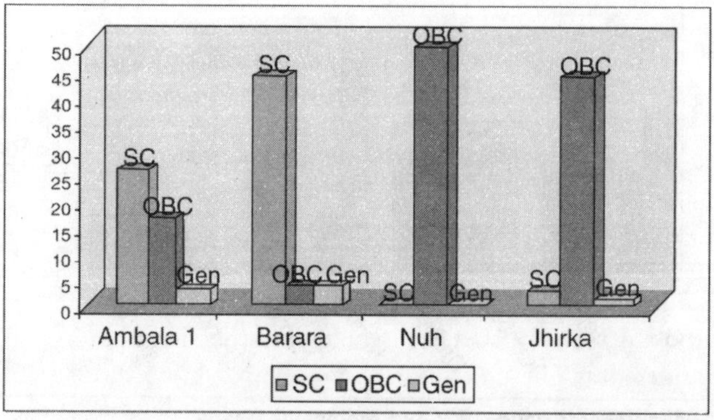

X-Axis represents caste status and Y-Axis represents studied blocks

Adult Males and Females in the Worker's Households

The overall sample data indicate that 68 per cent of the households had one male adult member, 18.5 per cent had two adult members, 8.5 per cent had three adult members, 1.5 per cent had four adult members, and 3.5 per cent households had no adult members (Table 9). Thus majority of the households had one adult member and 27 per cent had two to three adult members. Similarly, 82 per cent households had one adult female member, 13.5 per cent had two, 3.5 per cent had three, and only 1 per cent household had no female adult member (Table 10).

Table 9 Household Size Adult Males

District	Block	Village	0	1	2	3	4	Total
Ambala	Ambala-I	Sullar	–	9	10	5	–	**24**
		Tejan	–	18	4	3	–	**25**
	Barara	Kambasi	2	12	6	5	–	**25**
		Dadupur	1	16	6	1	2	**26**
Mewat	Nuh	Marora	–	20	2	3	–	**25**
		Namak	3	21	1	–	–	**25**
	Jhirka	Hirwari	–	20	4	–	1	**25**
		Jharpuri	1	20	4	–	–	**25**
Total			**7**	**136**	**37**	**17**	**3**	**200**

Table 10 Household Size Adult Females

District	Block	Village	0	1	2	3	Total
Ambala	Ambala-I	Sullar	1	15	5	3	**24**
		Tejan	–	17	6	2	**25**
	Barara	Kambasi	–	20	4	1	**25**
		Dadupur	–	20	6	–	**26**
Mewat	Nuh	Marora	–	22	2	1	**25**
		Namak	–	24	1	–	**25**
	Jhirka	Hirwari	1	23	1	–	**25**
		Jharpuri	–	23	2	–	**25**
Total			**2**	**164**	**27**	**7**	**200**

The number of male adults is slightly more than female adults. For the purpose of MGNREGA, households with one male and female adult are considered as one unit for 100 days employment; households with more than one male/one female have to be considered as a separate unit for MGNREGA.

Occupational Status

In the overall sample, cultivators were only 2.5 per cent, agricultural labourers were 20 per cent, non-agricultural labourers were 75 per cent, and the rest 2.5 per cent were artisans (Table 11). This pattern was consistent in all eight village Panchayats. This again reinforces the fact that the employment in MGNREGA programme was exclusively availed by the labouring population consisting of 95 per cent of the sample cases.

Table 11 Occupational status in the studied villages

District	Block	Village	Cultivator	Agriculture Labour	Non-Agriculture Labour	Artisan	Total
Ambala	Ambala-I	Sullar	0	5 (20.8)	19 (79.2)	0	**24**
		Tejan	0	2 (8.0)	21 (84.0)	2 (8.0)	**25**
	Barara	Kambasi	0	1(4.0)	24 (92.0)	0	**25**
		Dadupur	2 (7.7)	11 (42.3)	10 (38.5)	3 (11.5)	**26**
Mewat	Nuh	Marora	2 (8.0)	2 (8.0)	21 (84.0)	0	**25**
		Namak	0	3 (12.0)	22 (88.0)	0	**25**
	Jhirka	Hirwari	1 (4.0)	3 (12.0)	21 (84.0)	0	**25**
		Jharpuri	0	13 (52.0)	12 (48.0)	0	**25**
Total			**5 (2.5)**	**40 (20.0)**	**150 (74.5)**	**5 (2.5)**	**200**

Note: Figures in parentheses represent percentage.

Children in the Sample Households

The respective position of number of children per household is shown in Table 12.

Table 12 Number of children per household

No. of Children (per HH)	Ambala (No. of HH)	Mewat (No. of HH)
0	23	8
1	18	4
2	36	9
3	19	15
4	1	10
5	2	20

Contd...

...Cont'd

No. of Children (per HH)	Ambala (No. of HH)	Mewat (No. of HH)
6	0	9
7	0	5
8	1	8
9	0	7
10	0	4
11	0	1
	100	**100**

Graph 4 Districts and Number of Children per Household

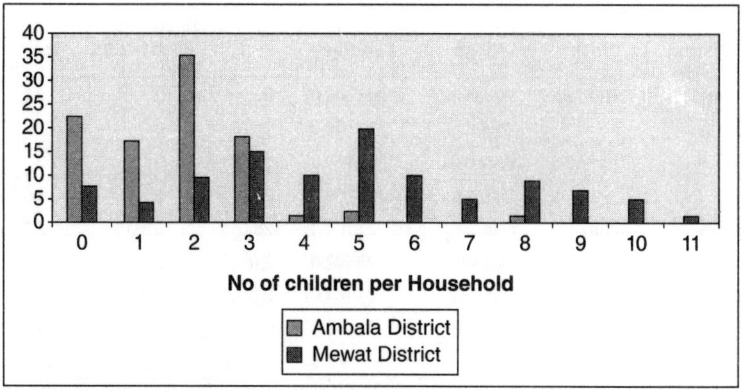

X Axis-Number of Household
Y Axis-Number of Children

There is a distinct pattern of number of children among the workers' households in Ambala and Mewat districts. The number of children per household in Ambala District range from one to five, while in Mewat District it ranges from 1 to 11. The majority of households in villages of Ambala District consist of scheduled castes, whereas in Mewat District it is overwhelmingly Muslims. This indicates that the number of children among the scheduled castes is lower than Muslims. In the Ambala District, 23 per cent of the households had no children, 73 per cent had between one and three children, and 3 per cent had between four and five children. In the Mewat District, 8 per cent of the households had no children, 28 per cent had between one and three children, 30 per cent between four and five children, and 34 per cent had larger number of children, i.e. ranging from 6 to 11 children. Thus workers in Mewat District had more children per household as compared to Ambala District.

Landholding Status

In the overall sample, 93.5 per cent are landless, 4.5 per cent have less than one acre, and only 2 per cent have between 1 and 2.5 acres in the studied villages (Table 13). It shows that overwhelming proportion of workers is landless and the rest have marginal holdings. It again reinforces the earlier observation that the beneficiaries of MGNREGA in both the districts are overwhelmingly belonging to weaker section landless households.

Table 13 Landholding Status (in Acres)

District	Block	Village	Landless	1	1.01–2.50	Total
Ambala	Ambala-I	Sullar	24 (100.0)	0	0	**24**
		Tejan	25 (100.0)	0	0	**25**
	Barara	Kambasi	25 (100.0)	0	0	**25**
		Dadupur	26 (100.0)	0	0	**26**
Mewat	Nuh	Marora	21 (84.0)	28.0%	2 (8.0)	**25**
		Namak	23 (92.0)	2 (8.0)	0	**25**
	Jhirka	Hirwari	21 (84.0)	2 (8.0)	2 (8.0)	**25**
		Jharpuri	22 (88.0)	3 (12.0)	0	**25**
			187 (93.5)	**9 (4.5)**	**4 (2.0)**	**200**

Note: Figures in parentheses represent percentage.

Economic Status (Annual Income)

In the overall sample, 82.50 per cent of the households have annual income of less than Rs 25,000 per annum and the remaining 17.50 per cent have annual income ranging from Rs 25,000 to Rs 60,000 (Table 14). The income level indicates that majority of the beneficiaries are below poverty line. This reinforces consistently that the workers in MGNREGA employment are vulnerable under several indicators, namely, labourers, landlessness, below poverty line, and lowest caste status. MGNREGA programme in Haryana thus amply substantiates that the beneficiaries of MGNREGA have been from the economically and socially vulnerable groups who have availed the benefits under this programme. It may further be pointed out that 16.5 per cent have annual income below Rs 15,000, 66 per cent between Rs 15,001

Table 14 Economic Status: Annual Income during 2006–2007

Village	< Rs 5,000	Rs 5,001–10,000	Rs 10,001–15,000	Rs 15,001–20,000	Rs 20,001–25,000	Rs 25,001–40,000	Rs 40,001–60,000	Rs 60,001 & Above	Total
Sullar	0	6	3	1	10	4	0	0	**24**
Tejan	1	5	2	0	13	3	1	0	**25**
Kambasi	1	3	1	1	10	6	3	0	**25**
Dadupur	0	0	0	9	9	6	1	1	**26**
Marora	0	0	0	8	15	2	0	0	**25**
Namak	0	3	7	9	6	0	0	0	**25**
Hirwari	0	0	1	9	10	5	0	0	**25**
Jharpuri	0	0	0	7	15	3	0	0	**25**
Total	**2**	**17**	**14**	**44**	**88**	**29**	**5**	**1**	**200**

Graph 5 Annual Family Income in the Studied Villages

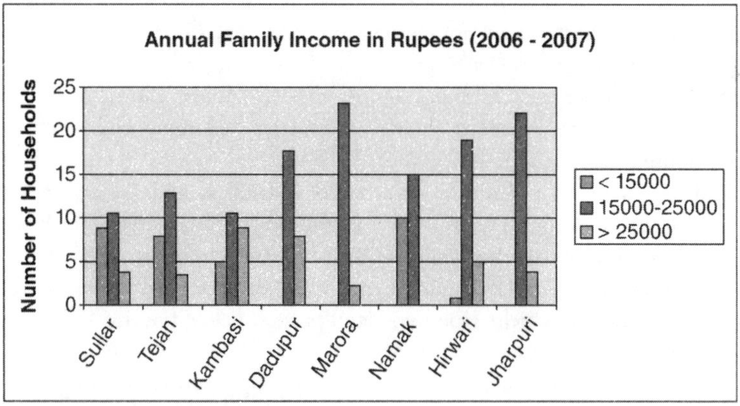

X-Axis denotes studied villages
Y-Axis denotes number of households

and Rs 25,000, and the remaining 17.5 per cent have annual income of more than Rs 25,000 per annum. This further validates the point that 38.5 per cent of the beneficiaries are absolutely poor, another 44 per cent are just below poverty line, and 17.5 per cent just above poverty line.

Features of the Social Profiles of Workers

1. The average age of workers in the overall sample of MGNREGA beneficiaries in Ambala and Mewat districts was 37.53 years.
2. Of the total 200 sample workers, 68.50 per cent were males and 31.50 per cent were females.
3. The participation of women workers was higher in Ambala District (41 per cent) as compared to Mewat District (22 per cent).
4. There is significant difference in the caste composition of workers in the two districts. In Ambala District, SC workers were predominant (72 per cent) and in Mewat District, OBC workers were overwhelming (97 per cent), who were invariably Muslims.
5. The majority of the HHs had one adult member and 27 per cent had two to three adult members.
6. Similarly, 82 per cent households had one adult female member, 13.5 per cent had two, 3.5 per cent had three, and only 1 per cent household had no female adult member.
7. The number of male adults is slightly more than female adults.
8. In the overall sample, cultivators were only 2.5 per cent, agricultural labourers 20 per cent, non-agricultural labourers 75 per cent, and the rest 2.5 per cent were artisans.
9. The number of children among the scheduled castes is lower than Muslims. Muslims in Mewat District had more children per household.
10. Overwhelming proportion of workers is landless and the rest have marginal holdings. The income level indicates that majority of the beneficiaries are below poverty line. This reinforces consistently that the workers in MGNREGA employment are under several indicators of vulnerability, namely, labourers, landlessness, below poverty line, and lowest caste status.
11. MGNREGA programme in Haryana thus amply substantiates that the beneficiaries of MGNREGA have been from the economically and socially vulnerable groups who have availed the benefits under this programme.

AWARENESS OF MGNREGA PROGRAMME

Awareness of Entitlement

The workers were asked about the provision in MGNREGA, e.g., on entitlements, 100 days guaranteed employment, unemployment allowance, wages to be paid if work is given beyond 5 km, time limit for providing employment after submission of application, etc. Their responses to these items are shown in tables below.

Table 15 Are You Aware of Entitlements under MGNREGA

District	Block	Village	Yes	%	No	%	Total
Ambala	Ambala-I	Sullar	20	83.33	4	16.67	**24**
		Tejan	16	64.00	9	36.00	**25**
	Barara	Kambasi	16	64.00	9	36.00	**25**
		Dadupur	8	30.77	18	69.23	**26**
Mewat	Nuh	Marora	5	20.00	20	80.00	**25**
		Namak	1	4.00	24	96.00	**25**
	Jhirka	Hirwari	0	0.00	25	100.00	**25**
		Jharpuri	0	0.00	25	100.00	**25**
Total			**66**	**33.00**	**134**	**67.00**	**200**

In the overall sample, only 33 per cent are aware of various entitlements under MGNREGA and the remaining 67 per cent are not aware of the entitlements indicating a low level of awareness. The awareness is higher relatively in the villages of Ambala District (60 per cent) and extremely low in the villages of Mewat District (6 per cent). Even in Ambala District, awareness is higher in villages (73.47 per cent) of Ambala-I block as compared to Barara block (47.06 per cent); the awareness is marginally higher in the village of Kambasi and relatively low in the village of Dadupur. In Mewat District, the awareness level is extremely low as only 6 per cent are aware of the MGNREGA programme. This indicates that the awareness campaign at the grassroots Panchayat level is an important requirement in both the districts but much more so in the villages of Mewat District.

Awareness about 100 Days Employment

The awareness of 100 days of guaranteed employment under MGNREGA is known to 75 per cent respondents which is one of the most important provisions in MGNREGA. Awareness on this item is higher in villages of Mewat District (83 per cent) as compared to villages of Ambala District (66 per cent) (Table 16). The relatively low awareness is witnessed particularly in village Tejan (56 per cent) of Ambala-I block and village Namak (40 per cent) block of Mewat District. However, awareness of this entitlement of 100 days of guaranteed employment is also one of the key ingredients of entitlements under MGNREGA.

Table 16 Maximum Number of Days of Guaranteed Employment (100 Days)

District	Block	Village	Yes	%	No	%	Total
Ambala	Ambala-I	Sullar	17	70.83	7	29.17	**24**
		Tejan	14	56.00	11	44.00	**25**
	Barara	Kambasi	16	64.00	9	36.00	**25**
		Dadupur	19	73.08	7	26.92	**26**
Mewat	Nuh	Marora	24	96.00	1	4.00	**25**
		Namak	10	40.00	15	60.00	**25**
	Jhirka	Hirwari	25	100.00	–	0.00	**25**
		Jharpuri	24	96.00	1	4.00	**25**
Total			**149**	**74.50**	**51**	**25.50**	**200**

Awareness about Unemployment Allowances

The MGNREGA programme provides that on demand from the villagers employment should be made available to them within 15 days, and in case of default, the workers are entitled for unemployment allowance (Table 17). Overwhelming proportion of the village people are not aware that employment should be provided to them within 15 days of demand. This is an important directive to which people must be made aware.

Table 17 Unemployment Allowance: Awareness

District	Block	Village	Yes	%	No	%	Total
Ambala	Ambala-I	Sullar	3	12.50	21	87.50	**24**
		Tejan	0	0.00	25	100.00	**25**
	Barara	Kambasi	0	0.00	25	100.00	**25**
		Dadupur	2	7.69	24	92.31	**26**
Mewat	Nuh	Marora	1	4.00	24	96.00	**25**
		Namak	0	0.00	25	100.00	**25**
	Jhirka	Hirwari	0	0.00	25	100.00	**25**
		Jharpuri	0	0.00	25	100.00	**25**
Total			**6**	**3.00**	**194**	**97.00**	**200**

Over 97 per cent of the respondents are not aware that they are entitled for unemployment allowance if employment is not provided to them within 15 days.

Graph 6 Do Workers Know about Unemployment Allowance

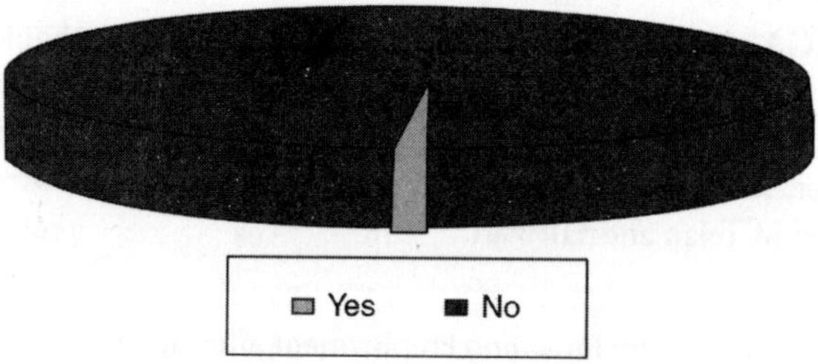

Awareness of Wage Rates if Work is Given beyond Five Kilometres

MGNREGA programme provides that the minimum wages should be paid for works undertaken within the village boundary and if it exceeds five kilometres than 10 per cent more wages has to be given to the workers. The data indicate that there is very low awareness with respect to the provision of 10 per cent more wages in case the work is undertaken beyond 5 km of the village boundary (Table 18). Overwhelming proportion of 94 per cent respondents are not aware of this provision. This low awareness is uniformly shared across all the eight sampled villages and accordingly it can be surmised that low awareness with respect to this provision would be widely prevalent in both the districts.

Table 18 Wages to be Paid if Work is Given beyond Five Kilometres (10 Per Cent More): Awareness

District	Block	Village	Yes	%	No	%	Total
Ambala	Ambala-I	Sullar	2	8.33	22	91.67	**24**
		Tejan	3	12.00	22	88.00	**25**
	Barara	Kambasi	4	16.00	21	84.00	**25**
		Dadupur	4	15.38	22	84.62	**26**
Mewat	Nuh	Marora	0	0.00	25	100.00	**25**
		Namak	0	0.00	25	100.00	**25**
	Jhirka	Hirwari	0	0.00	25	100.00	**25**
		Jharpuri	0	0.00	25	100.00	**25**
Total			**13**	**6.50**	**187**	**93.50**	**200**

Awareness about Time Limit for Providing Employment after Application

MGNREGA programme provides that the employment should be provided to the workers within 15 days of submission of application and 76.5 per cent of the workers are not aware of this provision (Table 19). The low awareness is equally shared in all the villages of the two districts except the villages of Tejan and Hirwari.

Table 19 Time Limit for Providing Employment after Application (within 15 Days): Awareness

District	Block	Village	Yes	%	No	%	Total
Ambala	Ambala-I	Sullar	3	12.50	21	87.50	**24**
		Tejan	12	48.00	13	52.00	**25**
	Barara	Kambasi	5	20.00	20	80.00	**25**
		Dadupur	4	15.38	22	84.62	**26**
Mewat	Nuh	Marora	4	16.00	21	84.00	**25**
		Namak	6	24.00	19	76.00	**25**
	Jhirka	Hirwari	10	40.00	15	60.00	**25**
		Jharpuri	3	12.00	22	88.00	**25**
Total			**47**	**23.50**	**153**	**76.50**	**200**

Time Limit for Payment of Wages

Over 55 per cent of the workers were not aware of this provision that wages should be paid within 15 days (Table 20). The awareness level of workers was relatively better in two villages, namely, Jharpuri (Mewat) (84 per cent) and Tejan (Ambala) (60 per cent). Thus on the provisions of awareness of MGNREGA programme, the workers were relatively better aware of entitlements to 100 days of guaranteed employment and to some extent about the time limit of payment of wages within 15 days. The awareness was quite low with respect to important provisions, e.g. entitlement to unemployment allowance, 10 per cent more wages if work is given beyond 5 km, providing employment within 15 days of submission of application, and time limit for payment of wages within 15 days. The low awareness to these important entitlements would have its impact on lower effectiveness of MGNREGA programme.

Table 20 Time Limit for Payment of Wages (15 Days): Awareness

District	Block	Village	Yes	%	No	%	Total
Ambala	Ambala-I	Sullar	9	37.50	15	62.50	**24**
		Tejan	15	60.00	10	40.00	**25**
	Barara	Kambasi	9	36.00	16	64.00	**25**
		Dadupur	4	15.38	22	84.62	**26**
Mewat	Nuh	Marora	9	36.00	16	64.00	**25**
		Namak	10	40.00	15	60.00	**25**
	Jhirka	Hirwari	12	48.00	13	52.00	**25**
		Jharpuri	21	84.00	4	16.00	**25**
Total			**89**	**44.50**	**111**	**55.50**	**200**

Awareness about RTI Act

There is total lack of awareness about RTI Act amongst the workers (Table 21). This is a very important tool provided to the people for asserting their rights and entitlements. The low awareness of several MGNREGA provisions along with complete lack of awareness of RTI Act would lead to low effectiveness of MGNREGA programme.

Transparency, Accountability, and Elimination of Corruption

MGNREGA programme stresses on transparency, e.g., retention of job cards with workers (both during work and after work), entries in job cards of day-to-day employment provided and wages paid, and other connected aspects. The workers responses were also elicited on some of these items whose responses have been analysed here.

Table 21 Awareness regarding RTI

District	Block	Village	Yes	%	No	%	Total
Ambala	Ambala-I	Sullar	1	4.17	23	95.83	**24**
		Tejan	1	4.00	24	96.00	**25**
	Barara	Kambasi	–	0.00	25	100.00	**25**
		Dadupur	–	0.00	26	100.00	**26**
Mewat	Nuh	Marora	1	4.00	24	96.00	**25**
		Namak	–	0.00	25	100.00	**25**
	Jhirka	Hirwari	–	0.00	25	100.00	**25**
		Jharpuri	–	0.00	25	100.00	**25**
Total			**3**	**1.50**	**197**	**98.50**	**200**

Job Cards of the Workers

The data provide a very critical information that only 16.28 per cent of the workers are keeping the job cards with themselves and the remaining 83.72 per cent of the job cards are invariably kept with the Sarpanch or rozgar sahayak (Table 22). However, in our field work the workers did not complaint of manipulation or corruption in view of job cards remaining with the Sarpanch or rozgar sahayak. The usual reply is that the rozgar sahayak and Sarpanch need the job cards for feeding the data in the computer. However, this aspect needs to be monitored closely by the officials and the workers also need to be made aware of this right.

Table 22 Job Card Holders in the Studied Blocks

Block	Village	Self	%	Sar-panch	%	Rojgar Sahayak	%	Total
Ambala-1	Sullar	–	0.00	23	95.83	1	4.17	**24**
	Tejan	–	0.00	12	48.00	13	52.00	**25**
Barara	Kambasi	16	64.00	5	20.00	4	16.00	**25**
	Dadupur	1	4.00	24	96.00	1	4.00	**25**
Nuh	Marora	4	19.05	21	100.00	–	0.00	**21**
	Namak	7	38.89	18	100.00	–	0.00	**18**
Jhirka	Hirwari	–	0.00	25	100.00	–	0.00	**25**
	Jharpuri	–	0.00	25	100.00	–	0.00	**25**
Total		**28**	**16.28**	**153**	**88.95**	**19**	**11.05**	**172**

Expenditure Incurred for Getting Job Cards

There is overwhelming satisfactory response to incurring expenditure for getting job cards, as 98.5 per cent of the workers have stated that they did not have to incur any expenditure for getting job card (Table 23). This makes the whole system transparent. The usual complaints of corruption in the implementation of rural development programmes have not been witnessed in case of MGNREGA programme. This is indeed a great silver lining in the light of overall prevalence of corruption in public life in India.

Table 23 Expenditure Incurred for Getting Job Cards

District	Block	Village	Yes	%	No	%	Total
Ambala	Ambala-I	Sullar	–	0.00	24	100.00	**24**
		Tejan	2	8.00	23	92.00	**25**
	Barara	Kambasi	–	0.00	25	100.00	**25**
		Dadupur	–	0.00	26	100.00	**26**
Mewat	Nuh	Marora	1	4.00	24	96.00	**25**
		Namak	–	0.00	25	100.00	**25**
	Jhirka	Hirwari	–	0.00	25	100.00	**25**
		Jharpuri	–	0.00	25	100.00	**25**
Total			**3**	**1.50**	**197**	**98.50**	**200**

Job Cards at Work Place

Nearly 57 per cent of the workers responded positively to this item (Table 24). However, in the three villages of Ambala, i.e. Sullar, Tejan, and Kambasi, the workers stated that they do not carry job cards when going for MGNREGA work. This is not a desirable thing. The workers need to be made aware of its necessity. An overwhelming proportion of respondents in the four villages of Mewat District has responded positively to this item. Generally, Mewat is considered to be a backward district and Ambala is considered to be a more literate and forward district. This aspect needs to be probed further and also needs to be closely monitored by the district and block officials as also during social audit.

Table 24 Job Cards at Work Place in the Studied Villages

District	Block	Village	Yes	%	No	%	NA	%	Total
Ambala	Ambala-I	Sullar	–	0.00	23	95.83	1	4.17	**24**
		Tejan	–	0.00	24	96.00	1	4.00	**25**
	Barara	Kambasi	6	24.00	17	68.00	2	8.00	**25**
		Dadupur	17	65.38	6	23.08	3	11.54	**26**
Mewat	Nuh	Marora	18	75.00	5	20.83	1	4.17	**24**
		Namak	23	92.00	1	4.00	1	4.00	**25**
	Jhirka	Hirwari	24	100.00	–	0.00	–	0.00	**24**
		Jharpuri	25	100.00	–	0.00	–	0.00	**25**
Total			**113**	**57.07**	**76**	**38.38**	**9**	**4.55**	**198***

** Of the total, two respondents refused to answer.*

Employment and Wages Paid Entries

The responses to this item is on the positive direction as nearly 66 per cent of the workers stated that employment days and wages paid are entered into the job cards (Table 25). However, 30 per cent have stated that they have no knowledge about this. This was particularly noticed in the four villages of Ambala District. This also needs to be monitored and probed.

Table 25 Entries of Employment and Wages Paid in the Studied Villages

District	Block	Village	Yes	%	No	%	NA	%	Total
Ambala	Ambala-I	Sullar	7	29.17	–	0.00	17	70.83	**24**
		Tejan	9	36.00	1	4.00	15	60.00	**25**
	Barara	Kambasi	14	56.00	1	4.00	10	40.00	**25**
		Dadupur	10	38.46	4	15.38	12	46.15	**26**
Mewat	Nuh	Marora	20	83.33	1	4.00	3	12.50	**24**
		Namak	23	92.00	–	0.00	2	8.00	**25**
	Jhirka	Hirwari	24	100.00	–	0.00	–	0.00	**24**
		Jharpuri	25	100.00	–	0.00	–	0.00	**25**
Total			**132**	**66.67**	**7**	**3.50**	**59**	**29.80**	**198***

** Of the total, two respondents refused to answer.*

Applying for Work

The data in this respect show that about 80 per cent of the respondents are not aware that they have to give applications for work (Table 26). One of

Table 26 Applying for Work in the Studied Villages

District	Block	Village	Yes	%	No	%	Total
Ambala	Ambala-I	Sullar	6	25.00	18	75.00	**24**
		Tejan	5	20.00	20	80.00	**25**
	Barara	Kambasi	1	4.00	24	96.00	**25**
		Dadupur	3	11.54	23	88.46	**26**
Mewat	Nuh	Marora	3	12.50	21	87.50	**24**
		Namak	5	20.00	20	80.00	**25**
	Jhirka	Hirwari	6	25.00	18	75.00	**24**
		Jharpuri	11	44.00	14	56.00	**25**
Total			**40**	**20.20**	**158**	**79.80**	**198***

** Of the total respondents, two refused to answer.*

the important features of the MGNREGA programme is that it is demand driven. The knowledge about this seems to be low among the workers. This aspect also needs to be carefully monitored and the workers need to be made aware about the demand-driven content of the MGNREGA programme.

Job Cards and Availability of Work

The response with respect to this item is ambiguous. The data indicate that 42 per cent of the respondents believe that they can get work without job cards (Table 27). On the other hand, 58 per cent of the respondents are aware that work will not be available without job card. During our visit to village Sullar, the Sarpanch said that on certain days for specific work there was requirement of large number of workers and on such occasion even if the workers did not have the job cards initially, they were given the work but very soon job cards were made available for them. This is an anomalous situation which needs to be monitored closely by the implementing officials.

Table 27 Availability of Work & Job Cards in the Studied Villages

District	Block	Village	Yes	%	No	%	Total
Ambala	Ambala-I	Sullar	11	45.83	13	54.17	**24**
		Tejan	7	28.00	18	72.00	**25**
	Barara	Kambasi	7	28.00	18	72.00	**25**
		Dadupur	12	46.15	14	53.85	**26**
Mewat	Nuh	Marora	13	54.17	11	45.83	**24**
		Namak	9	36.00	16	64.00	**25**
	Jhirka	Hirwari	12	50.00	12	50.00	**24**
		Jharpuri	12	48.00	13	52.00	**25**
Total			**83**	**41.92**	**115**	**58.08**	**198**

Applying for Work

Similar response was discerned even in this case as 63 per cent of the respondents have stated that they can get work without giving application (Table 28). However, 37 per cent stated that they cannot get work without application. This could also be noticed in the field as many of the workers got jobs when the demand for labour was very high for certain works.

Table 28 Getting Work without Application

District	Block	Village	Yes	%	No	%	Total
Ambala	Ambala-I	Sullar	20	83.33	4	16.67	**24**
		Tejan	11	44.00	14	56.00	**25**
	Barara	Kambasi	16	64.00	9	36.00	**25**
		Dadupur	22	84.62	4	15.38	**26**
Mewat	Nuh	Marora	16	66.67	8	33.33	**24**
		Namak	11	44.00	14	56.00	**25**
	Jhirka	Hirwari	12	50.00	12	50.00	**24**
		Jharpuri	16	64.00	9	36.00	**25**
Total			**124**	**62.63**	**74**	**37.37**	**198**

The respondents were asked whether they gave application for work. Only 7 per cent of the respondents reported in affirmation (Table 29). The overwhelming response of getting work even without application is intriguing. This needs to be closely monitored. There apparently appears to be a consistency in the responses to the items, namely, getting work without job card and without application. It apparently transpires that the workers were called by the Sarpanch/other PRI representatives when a particular work had to be executed within a specific time on priority basis.

Table 29 Respondents Applying for Work

District	Block	Village	Yes	%	No	%	NA	%	Total
Ambala	Ambala-I	Sullar	–	0.00	24	100.00	–	0.00	**24**
		Tejan	1	4.00	24	96.00	–	0.00	**25**
	Barara	Kambasi	2	8.33	21	87.50	1	4.17	**24**
		Dadupur	1	3.85	25	96.15	–	0.00	**26**
Mewat	Nuh	Marora	1	4.17	17	70.83	6	25.00	**24**
		Namak	4	16.67	19	79.17	1	4.17	**24**
	Jhirka	Hirwari	–	0.00	24	100.00	–	0.00	**24**
		Jharpuri	5	20.00	16	64.00	4	16.00	**25**
Total			**14**	**7.14**	**170**	**86.73**	**12**	**6.12**	**196***

** Of the total respondents, four refused to answer.*

Nature of Work and Wages

The respondents were asked whether they were given piece rate or time rate wages. The data show that over 80 per cent of the respondents have replied that they were given piece rate wages. As a matter of fact, during our field visit we could observe that the respondents had invariably stated that the payment was based on piece rate, but most of them received the minimum wages as prescribed for eight hours work. There were, however, some complaints of getting less than the minimum wage as according to piece rate formula the workers had not done the amount of work which was required on piece rate basis. In this respect, there are some inherent problems. We inquired about this issue with the XEN, SDO, JE, and the BDPO of Ambala-I and Barara block regarding the technicality of deciding the methodology of piece rate wage. They informed us that *Time and Motion Study* was conducted in different parts of Haryana by examining eight hours piece work output in hard soil and soft soil. The different piece rate was fixed for the two (hard and soft soil) in the entire state and that formula was stated to be applicable in all the villages of Haryana state.

Another problem encountered by the workers is that the female workers were not able to do the equivalence of hard work which the male members undertake. During the course of interview, the workers did complaint about the low payment in spite of working for eight hours. This was particularly noticed in village Sullar and also substantiated by the Sarpanch of the village. This matter was also discussed by us with the XEN who confirmed that the actual work done was below the required norm and hence the payment was done according to work output.

This aspect needs to be thoroughly looked into. Our field observations lead us to believe that the XEN and the technical staff have not properly communicated with the workers, of the methodology of evolving the piece rate work and its compatibility with the time rate wages. It is necessary that the 'Time-and-Motion-Study' should be conducted while the workers are doing their job in the field so that there is not only transparency, but it will also convince the workers about the genuineness of the scientific methodology adopted for deciding piece rate.

Gender and Nature of Work

The respondents were asked whether piece rate work is disadvantageous to the females. Approximately 70 per cent of the workers responded in affirmation (Table 30). This aspect also needs to be probed and examined carefully.

Table 30 Opinion on Nature of Work Disadvantageous to Females

District	Block	Village	Yes	%	No	%	Total
Ambala	Ambala-I	Sullar	15	62.50	9	37.50	**24**
		Tejan	20	80.00	5	20.00	**25**
	Barara	Kambasi	19	76.00	6	24.00	**25**
		Dadupur	21	80.77	5	19.23	**26**
Mewat	Nuh	Marora	12	50.00	12	50.00	**24**
		Namak	13	61.90	8	38.10	**21**
	Jhirka	Hirwari	18	72.00	7	28.00	**25**
		Jharpuri	19	76.00	6	24.00	**25**
Total			**137**	**70.26**	**58**	**29.74**	**195***

** Of the total respondents, five refused to answer.*

Facilities Provided at the Worksite

Nearly 77 per cent of the respondents reported that muster rolls were kept at the worksite (Table 31). However, 18.5 per cent of the respondents indicated their ignorance about this. We also verified this in the field situation and observed that the muster rolls were kept at the worksite. This needs to be checked during social audit as well.

Most of the labours reported that mandatory facilities were provided at the worksite during the MGNREGA works. About 76 per cent of the respondents agreed that one of the mandatory facilities of making first aid available at the worksite was invariably done (Table 32). Similarly, 87 per cent respondents said that the mandatory facility of providing drinking water at the worksite was complied. With respect to the provision of crèche facility, only 44 per cent agreed affirmatively and the remaining 56 per cent replied that this facility was not provided. This aspect needs closer monitoring as over 40 to 50 per cent of the workers are females who are married and their younger kids need crèche facility. Similarly, 54 per cent stated that shed is also arranged at the worksite as the MGNREGA work is also undertaken during the summer season. This aspect also needs to be probed during social audit. About 76 per cent of labourers reported that first aid facility was available at worksite and remaining 24 per cent complained about the lack of first aid facility at worksite.

Table 31 Muster Rolls Were Kept at the Worksite

District	Block	Village	Yes	%	No	%	Don't Know	%	Total
Ambala	Ambala-I	Sullar	8	33.33	5	20.83	11	45.83	**24**
		Tejan	12	48.00	–	0.00	13	52.00	**25**
	Barara	Kambasi	20	80.00	1	4.00	4	16.00	**25**
		Dadupur	21	80.77	1	3.85	4	15.38	**26**
Mewat	Nuh	Marora	20	86.96	1	4.35	2	8.70	**23**
		Namak	23	92.00	–	0.00	2	8.00	**25**
	Jhirka	Hirwari	24	96.00	–	0.00	1	4.00	**25**
		Jharpuri	25	100.00	–	0.00	–	0.00	**25**
Total			**153**	**77.27**	**8**	**4.04**	**37**	**18.69**	**198***

** Of the total respondents, two refused to answer.*

Table 32 Facilities Provided at the Worksite

District	Block	Village	Yes	%	No	%	Total
Ambala	Ambala-I	Sullar	19	90.48	2	9.52	**21**
		Tejan	12	50.00	12	50.00	**24**
	Barara	Kambasi	20	80.00	5	20.00	**25**
		Dadupur	18	69.23	8	30.77	**26**
Mewat	Nuh	Marora	14	60.87	9	39.13	**23**
		Namak	25	100.00	–	0.00	**25**
	Jhirka	Hirwari	15	60.00	10	40.00	**25**
		Jharpuri	24	96.00	1	4.00	**25**
Total			**147**	**75.77**	**47**	**24.23**	**194***

** Of the total respondents, six refused to answer.*

MGNREGA Work Information in the Village

Nearly 50 per cent of the respondents stated that the works undertaken under MGNREGA are displayed in Gram Panchayat; 44 per cent of the respondents are not aware of this (Table 33). During our field visit in all the eight villages of both the districts, we could observe that there was prompt display of the MGNREGA programme by indicating the name of work, amount spent, number of man-days generated, and other information. The lack of awareness is obviously because of the low level of literacy of many of the male and female workers. This aspect also needs to be taken up in the awareness programme at the Gram Sabha level.

Table 33 Information Relating to the MGNREGA Works Displayed in Gram Panchayat

District	Block	Village	Yes	%	No	%	NA	%	Total
Ambala	Ambala-I	Sullar	11	45.83	5	20.83	8	33.33	**24**
		Tejan	14	56.00	2	8.00	9	36.00	**25**
	Barara	Kambasi	10	40.00	1	4.00	14	56.00	**25**
		Dadupur	5	19.23	3	11.54	18	69.23	**26**
Mewat	Nuh	Marora	11	52.38		0.00	13	61.90	**24**
		Namak	13	52.00	–	0.00	12	48.00	**25**
	Jhirka	Hirwari	17	68.00	1	4.00	7	28.00	**25**
		Jharpuri	19	76.00		0.00	6	24.00	**25**
Total			**100**	**51.02**	**12**	**6.12**	**87**	**44.39**	**199***

** Of the total respondents, one refused to answer.*

MGNREGA Wages Impact

Around 78.5 per cent of the respondents stated that the wage rates fixed for the MGNREGA programme also impacted other works in the village, particularly agriculture wages (Table 34). It is necessary in this context to point out that in the initial stages of work during 2007–2008, the minimum wage rate in Haryana was fixed at Rs 99 which was subsequently raised to Rs 136. This is one of the highest minimum wage rates prevalent in the MGNREGA programme in the country. Wherever there was difference in payment in respect to the minimum wages, it was later on paid to the workers in the form of arrears. During the course of our field work, we could not notice any complaint made by the workers on the short payment or less payment than the minimum wages prescribed.

However, the MGNREGA work did impact the agricultural work in the village as the farmers were finding it difficult to get adequate labourers during peak season of farm operations. The workers were demanding higher wages than the earlier rates. The farmers had to invariably agree to increase the wages. Now, apparently there is an informal understanding and agreement between the farmers and the officials that the MGNREGA programme should be kept in abeyance during the peak agricultural season. However, it is a positive point that the implementation of MGNREGA has increased the agricultural wages. Another related impact is that the

Table 34 Impact on Wages of Unskilled Workers in Other Works/Activities

District	Block	Village	Yes	%	No	%	Total
Ambala	Ambala-I	Sullar	17	70.83	7	29.17	**24**
		Tejan	25	100.00	–	0.00	**25**
	Barara	Kambasi	23	92.00	2	8.00	**25**
		Dadupur	23	88.46	3	11.54	**26**
Mewat	Nuh	Marora	8	33.33	16	66.67	**24**
		Namak	19	76.00	6	24.00	**25**
	Jhirka	Hirwari	20	80.00	5	20.00	**25**
		Jharpuri	22	88.00	3	12.00	**25**
Total			**157**	**78.89**	**42**	**21.11**	**199***

** Of the total respondents, one refused to answer.*

migrant labourers who used to flock on a big scale in Punjab and Haryana were available less in number during the agricultural season of 2007–2008. This may be partly due to the impact of MGNREGA in the state of Bihar, Jharkhand, etc. which might have arrested the flow of the migrant labour to Punjab and Haryana.

Usefulness of MGNREGA Work

The nature of work undertaken for MGNREGA has been clearly specified in the MGNREGA programme. Most of the works are related to earthwork of digging ponds, constructing village roads, undertaking watershed works, afforestation, etc. Nearly 81 per cent of the respondents were in agreement that MGNREGA work is useful to the village (Table 35). However, there are certain issues which we noticed during our field work. The nature of earthwork to be undertaken in MGNREGA is mostly confined to the Shamlat land/Panchayat land. There is apparently very minimal scope of undertaking MGNREGA programme in villages with less of Shamlat land or no Shamlat land. It is for this reason that the MGNREGA work is not undertaken in all the villages, particularly in Ambala District where there is less of Shamlat land. Another reason for the coverage of lesser number of villages in Ambala District is because of high incidence of urbanisation as compared to the Mewat District which has low level of urbanisation. Some of the officials and PRI representatives also expressed concern about raising the scope and nature of work under MGNREGA so that it can have the flexibility of undertaking other works which the Gram Sabha and the PRI representatives consider useful and beneficial.

Table 35 Usefulness of MGNREGA Work

District	Block	Village	Yes	%	No	%	Don't Know	%	Total
Ambala	Ambala-I	Sullar	21	87.50	1	4.17	2	8.33	**24**
		Tejan	23	92.00	–	0.00	2	8.00	**25**
	Barara	Kambasi	22	88.00	–	0.00	3	12.00	**25**
		Dadupur	18	69.23	3	11.54	5	19.23	**26**
Mewat	Nuh	Marora	16	66.67	–	0.00	8	33.33	**24**
		Namak	18	85.71	–	0.00	3	14.29	**21**
	Jhirka	Hirwari	22	88.00	1	4.00	2	8.00	**25**
		Jharpuri	18	72.00	2	8.00	5	20.00	**25**
Total			**158**	**81.03**	**7**	**3.59**	**30**	**15.38**	**195***

** Of the total respondents, five refused to answer.*

Effectiveness of MGNREGA in the Studied Villages

The respondents were asked about the level of effectiveness of MGNREGA programme. The data indicate that nearly 75 per cent of the respondents considered MGNREGA programme as effective and only 17 per cent considered it as less effective (Table 36). It is necessary in this context to point out that the village women, particularly belonging to the SC and BC category, considered MGNREGA programme as a boon for them. It has done a positive service by raising the dignity of women as they were earlier paid very low wages with the farmers. Many of the women workers even considered MGNREGA work as highly dignified as compared to the dependency syndrome inherent in working with the farmers.

There is a clear-cut class divide in terms of the effectiveness of the MGNREGA work. The Dalits and weaker sections consider it as very effective, whereas the agriculturists and the prosperous among them have generally a hate attitude towards MGNREGA as it affects their labour requirement and higher payment of wages. The officials and politicians, in general, are also not well disposed towards MGNREGA programme and their blunt response is that MGNREGA cannot be effective and useful in Punjab and Haryana. It has also led to the spread of negative and adverse rumour that 'MGNREGA, KAREGA, MAREGA'. This has reverberated into a great dissonance in the mindset of the affluent section.

Table 36 Effectiveness of MGNREGA

District	Block	Village	Most Effective	Effective	Less Effective	Not Effective	Can't Say	Total
Ambala	Ambala-I	Sullar	2	13	8	1		**24**
		Tejan	–	17	1	–	7	**25**
	Barara	Kambasi	4	15	4	–	2	**25**
		Dadupur	1	13	10	–	2	**26**
Mewat	Nuh	Marora	2	15	6	–	1	**24**
		Namak	1	20	2	–	2	**25**
	Jhirka	Hirwari	2	21	2	–	–	**25**
		Jharpuri	3	22	–	–	–	**25**
Total			**15**	**136**	**33**	**1**	**14**	**199***

** Of the total respondents, one refused to answer.*

Graph 9 Effectiveness of MGNREGA in the Studied Villages

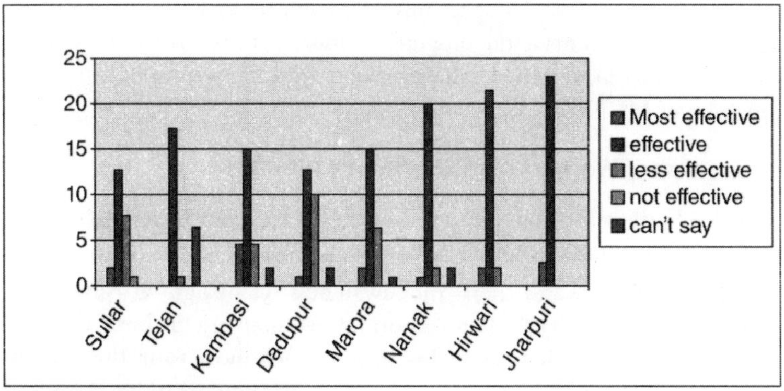

X-Axis denotes studied villages
Y-Axis denotes extent of effect

Implications

There were few questions on the transparency of MGNREGA programme and on its effective functioning. There were several positive indicators of transparent functioning of MGNREGA scheme, e.g. no expenditure incurred on job cards, entries of employment days and wages done in job cards, social audits undertaken, and display of MGNREGA works on the boards. Certain indicators were not very satisfactory with respect to transparency, e.g. retention of job cards with Sarpanch/rozgar sahayak and functioning of vigilance/monitoring committees. There were few items on factual indicators of effectiveness, e.g. payment of time-rate/piece-rate, display of muster rolls, provision of mandatory facilities like first aid, drinking water, crèche, and shed. The workers faced some problems between the matching of time-rate with piece-rate wage in village Sullar, as they were made lesser payment than the minimum wage. However, display of muster rolls and working of mandatory facilities were satisfactory. There were also two direct questions on impact of MGNREGA, e.g. wages in agriculture and the usefulness of MGNREGA work. The response indicated that MGNREGA has led to increase in agricultural wages causing anxiety to the farmers. The work done under MGNREGA is considered useful for the village which is also reinforced through the quantitative information on effectiveness.

Thus as per the perception of the workers, MGNREGA programme is effective as it has provided employment and created assets, led to development of the village, and stood the test of transparency and accountability. The programme has benefited the most vulnerable sections that are placed at the rock bottom with respect to caste, land, occupation, income, and gender. In order to make the programme more effective, some more work has to be undertaken to make the grassroots workers aware about the basic provision of MGNREGA.

Awareness of Workers of MGNREGA Programme

- In the overall sample only 33 per cent are aware of various entitlements under MGNREGA.
- This indicates that the awareness campaign at grassroots Panchayat level is an important requirement in both the districts of Ambala and Mewat, but much more so in the villages of Mewat District.
- The awareness of 100 days of guaranteed employment under MGNREGA is known to 75 per cent respondents which is one of the most important provisions in MGNREGA.
- The awareness about entitlement of 100 days of guaranteed employment is also one of the key ingredients of entitlements under MGNREGA.
- An overwhelming proportion of the village people are not aware that employment should be provided to them within 15 days of demand. This is an important provision of which people must be made aware.

- Over 97 per cent of the respondents are not aware that they are entitled for unemployment allowance if employment is not provided to them within 15 days.
- The data indicate that there is very low awareness with respect to the entitlement of 10 per cent more wages in case the work is undertaken beyond 5 km of the village boundary.
- MGNREGA programme provides that the employment should be provided to the workers within 15 days of submission of application and 76.5 per cent of the workers are not aware of this provision.
- Thus on the provisions of awareness of MGNREGA programme, the workers were relatively better aware of entitlements to 100 days of guaranteed employment and about the time limit of payment of wages within 15 days. The awareness was quite low with respect to important provisions, e.g. entitlement to unemployment allowance, 10 per cent more wages to be paid if work is given beyond 5 km of village boundary, time limit of providing employment within 15 days of submission of application, and time limit for payment of wages within 15 days. The low awareness to these important entitlements would have its impact on lower effectiveness of MGNREGA programme.
- The low awareness of several MGNREGA provisions along with complete lack of awareness of RTI Act would lead to low effectiveness of MGNREGA programme.
- The data provide very critical information that only 16.28 per cent of the workers are keeping the job cards with themselves and the remaining 83.72 per cent of the job cards are invariably kept with the Sarpanch or rozgar sahayak.
- There is overwhelming satisfactory response (98.5 per cent) of the workers who stated that they did not have to incur any expenditure for getting job card. This makes the whole system transparent.
- This is indeed a great silver lining in the light of overall prevalence of corruption in public life in India.
- The respondents were asked whether they carried the job cards to the work place in the field. Nearly 57 per cent of the workers responded positively to this item. However, the overwhelming proportion of respondents in the four villages of Mewat District has responded positively.

- The responses are on the positive direction as nearly 66 per cent of the workers stated that employment days and wages paid are entered into the job cards.
- Seventy-nine per cent of the respondents are not aware that they have to give applications for getting employment under MGNREGA programme.
- The data indicate that 42 per cent of the respondents believe that they can get work without job cards. This is an anomalous situation which needs to be monitored closely by the implementing officials and PRI representatives during social audit.
- Sixty-two per cent of the respondents have stated that they can get work without giving application. The respondents were asked whether they gave application for work. Only 7 per cent of the respondents stated in affirmation.
- The respondents were asked whether they were given piece-rate or time-rate wages. The data show that over 80 per cent of the respondents have replied that they were given piece-rate wages.
- During the course of our interview, the workers did complaint about the low payment of wages, in spite of working for eight hours. This was particularly noticed in village Sullar and also substantiated by the Sarpanch of the village. This matter was discussed by us also with the XEN who confirmed that the actual work done was below the required norm and hence the payment was done according to work output.
- In fact under MGNREGA, the role of Gram Sabha is very pre-eminent and therefore, the awareness level of Gram Sabha members needs to be increased on all ingredients of MGNREGA programme.
- During our field visit, in all the eight villages of both the districts, we could observe that there was prompt display of the MGNREGA programme by indicating the name of work, amount spent, number of man-days generated, and other information.
- Around 78.5 per cent of the respondents stated that the wage rates fixed for the MGNREGA programme also impacted other works in the village, especially agriculture wages.
- The prevalent wage rate for MGNREGA in Haryana is Rs 138 per day, which is one of the highest minimum wage rates prevalent in the MGNREGA in the country.

- During the course of field work we could not notice any complaint made by the workers on the short payment or less payment than the minimum wages prescribed.
- However, the MGNREGA work did impact the agricultural work in the village as the farmers were finding it difficult to get adequate labourers during peak season of farm operations.
- The farmers had to invariably agree to increase the wages.
- Another related impact is that the migrant labourers who used to flock on a big scale in Punjab and Haryana were available less in number during the agricultural season of 2007–2008. This is one of the impacts of MGNREGA programme on the source of origin state of migrants particularly Bihar and Jharkhand.
- The nature of earthwork to be undertaken in MGNREGA is mostly confined to the Shamlat land/Panchayat land. There is apparently very minimal scope of undertaking MGNREGA programme in villages with less Shamlat land or no Shamlat land. It is for this reason that the MGNREGA work is not undertaken in all the villages particularly in Ambala District where there is less of Shamlat land. Another reason for the coverage of lesser number of villages in Ambala District is because of high incidence of urbanisation as compared to the Mewat District which has low level of urbanisation.
- It is necessary in this context to point out that the village women, particularly belonging to the SC and BC category, considered MGNREGA programme as a boon for them. It has done a positive service by raising the dignity of women, as they were earlier paid very low wages by the farmers. Many of the women workers even considered MGNREGA work as highly dignified as compared to the dependency syndrome inherent in working with the farmers.

CHAPTER 7

FROM CASTE ASSOCIATIONS TO KHAP PANCHAYATS: THE JATS OF HARYANA

Bhupendra Yadav

Formed on November 1, 1966, Haryana is a young, modern state. Its story of development is wonderful. It is also the state where the vibrant people are subjected to traditional institutions and their barbaric injustice. This paradox in Haryana reminds us that if it does not change the culture and thought, development can sometimes be a misnomer.[1] Haryana marks the failure of a successful model in a way few provinces do.

Jats are the dominant caste in Haryana. In the absence of any caste enumeration since independence, the various estimates of Jat population in Haryana range from 20 to 25 per cent. This is vastly higher than Rajasthan where Jat population is estimated to constitute nine per cent of that province's population and Uttar Pradesh where this figure was slightly higher than one per cent. Haryana constitutes five districts of colonial Punjab, i.e. Hisar, Rohtak, Gurgaon, Karnal, and Ambala, and the princely state of Jind. In 1931, Jats constituted 28.48 per cent of Hisar's and 36.80 per cent of Rohtak's population.[2] These districts have since become administrative divisions, meaning they are composed of several districts led by a commissioner. Hence, within Haryana, the highest concentration of Jat population is in the Rohtak and Hisar divisions.

---

[1] Distinguishing westoxication (meaning intoxication with brands and styles of Western culture) from modernisation is the first step in defining a modern society in ex-colonies like ours. The second thing is to realise that a modern society uses automobiles or electronic gadgets but this alone is not modernity. A modern society insists on four things, i.e. 'the dignity of the individual, adherence to universalistic norms, preference for individual achievement over privileges of birth and accountability in public life'. See Gupta, D. (2000). *Mistaken Modernity: India between Worlds* (New Delhi: HarperCollins India & *India Today*).

[2] Chowdhry, P. (1994). *The Veiled Women: Shifting Gender Equations in Rural Haryana 1880–1980* (Delhi: Oxford University Press).

Like the world in which we live, the Jats of Haryana are moving. The pace of this change may not be 8 per cent like the celebrated growth of the post-Liberalisation Indian economy. In fact instead of saying that they are lunging forward, it could also be said that the change among Jats in Haryana is negative. We notice two trends in this negative change, i.e. demand for OBC status by a section of the Jats and restoration of the importance of Khap Panchayats widely in the Rohtak division. On the face of it, this is social decay. The reason for this decay may be attributed to the proverbial tribal clannishness and inherent evil genius of Jats. But we think there are sound political and economic reasons to understand the panic and despair engulfing Jats. Therefore, the demand for quotas and restoration of Khap Panchayats is a sign of desperation and not degeneration of these Jats in Haryana.[3]

Is there politics behind these phenomena? Of course, there is. The Khaps are barbaric in Rohtak but the ones in Hisar are more compassionate. In the recent spate of quota politics, Hisar has led whereas Rohtak has stayed quiet or peaceful. Hisar is the region of relatively large landholdings and commercial crops to which the wily Om Prakash Chautala belongs. Rohtak is the area of the small landholdings and subsistence farming to which the relatively restrained Bhupender Singh Hooda belongs.[4] Chautala and Hooda are not just two different individuals, they represent two different political parties and they have different political styles.

The Khaps are everywhere in the region where the Hindu Jats preponderate. But the Khaps in the erstwhile Rohtak District appear most inspired in spirit and obnoxious in deed. The ones in Hisar are more subdued. In matters of love and cohabitation the Khaps of Rohtak are tyrannical whereas the ones in Hisar are lenient. This is because that Hisar is at the cusp of two regions, i.e. Punjab and Rajasthan. This area has seen the intermixing of cultures in a way Rohtak has not. Moreover, there has been an influx of people both from Punjab and Rajasthan in Hisar till late eighteenth century because the arid land here had few takers.[5]

[3] This desperation is captured best in Chowdhry, P. (2009). '"First Our Jobs Then Our Girls": The Dominant Caste Perceptions on the "Rising" Dalits', *Modern Asian Studies* 43(2): 437–479.

[4] In 2000–2001, the average size of landholdings in Haryana was 2.32 hectares. In Rohtak, the size of average landholdings was 2.29 hectares whereas in Hisar it was 2.96 hectares. Government of Haryana, *Statistical Abstract, Haryana, 2007–08 Publication No. 910* (Department of Economic and Statistical Analysis, Haryana, 2009): 226–229.

[5] Darling, M. (1925). *Punjab Peasant in Prosperity and Debt* (London: Oxford University Press).

POLITICO-SOCIAL CHANGES IN JAT LIFE

Let us begin with the changes in Jat politics. Firstly, some sections of the Jats of Haryana are moving away from *Kisan* politics to quota politics.[6] Quota politics has been the mainstay of socialists since the 1960s. Jat Arakshan Samiti is not socialist in any way. Moreover, quota politics among Jats looks odd due to two reasons. Firstly, the Jats are the dominant caste in Haryana and it sounds odd that a dominant caste is also claiming social and educational backwardness. Secondly, a big section of Jats were in the forefront of the Anti-Mandal agitation in 1990–1991. The implementation of Mandal Commission meant giving 27 per cent job reservation in public sector to the Other Backward Classes (OBCs). The logic of Jat opposition then was, why dilute merit and why not an economic criterion be had for job reservations. Now, a section of Jats are seeking OBC status for themselves. The implied logic now is that if you cannot beat the quota beneficiaries, then it is best to just join them.

The second negative change we notice is that some sections of Jats have embraced old style Khap Panchayats just as strongly as they once clung to their caste associations.[7] Caste associations have conducted internal social reforms like insisting on dowry-less marriages, cost-effective marriages with small celebrations, simplifying death rituals, etc. Caste associations have also been doing some salutary work in the sphere of education, especially secondary school and college education. Non-government colleges in Haryana are usually full of region-specific caste-based colleges like All India Jat Heroes Memorial Jat School and College in Rohtak or Ahir College in Rewari. Rohtak is also dotted by Gaur Brahmin College and Vaishya College. Education and reform is a thing of the past because caste associations proliferated but lost focus along the way. Khap Panchayats are custodians of tradition and their protagonists look upon themselves as saviours of culture and customs.

Why have these negative changes surfaced so strongly now? We can think of two reasons. Firstly, opportunities are on the decline in both agriculture and the public sector jobs. Secondly, politics is hostage to social networks. Incapable of solving substantive problems or disinterested in serious issues,

---

[6] The expression Quota Politics and *Kisan* politics used in Christophie Jaffrelot (2000), 'The Rise of Other Backward Classes in the Hindi Belt', *The Journal of Asian Studies*, Vol. 59, No. 1 (Feb. 2000): 86–108.

[7] A rather old but useful research article on this subject, see Lloyd I. Rudolph and Susanne Hoeber Rudolph (1960), 'The Political Role of India's Caste Associations', *Pacific Affairs*, Vol. 33, No. 1 (March 1960): 5–22.

the discredited political leaders will do anything to pander to the whims of their constituents. Khaps happen to be area-specific and electoral constituencies are also territorial. This overlap means that geography plays an important part when the traditional clan and modern electoral constituency are spread over the same territory.

Landholdings in Haryana have been small since the twentieth century. A steady decline in the size of the already small landholdings has messed up life for a large section of those dependent on agriculture. On the other hand, ruralites of Haryana have, since colonial times, been in need of alternative employment and they prefer the army or government jobs. The situation here has worsened because public sector jobs are decreasing and the share of quota beneficiaries is increasing. Pending an in-depth analysis of the nature and activities of the Jat Arakshan Samiti and different Khap Panchayats, only guesses can be made. My guess is that lower class Jats are behind the demand for quotas and the restoration of Khap Panchayats.

Let us now look at the context and go through the evidence on the basis of which the aforementioned claims are made.

THE CONTEXT

Till the medieval times, the peasants appeared only as targets of land tax or as brutal rebels against the Royal Lord who was the shadow of God. Peasants were portrayed as stupid or evil in the West as well. The *Declinatio Rustico*, a thirteenth-century dictionary, defined the six declensions of the word *peasant* to be 'villain, rustic, devil, robber, brigand and looter and in plural wretches, beggars, liars, rogues, trash and infidels'. *Smerd*, the Russian term for peasant was derived from the verb *smerdet*, which means 'to stink'. The Polish term *cham* means crudity. In the eighteenth-century English, peasant meant a brute and an illiterate and the verb 'to peasant' meant 'to subjugate and slave'.[8] To cap it all, Karl Marx from whom some empathy was to be expected, disappointed more badly. He dismissed the peasantry as '...the class that represents barbarism within civilization'.

The bad-mouthing of Jats in proverbs can, therefore, be called a part of this global phenomenon. In capitalist societies, like the one we have been building since independence, the peasantry was expected to polarise

[8] Shanin, T. (1987). 'Short Historical Outline of Peasant Societies', in idem (ed.), *Peasants and Peasant Societies: Selected Readings* (Oxford: Basil Blackwell): 467.

into rich farmers and landless wage labourers. It has not. Politically, it was expected that a self-aware and cohesive peasantry would successfully get the legislation to protect its interests. This also has not happened. Hence, Teodor Shanin (1972) called the peasantry in Russia's developing society 'The Awkward Class'.[9]

We have agrarian capitalism in Haryana. Agrarian capitalism in most of India is not of the large-scale corporation or landlord variety. It is a mix of commercial capitalism and peasant capitalism.[10] Thanks to commercial capitalism, we have labour, commodity, credit, and land markets. On the other hand, production under peasant capitalism is geared for the market. The capitalist farmers are concerned with productivity in a way feudal lords were not. The capitalist farmers are also different from feudal chiefs because they till their own land and are keen to adopt new technology.

Interestingly, peasant capitalism is not defined by use of hired labour. Only some sections of the peasants of the intermediate dominant castes may hire labour but most of them may do with family labour. Hence, they are sometimes also called family farmers. Jats are/were neither big nor wealthy farmers. They are mostly family farmers. Not rich enough to employ agricultural labourers in a big way and thereby exploit family labour.

There is an unprecedented consolidation of agricultural castes since the nineteenth century from the Patidars in Gujarat, the Kammas in Andhra, and the Jats in north-western India. The Jats in Uttar Pradesh were able to evolve a more inclusive approach, thanks to their enlightened, educated leadership under Chaudhri Charan Singh. Charan Singh may also have felt compelled to adopt this approach because Jats constituted a little more than 1 per cent of the population in Uttar Pradesh.[11]

Global movement is not much but it is not new to the people of Haryana. Unlike neighbouring Punjab, there is not much out-migration for work from any part or caste in Haryana. The ranks in the British colonial army, however, had a good representation from people of Haryana. Before independence, the soldiers were sent abroad to enlarge the British Empire and

[9] Quoted on the title page of Shanin, T. (1972). *The Awkward Class: Political Sociology of Peasantry in a Developing Society: Russia 1910–1925* (Oxford: Oxford University Press).

[10] For a discussion on academic approaches to different kinds of agrarian capitalism, see Banaji, J. (1999). 'Metamorphoses of Agrarian Capitalism', *Economic and Political Weekly*, 34(40): 2850–2858.

[11] Jaffrelot, C. (2000). 'The Rise of the Other Backward Classes in the Hindi Belt', *Journal of Asian Studies*, 59(1): 91.

to secure its interests. Those that survived were dutifully brought back, given medals, and pensioned off to die in their land. But this, as we know, was the nature of the labour market for soldiers in the colonial period.

The economy in independent India also saw the growth of some new sectors and these emerging arenas have provided opportunities far and wide. There has been little investment of the agrarian surplus in non-agricultural sectors. A few Jats, however, have availed the new opportunities in the emerging sectors. A corporation was created by a Jat entrepreneur due to community support and this deserves recounting here. Delhi Land and Finance (DLF) is an enterprise founded in 1946 by Chaudhry Raghvendra Singh (1910–2000). Raghvendra Singh was the son of the first 'Jat graduate' Rai Bahadur Lal Chand who was a lawyer and a leader in the Unionist Party like Sir Chhotu Ram. The Unionist Party was formed in 1923 as an interest group to lobby for concessions to the so-called agriculturist castes in united colonial Punjab.

DLF got into real estate and grew rapidly in the years before 1957, when Delhi Development Authority (DDA) was started. DDA had monopoly rights to develop residential and commercial property in Delhi and this put private players out of business. However, on the basis of 5,800 acres acquired in the early 1950s in Delhi, DLF developed some colonies in Delhi to meet the growing demand of housing. Raghvendra Singh was joined by Kushal Pal Singh, his son-in-law, in 1961. In a meeting, Kushal Pal Singh convinced Rajiv Gandhi that private corporations should be allowed to develop housing colonies in the 1980s. On instructions from Bhajan Lal, the contemporary chief minister of Haryana, DLF acquired 3,500 acres in Gurgaon from 1980 to 1997.[12]

---

[12] In the 1950s, DLF developed Hauz Khas, Greater Kailash Part I and II (on land belonging to peasants of Yaqudpur and Bahapur villages), Kailash Colony (previously Zamrudpur Village), South Extension (previously Kotla Mubarakpur Village), and Shivaji Park (previously Madipur Village). The colonies in Gurgaon had to be initially called Qutab Enclave to show its proximity to Delhi. But, then, DLF city has grown in several phases and it has built luxury condominiums named Silver Oaks, Beverly Park I, Ridgewood, Windsor, Regency, Richmond Park, and Hamilton Park (in what were previously Sikanderpur Ghosi and Chakkerpur villages), Oakwood, Belvedere Tower, and Beverly Park II (in previously Sarhaul and Shahpur villages); Nathupur Village has become Belvedere Park and Wazirabad village hosts a golf course and commercial/residential areas named Princeton, Carlton, Aralias, Westend Heights, Royalton Towers, Icon, and Pinnacle. See Damodaran, H. (2008). *India's New Capitalists: Caste, Business, and Industry in a Modern Nation* (Ranikhet: Permanent Black): 284–287.

The model of land acquisition started by Raghvendra Singh was called the 'land bank-partnership model'. Raghvendra Singh used his community connections to get the land of the farmers on credit. He then developed this land and sold it, obviously on a premium. The farmers who gave their land to DLF were looked after rather well. To begin with, the farmers were given plots on the land developed for sale. Moreover, they were paid for their land but Raghvendra got the farmers to re-invest up to 90 per cent of their proceeds in DLF. Interest on the money invested by farmers was paid on the 3rd of every month and farmers also got a small share in the profits of the company as well. On these payments the company never faltered, and hence, it was able to retain the trust of the farmers/investors. Hence, community was the bond on which DLF built its corpus of a land bank, but this initial trust was cemented by regular payment of interests and profits to farmers. 'I have occasionally mediated in family disputes and even helped in arranging marriage alliances', says Kushal Pal Singh the present boss of DLF.[13]

Information, communication and entertainment are also the new, highly visible areas in the globalising world. Films are the most glamorous part of this sector. A few individuals, who happen to be Jats from Haryana, shine in this sector as well. Mallika Sehrawat and Randeep Hooda are good examples of them. Few female actors are considered more than eye-candies, and Sehrawat has made no effort to give the impression of being anything other than a beauty with a shapely body. Hence, probably, no one asks her what fills her mind and what she reads. But when Randeep Hooda was asked, he replied, 'I read everyday. I think reading makes your imagination big. My favourite book is *Papillion* by Henri Charriere. It's a very old book about prison escape. Then I like *The Alchemist* by Paulo Coelho and there are a number of others.'[14]

WHAT'S HAPPENING IN AGRICULTURE? WHICH WAY ARE THE JAT HOUSEHOLDS GOING? UPWARDS OR DOWNWARDS?

Like elsewhere, agriculture is the biggest employer in Haryana. In the areas of the Green Revolution, 8 acres (or slightly more than 3 hectares)

[13] See Damodaran, H. (2008). *India's New Capitalists: Caste, Business, and Industry in a Modern Nation* (Ranikhet: Permanent Black): 284, 286.

[14] 'Bollywood Booked', HT City *Hindustan Times*, August 22, 2010, p. 2. The other Jat asked about his readings was Bobby Deol. Being Dharamendra's son, Deol is a second-generation actor. But when asked what he was reading, Deol replied, 'I haven't read a book in some time, but I used to love vampire books. I love *Interview With a Vampire* by Anne Rice.' *Ibid.*

of land was considered viable for raising a family. But, between early 1970s and 1991, the percentage of unviable marginal and small cultivators (who owned from less than 1 up to 2 hectares of land) increased from 30 to 74.6 per cent in Punjab and from 35 to 63.5 per cent in Haryana. This may not be considered too bad because, in 1991, the all India average of small and marginal cultivators was 78 per cent.[15]

As compared to Punjab, the size of landholdings in Haryana was much smaller. In 2000–2001, the average size of landholdings in Haryana was merely 2.32 hectares as compared to 4.04 hectares in Punjab.[16] The size of holdings in Haryana was skewed to begin with. These inequalities of property got worse with time. The total number of landholdings increased from 9.98 lakhs in 1976–1977 to 13.4 lakhs in 1985–1986 to 17.2 lakhs in 1995–1996. But this did not create more employment because the size of holdings got smaller and hence agriculture became unviable for the small cultivators. The number of small and marginal cultivators (i.e. people possessing less than 2 hectares of land) in 1985–1986 was 56.92 per cent and this increased to 66.74 per cent by 1995–1996. These two groups of small and marginal farmers together owned just 24 per cent of the arable land in Haryana. On the other hand, in 1995–1996, 15 per cent of the large cultivators (i.e. peasants possessing more than 4 hectares of land) of Haryana possessed 51 per cent of the agricultural land while middle cultivators (i.e. peasants possessing between 2 to 4 hectares) formed 19 per cent of the total cultivators and possessed about as much land (i.e. 25 per cent) as their less fortunate folks.[17]

In 1995–1996 in Haryana, therefore, the large cultivators formed 15 per cent of the population but possessed 51 per cent of the land whereas 85 per cent of the rest had to make do with 49 per cent of the land. The land possessed by Jats in all this cannot be known specifically because such data are not available. But it stands to reason that the law of averages does apply to Jats – the leading agriculturist caste in the land of the Green Revolution. The law of averages may not apply to scheduled castes that traditionally form the core of the landless section everywhere.

SCs mostly live in villages but not many among them are landowners. According to provisional figures for 2000–2001, SCs in Haryana have 26,729

---

[15] Table (2R), NSS Report No. 407, 48th Round, 1991–1992. As quoted in Frankel, F. R. (2005). *India's Political Economy, 1947–2004: The Gradual Revolution*, Second Edition (New Delhi: Oxford University Press), pp. 582–583.

[16] Government of Haryana, *Statistical Abstract, Haryana, 2007–08*. Publication No. 910 (Department of Economic and Statistical Analysis, Haryana, 2009): 232

[17] See Kumar, S. (2005). *Haryana: Dasha Aur Disha* (Rohtak: Sahar Prakashan), p. 95.

holdings and these holdings are spread over 41,810 hectares. The number of small and marginal proprietors (meaning those with holdings of less than 2 hectares) among SC landholders is 76.43 per cent and the land they cultivate is 38.55 per cent of the land held by SCs. Big landlords (meaning those holding more than 4 hectares) among the SCs form 7.5 per cent of the total SC landholders in Haryana and the area they control is 32.42 per cent of the SC holdings. The middle peasants (meaning landholders with more than 2 but less than 4 hectares) among SCs are 16.06 per cent and the area under their command is 29 per cent of all the SC holdings in Haryana.[18]

According to the provisional figures of 2000–2001, the total number of landholdings in Haryana was 15.27 lakh and the area over which they were spread was 35.49 lakh hectares. The number of small and marginal proprietors (meaning those with holdings up to 2 hectares) among these were 66.33 per cent and they jointly cultivated 20.80 per cent of the arable land in Haryana. On the other hand, in 2000–2001, the 16.47 per cent of the large cultivators (meaning the peasants possessing more than 4 hectares of land) owned 57.19 per cent of the landholdings in Haryana. The middle peasants (peasants with holdings from 2 to 4 hectares) formed 18.19 per cent of the owners of land and they possessed 21.99 per cent of the landholdings in Haryana.[19]

This shows that by 2000–2001, land possessed by the general cultivators was getting into the hands of the large cultivators whose number went up slightly. Hence, 16.47 per cent of the large cultivators came to acquire 57 per cent of the land whereas the remaining 83.5 per cent of the rest were left with 42 per cent of it.

DECLINING PUBLIC SECTOR EMPLOYMENT LEADING TO DESPERATION IN JATS AND DEVALUATION LEADING TO CRIES OF DISCRIMINATION AMONG SCS/OBCS

We know that organised sector jobs are valued more because they ensure a reasonable salary, some security of employment and other benefits/allowances for housing, health care, etc. At the outset, it should be noted that since the inception of Haryana on November 1, 1966, the public sector (consisting of central and state governments, the quasi-government organisations,

[18] Government of Haryana, *Statistical Abstract, Haryana, 2007–08*. Publication No. 910 (Department of Economic and Statistical Analysis, Haryana, 2009): 231.

[19] Calculated from Government of Haryana, *Statistical Abstract, Haryana, 2007–08*. Publication No. 910 (Department of Economic and Statistical Analysis, Haryana, 2009): 230.

and local bodies) has been the biggest employer in the organised sector. But the employment provided by this sector is decreasing over the 44 years of Haryana's history. The public sector employed 60.42 per cent of the total workforce in the organised sector in 1967; this figure increased to 63 per cent in 1981 and went up to 65 per cent in 1991. But after the reforms in 1991, the share of public sector in total organised sector employment fell to 57 per cent in 2007.[20] (See Table 1)

Growth of employment in the organised sector has not been consistent or confined to the public sector. During the first fourteen years after its formation till 1981, there was a huge overall growth of employment in the organised sector in Haryana, i.e. 234 per cent. The share of public sector in this employment growth was 246 per cent whereas the share of the private sector was 216 per cent. In the next decade, from 1981 to 1991, there was moderate overall growth in the organised sector employment, viz. 119 per cent, with employment growth in the public sector (123 per cent) again being more than in the private sector (111 per cent). Since the Reforms in 1991 to 2007, overall employment growth rate slowed down (110 per cent) with employment increasing in the private sector (138 per cent) but actually declining by around 4 per cent in the public sector.[21] (See Table 1)

Table 1 Employment in Organised Sector in Haryana

Employment	**1967**	**1981**	**1991**	**2001**	**2007**
			Public Sector		
Central Government	19,980	28,581	32,667	30,950	23,445
State Government	86,323	1,95,932	2,34,260	2,53,476	2,45,552
			Quasi-Government		
Central	13,364	25,162	43,865	42,535	37,859
State	–	56,923	69,894	71,691	61,460
Local Bodies	10,892	14,231	15,381	17,227	14,557
Total	**1,03,559**	**3,20,829**	**3,96,067**	**4,15,879**	**3,82,873**

Cont'd...

[20] Calculated from Government of Haryana, *Statistical Abstract, Haryana, 2007–08.* Publication No. 910 (Department of Economic and Statistical Analysis, Haryana, 2009): 508.

[21] Calculated from Government of Haryana, *Statistical Abstract, Haryana, 2007–08.* Publication No. 910 (Department of Economic and Statistical Analysis, Haryana, 2009): 508.

...Cont'd

Employment	1967	1981	1991	2001	2007
			Private Sector		
Act	–	1,64,484	1,83,131	2,13,311	2,61,090
Non-Act	–	20,675	22,611	23,081	23,311
Total	**85,523**	**1,85,159**	**2,05,742**	**2,36,392**	**2,84,401**
Grand total	**2,16,082**	**5,05,988**	**6,01,809**	**6,52,271**	**6,67,274**

Source: Calculated from Government of Haryana, *Statistical Abstract, Haryana, 2007–08*. Publication No. 910 (Department of Economic and Statistical Analysis, Haryana, 2009): 508.

Jobs in the public sector are declining, as we have just seen, especially in the period of economic reforms since 1991. But evidence also shows that the share of scheduled castes and, more especially, the share of OBCs are increasing in the shrinking employment provided by Haryana government. The caste breakup of the 97,385 employees of Haryana government in 1967 is not available. But the number of OBCs out of the 1.97 lakh employees in Haryana government in 1981 was just 7.8 per cent and this almost doubled to 14.76 per cent in 2001 and stood at 16.68 per cent in 2007. The proportion of SCs out of the 1.97 lakh employees in Haryana government in 1981 was 15.4 per cent and this marginally increased to 15.85 per cent in 1991 but it went up to 19.92 per cent in 2007. This would seem to be adequate representation to SCs in government employment because, according to the Census of 2001, the proportion of these castes in Haryana's population was 19.35 per cent (see Table 2).[22]

Table 2 Employment in Haryana Government Offices

Category	1967	1981	1991	2001	2007
Total	97,385	1,97,832	2,78,040	3,19,027	3,11,340
OBCs	–	15,431	30,342	47,112	51,949
SCs	–	30,492	44,071	59,162	62,049

Source: Calculated from Government of Haryana, *Haryana Economy, 2008*. Publication No. 891 (Economic and Statistical Adviser, Planning Department, Haryana): 17.

---

[22] Government of Haryana, *Haryana Economy, 2008 Publication No. 891* (Economic and Statistical Adviser, Planning Department, Haryana): 17.

The aforementioned data might lead one to believe that SCs and OBCs are happy with the employment pattern in government. This, however, may not be the case. The OBCs could be unhappy that though their quota for government jobs is 27 per cent, all that they have been forked out is 16.68 per cent of the jobs in the Haryana government. On the other hand, SCs could be dissatisfied that their numbers have been ostensibly filled but they have been deprived of better government jobs. It should be noted that in 2007, there were few SCs in the Class I (only 10.15 per cent), Class II (only 10.73 per cent), and Class III (only 14.37 per cent) jobs of Haryana government. But, at almost 33 per cent, the SCs are over-represented in the Class IV jobs and they constitute more than 28 per cent of others in government employment. These others consist of ad hoc, contingency paid, work charged, and contractual employees (see Table 3).[23]

Table 3 Class and Caste of Government Employees in 2007

Class	Total	SC	OBC
Class I	**3,102**	**315**	**184**
Class II	**16,078**	**1,700**	**866**
Class III	**1,86,609**	**26,816**	**30,864**
Class IV	**63,198**	**20,816**	**11,119**
Others	**45,258**	**12,778**	**8,458**
Ad hoc	**67**	**5**	**8**
Contingency paid	**38,761**	**11,565**	**7,174**
Work charged	**297**	**31**	**13**
Contract basis	**9,133**	**1,177**	**1,263**

Source: Calculated from Government of Haryana, *Statistical Abstract, Haryana, 2007–08.* Publication No. 910 (Department of Economic and Statistical Analysis, Haryana, 2009): 674–675.

SUMMING UP

The process of social transformation experienced in Haryana state has not been very cheerful experience. Though after acquiring statehood in 1966 it

[23] Calculated from Government of Haryana, *Statistical Abstract, Haryana, 2007–08.* Publication No. 910 (Department of Economic and Statistical Analysis, Haryana, 2009): 674–675.

has made rapid strides in various fields, the success of the green revolution, its first rate physical and social infrastructure, rapid expansion in the field of education, health services etc. are the parameters used to project the state of modern and progressive. The official version hides as much as it reveals. We have examined Haryana's path of social transformation, which provided a wide gap between appearance and reality. The emphasis on meterial growth and callous neglect of cultural advancement has triggered the major contradiction, which is the mother of many ills afflicting Haryana society today. Harmony between material growth and cultural advancement is the prerequisite for a healthy state. However, in Haryana, there has been a dissonance between the two. Civil society in Haryana is very fragile. Authoritarianism operates at every level-from the family to the government. Haryana appears to be in need of a cultural renaissance, a battle of ideas to come to terms with its historical backlog in terms of identity and culture.

CHAPTER 8

MARRIAGE NORMS, NOTION OF HONOUR, AND KHAPS IN HARYANA

Neerja Ahlawat

The institution of marriage has emerged as a subject of critical investigation in the social sciences due to its close links with processes of historical change and forms of social organisation. In that large segment of an individual's life, which constitutes his social life and involves relationship with another individual, this institution assumes extreme significance. The family unit is not frozen nor is it immune from changes in the political and economic organisation of the concerned society at any specific point of time in history. In addition, given the diversity of the South Asian region, the changing form of the family reflects this linkage in myriad ways (Dube 1997).

The institution of caste plays a very crucial role with regard to marriage in India. It is generally believed that caste is characterised by the obligation to marry within the group, by endogamy. Thus, at first sight, the regulation of marriages is an expression of the principle of separation: castes separate themselves from one another by prohibiting marriage outside the group, just as they forbid contact and commensality between persons belonging to different groups. At a certain level of segmentation, caste prescribes endogamy and thus ensures its own reproduction. One belongs to the caste or sub-caste of one's parents. Although this view may seem satisfactory statistically, theoretically it is too simple and narrow. However, since caste formation itself is diverse in different parts of India, the customary patterns with regard to marriage and family are also varied (Dumont 1970). Although these divisions are most marked in terms of region and religion, often variations exist within regions and within castes. This diversity has been highlighted by the documentation conducted by the Anthropological Survey of India (Singh 1992). Although the majority of the marriages in the rural India are between different clans or different villages, they are nonetheless between the same castes. This is generally referred to as the pattern of caste endogamy and village exogamy in the social sciences. As regards hypergamy and hypogamy, the cases of hypergamy are more frequent than those of hypogamy. In rural India, the status and reputation of the family is of paramount importance in matters of match making, but of late there is some change in thinking and attitudes in this regard. In some villages, marriage may be contracted between villages 5 to 10 miles apart, whereas in some other villages this distance must not be less than 40 miles. There are certain families in the village that do not accept a match for marriage who is living within a hundred mile distance from the village; it should be more than hundred miles for these people (Jayapalan 2002).

In a caste group in North-Indian society, the principles of the hierarchy and equality are articulated in complex ways. The gotra is an exogamous patrilineal clan whose members share and claim patrilineal descent from a common ancestor. The gotra organisation also varies, with the Brahmins claiming origin from the seven sages. The gotra rules evolved and operate differently with regard to Brahmin and non-Brahmin castes and social groups. This is also determined by the fact that some of the tribes/groups are later entrants to the caste system. Yet, there is a social hierarchy within the caste and especially among different gotras within a village, which involves notions of dominant and subordinate gotra. The changes occurring in ideas about rank and equality, along with the increasing differentiation of status, power, and wealth developing within the each caste, recontribute to a re-evaluation of the relative status of different clans and the collapse of the earlier relativity coherent, internally consistent ideology within the caste group (Chowdhry 2004).

The present North-Indian family is patrilineal, patrilocal, and patriarchal. The marriage is generally outside of the kin group and the local group. It is a joint family in which the brides are brought from outside and the girls are given away. The behaviour is strictly regulated according to generations, according to whether one is born in the family or married into the family, and finally according to whether one is a man or a woman. Customs like levirate and sororate, by which a widow marries with the younger brother of her husband and a man marries the younger sister of his wife show that marriage is usually seen to be a relationship between two families rather than between two individuals.

Thus, a caste in a village is held to be patri-clan and so no inter-marriage is allowed in a village. Not only a 'village', but a 'group of villages' are supposed to be settled by a patrilineage and so marriage among its members is prohibited. However, more than one inter-marrying clan may live in one village and these may be known to practice inter-marriage for generations. The rules of marriage strictly enforced upon a person pertain to that (1) one must not marry in his patri-clan which can be called the patri-clan and in some cases also avoid marriage with the children of his mother's siblings and cousins and (2) with the children of his father's sisters and the children of his father's female cousins. This rule is the same as the one which was in vogue in ancient northern India. A person must not marry in his patri-family and must avoid marriage with the sapinda-kin. In almost all castes in northern India, the marriage of cousins is viewed with great disfavour though few cases occur as exceptions. This rule is elaborated in different ways of different communities. In northern India, mostly castes are agricultural and they are divided into exogamous gotras and the marriage rule is that a man must not marry into (1) his father's, i.e. his own gotra, (2) his mother's gotra, and (3) his dadi's gotra, i.e. his father's mother's gotra (Karve 1965).

CHANGING SOCIO-CULTURAL CONTEXT IN HARYANA

An important aspect of the institution of marriage is that it has undergone tremendous changes during the last few years. Marriage in India remains universal and nearly compulsory both for boys and girls as this is an indicator of one's overall position in the society. In case of girls/women, marriage is considered important to protect their sexuality and family honour. In case of men too, marriage is important as it is linked with reproduction, their masculinity, and having control on their wives and children. Haryana is fast urbanising, with extensive consumerist culture and individualism; education being emphasised for employment and marriage in better status families; particularly in case of girl's marriage resulting into higher age at marriage; changing family structure from joint to nuclear family system, where everyone would like to have one's own independent unit.

Census 2011 has shown sharp decline in child sex ratio (830 girls per 1,000 boys) in Haryana. The daughter aversion and son preference continues and this is expressed through rampant use of sex-selection technologies leading to abortions, neglect of female child, and female infanticide (Sudha and Rajan 1999). The aversion for daughters could be linked to inheritance rights of property, as the dominant landowning caste groups are strictly against girl's share in the property (Ahlawat 2012). The consequence of gender imbalance is reflected in the excess of males in the society leading to what demographers call the 'male marriage squeeze'. Scarcity of brides is a serious implication of skewed child sex ratio leading to non-marriage of young men in rural Haryana. The growing numbers of unmarried men is posing the biggest challenge ever felt, disturbing the very fabric of the society. The term *bare-branches* in China, to describe unmarried men without families, has a parallel in the term *malang* in Haryana, which simply indicates 'chronic bachelors' (Ahlawat 2013). As a result, many Haryanvi men are bringing wives from distant states such as Himachal Pradesh, Uttar Pradesh, Bihar, Bengal, Maharashtra, and even Kerala. There are combination of factors like skewed sex ratio, poverty, unemployment, addiction, etc. which are responsible for non-marriage of men (Kaur 2004).

There is a paradoxical situation in the sense that on the one hand Haryana is an economically developed state as it is reflected in the better standard of living, improved health care, increased life span, narrowed literacy level gaps between male and female, and growing opportunities for work for women/girls and on the other hand, there is shaming Haryana with the resurgence of rampant foeticide, honour killings, diktats by kangaroo Panchayats, violence against daughters in natal families on the choice of their marriage partners, etc. Since marriages are strictly marked by endogamy and exogamy and there is a prescribed social and spatial distance, therefore, in such a situation, inter-caste and gotra marriages are not only ridiculed and boycotted but sometimes the couples are eliminated too. There are numerous cases being reported in print and electronic media regarding the young couples in love who either eloped or sought police protection or committed suicide or they were killed in the name of 'family honour' and in extreme cases asked to tie *rakhi* (holy thread) and become brother–sister. This is the present-day scenario in contemporary Haryana. It seems that one of the affluent states of India appears to be more regressive than moving towards a modern egalitarian statehood and has not paved way for equalising gender relations (Chowdhry 1994). In such a situation where universality of marriage is the norm, the consequences of bride shortage, restrictions on marriage, and marriage squeeze become increasingly significant. Thus, there is limited choice of mate selection enforced due to marriage rules and already skewed sex ratio.

OBJECTIVES AND METHODOLOGY

In view of the emerging scenario in Haryana where issues such as skewed sex ratio, Khap diktat, and honour killings are important dimensions to be understood, an attempt has been made to examine marriage norms and restrictions across caste/class/community. How notion of honour or *izzat* is associated to women/girl. What is the social basis of Khaps in sustaining and enforcing marriage rules and prescriptions in the name of gotra and village? This study is based on the extensive ethnographic survey conducted in four villages, namely, Dobh and Bhali in Rohtak District and Kishanpura and Bibipur in Jind District of Haryana.

Obtaining information has been very arduous as people become very apprehensive particularly on issues related to Khaps. Keeping in mind the sensitivity of the issue, with great caution, information was collected using participant observations. Information on sensitive issues such as marriage norms, restrictions on marriage alliances, inter-caste marriages, functioning of traditional Panchayats and elected Panchayats, etc. were collected very carefully during group discussions with different set of people of different age groups. In all, there were 13 cases (from 2009 to 2012) where couples intended to marry against the wishes of parents but these alliances were treated as violations with regard to marriage rules. Both the boys and girls were in the age group of 19–23 years and studying in colleges. There were seven cases where the girls belonged to higher castes such as Brahmin and Jat who wanted to marry boys from Chamar caste. In four cases, Jat girls intended to marry Jat boys from adjoining villages where marriage alliance was prohibited. Except Chamar families who were engaged in occupations such as construction work or salesmanship, the higher caste families were engaged in agriculture. There were two more cases where Jat boys married girls from Punjabi community and Dhanak (SC) caste, respectively. They were excommunicated and not allowed to enter the village.

ARRANGING MARRIAGES IN HARYANA: RULES AND SOCIAL SANCTIONS

Significant aspect of marriage and kinship pattern pertains to certain rules and prescriptions observed while fixing marriage. Kinship system in a way reinforces the institution of marriage that gives the caste system its basic structure. Kinship relations through marriage and legitimacy strengthen caste. Caste endogamy, gotra exogamy, and village exogamy are strongly prescribed norms for marriage. Marriage and kinship regulations specify the norms and restrictions observed such as prohibition of marriage within the same or other prohibited gotras within the caste group called biradari (Chowdhry 2004).

There are specified ways through which these exogamous and endogamous units are identified and operate and bring residents of a village in direct relationship with other villages. In determining exogamous units, ties with a common ancestor with whom links can be traced provide the first step. It happens that a number of descendants become spread over a set of neighbouring villages claiming that they belong to a group of 8 villages or 24 villages. All members of the clan of the relevant caste (sub-caste) regard their fellow members of these villages as bhai-bandhi or those tied in fraternal bonds to an exogamous group. Clan organisations are common in North-West part of India among Rajput, Jat, Gujar, and Tyagi caste. Village exogamy is maintained in Haryana through brotherhood defined by a locality principle; a village may get linked by marriage by a hundred others. Villages touching the boundaries have exogenous status through 'fraternity of common boundary' (*seem ka bhaichara*) (Davis 1941).

Under the Hindu Marriage Act of 1955, except for the observation of the certain prohibited degree of relationship, legal restrictions on the choice of marriage partner are almost non-existent. This implies that under the law, both sagotra (kin in the patrilineal line of descent whose members claim descent from the same gotra ancestor) and inter-caste marriages are permitted (Gupta 1992). Yet, customarily, there are a variety of rules and practices and degrees of prohibited relationship observed in respect to marriage in different regions of India. This is specially marked in the North-South divide. Customary marriage rules in most part of North India upheld caste endogamy and adopt the rule of gotra or gotra exogamy. Most caste groups, upper or lower, follow a rule of three or four gotra exogamy (Lewis 1958). The violation in the observance of these prescribed rules of marriage changes the support structure of production and status not only of the immediate family or clan but also of the whole caste (Chowdhry 2007). This remains an important consideration while settling marriage, particularly in Haryana. Not only this, another important factor having tremendous influence is the control of women's sexuality through marriage which in turn is significantly linked with her production and reproduction capacities so crucial in patriarchal set-up. Claude Meillassoux (1978) in his analysis of the West African rural population argued that the social organisation of the peasantry first revolves around production and then around the necessity of reproduction of the producing unit as it is necessary for the survival of the unit. It implies that marriage must take place within the prescribed group that seeks to reproduce itself in terms of status and control over property. Thus, marriage is a social union of families rather than confined to an individual act. Keeping in view the wider considerations for settling marriages where issues such as caste, gotra, and bhaichara are necessary aspects, marriages are arranged by senior members of the family.

In the field site, it was observed that people strongly follow rules of caste endogamy, village exogamy, and gotra exogamy. In the villages, marriages are not at all allowed in the same village. Besides this, villagers are supposed to avoid neighbouring villages as well while settling marriages. An interesting observation is that except Kumhars, all caste groups leave three gotra, i.e. the gotra of mother, father, and paternal grandmother. Maternal grandmother's gotra is not considered saying *nani-kani kisne mani* (no one bothers about maternal grandmother's gotra). Among Kumhars, there is practice of prohibiting marriage alliances in four gotras. Earlier they used to skip seven gotras. It was also revealed that Kumhars do not have marriage alliances with 'mar-Kumhar' as they are considered lower to Kumhars in hierarchy. These rules are observed to keep village fraternity or bhaichara intact as stated by respondents from the village. Any change in observing such prescriptions are taken as serious violations, resulting in negative sanctions in the form of punishment such as torture, boycotting, and in extreme cases eliminating the couple in the name of honour killing inflicted either by Khap Panchayat or one's own family.

Another norm with regard to distance observed in settling marriage alliances was to marry their children particularly girls not to too far off villages or regions. The main reason attributed by higher caste is that if the distance is short, it takes less time to reach especially when there is some urgency. In case of boys' marriage, even long distance does not matter; 'everything depends on the availability of match' as pointed out by a 45-year-old agriculturist from Jat caste. In case of scheduled caste, it was observed that they did not want to marry their children to very close distance. Ram Prasad, aged 45 from Chamar caste, told that there should be sufficient distance so that relatives rarely visit them otherwise they will keep bothering every now and then (*Juti Jharkaienge*). This reflects the economic concern of poor scheduled caste households with regard to spending on entertaining affinal relations. On the other hand, this was not an issue among higher castes such as Brahmins, Jats, and Khatri/Arora.

KHAPS IN HARYANA: SUSTENANCE AND SURVIVAL

Khap Panchayats in rural Haryana are very well-known for playing the role of moral policing, of the couples who aspire for choice marriages particularly in rural set-up. Khap Panchayats have been in existence for a long time and there are evidences of their presence during Mughal ruler Akbar's regime. Khaps are the legacies of tribal councils that had been formed by various tribes for the resolution of disputes (Pradhan 1966).

Prem Chowdhry (2004) denotes them as caste Panchayats. In any case, these are traditional Panchayats that are patriarchal and revivalist in nature and having no constitutional base and reinforce traditions and norms especially in marriage practices in rural Haryana. Khaps are either in the name of clan or gotra which is dominant in that area such as Dahiya Khap, Hooda Khap, and Gathwala Khap, or by the name of geographical area such as Meham Chaubisi of 24 villages around Meham in Rohtak District and Bawal Chaurasi of 84 villages around Bawal in Rewari District. Although these Khaps claim to be multi-caste where they have representatives of all caste groups including backward castes, scheduled castes, in actual practice these Khaps are represented by Jats only. Women have never been included in any of their activities.

It has been observed through field survey that though people refrain from discussing the activities of Khaps, yet Khaps have their presence shown in terms of important decisions and restrictions imposed on marriage. On asking the role played by Khaps in the past and now, it was noted that across caste lines people do respect these Khaps saying that, 'Khaps have always played positive role in terms of solving marriage and property disputes. Khaps have played vital role in maintaining harmony in the village', stressed an elderly man aged 70 from Jat caste. It shows how these caste Panchayats are manoeuvring influence in rural Haryana by involving issues of day-today life. This is in a way an attempt to create space and legitimacy for their unconstitutional and revivalist actions.

ELOPING COUPLES, NOTION OF HONOUR, AND PUNISHMENT

This phenomenon needs to be understood in the context of patriarchal value system where the notion of *izzat* or honour is gendered, producing inequality and hierarchy, having different implications for men and women. For men, this notion of honour has to be regulated and guarded whereas woman is responsible for keeping the *izzat* (honour) intact. Any violation on the part of women is not just disobedience but stigmatises the whole family, clan, and community (Chowdhry 2007). The family is shamefaced and threatened in front of community/biradari and it justifies the killing of the couple or either of them. Throughout life, a woman is always under the guardianship of a male patriarch and any expression of selection of life partner, in a rural set-up by a woman, is taken as an assertion of her sexuality which is taken as threat to the society. Joseph (1911) has categorically explained that 'a female, minor or adult is always under guardianship; while single she is under the guardianship of her farther, if he be dead, of other relatives. When married, it is her husband who takes her charge and when old or if husband dies, her sons take over her.' The idea of love before marriage is considered feminised and thus unethical and immoral. For a man to be in love with a woman of her choice before marriage is a sure sign of lack of masculinity. As Veena Das (1976) puts it, 'the natural bonds of love and kinship are sacrificed for higher ends of morality and upkeep of honour. This behaviour is grounded on the belief that like social order, individual personality is also purified and lifted from a lower to a higher self by means of sacrifice. A combination of morality, sacrifice and honour absolves the criminals of this action and effectively takes away from the charge of killing the errant women and there is no condemnation of the crime or of the perpetrators.'

During field work, it was observed that inter-caste marriage or marriage in same village or gotra is forbidden, and if there is any violation, it is strictly dealt with. Despite factional politics, people have consensus with regard to marriage norms and practices, where violation of rules is taken serious offence resulting into losing family honour. An interesting observation was that though cases of 'eloping couples' were discussed, people refrained from disclosing the identities of household to avoid bad name to the families and the village.

At the same time there were quite a few households that strongly objected to the killings of boys and girls. Instead, they were of the opinion that they should not stay in the village to avoid unpleasantness as stated by Somraj, a 32-year-old Jat, an agriculturist. With regard to the functioning of Khaps, it was revealed during the field survey that initially parents resisted such marriages and tried to stop them from indulging in the affair but when boy and girl did not listen to their parents only then on the insistence of local caste Panchayat pardhan, a meeting was called where reputed elderly men of the village from different clans, (thola) immediate family members of both the parties, and elected Sarpanch of the village participated and the issue was discussed at length and finally the verdict was passed which was mostly acceptable to parents and community. Very rarely, if the parties showed distrust or dissatisfaction, then the case was passed to territorial Khap of adjoining villages as it was observed in a few cases where both the boy and girl belonged to Jat caste but due to territorial exogamy they were not allowed to marry each other.

Local caste Panchayats enforce strict sanctions against the couple/family. Punishment includes boycotting the family, asking the family to leave the village, and in extreme cases eliminating the girl. It was observed that across caste/class lines, people justify the actions of Khaps. Retired from army,

61-year-old Prem Singh said categorically that 'Khaps are doing the right thing by disciplining boys and girls who violate rules and regulations of marriage. Punishment is essential to create terror to stop such undesirable marriages; otherwise many others will follow them.' Shanti aged 65, from Chamar caste, told that 'boys and girls of this village as well as of adjoining villages are considered brother-sister. If they indulge in love affair or elope with boy/girl of prohibited gotras and villages then no one will tolerate. Who will marry these children? Rather, they will face the consequences and be punished severely so that no one in future dare repeat such shameful act.' She further told that such relationships/marriages bring bad name to the entire family and village. It is a stigma that the whole family suffers throughout ages. 'Media and excessive freedom given to children these days are basically responsible for this degradation in society', she emphasised. Birmati, aged 40, illiterate from Jat caste, mentioned that 'in our community, if there is any violation then it is seriously dealt with. In extreme cases, family is excommunicated and sometimes family is asked to kill the boy/girl.' Among Khatri/Arora, though they too observed restrictions such as village exogamy and follow rules and regulations prescribed by their forefathers since ages, at the same time they did not mind too seriously the inter-caste marriages particularly in case of boys marrying a girl of their choice. Naresh, aged 51 from Khatri/Arora caste, who worked as a mechanic in a factory told that 'in our community, the choice of boy/girl regarding marriage is sought. In case they elope or marry on their own then for few months, family shows anguish but afterwards things become normal and acceptable.'

During group discussion with elderly men and youth, it was observed that people take serious note of such marriages which are prohibited. It was asserted that such marriages disturb the social fabric of society and are black spot and result into loss of 'honour or izzat' of the family including the whole clan. These not only affect the relationships in their own village but also ruin their status and prestige in other adjoining villages. Elderly men very categorically stated that 'in rural set-up, it is one's izzat that is important and if it is gone then what else is left'. Breaching the caste, gotra, and village(s) barriers have been taken seriously, and negative sanctions were attached resulting into strict punishment. Expressing choice for marriage and breaking the prescribed code of conduct was enough ground for either killing the girl or boycotting the family/boy. It was the girl who was held responsible for going astray and eliminating her was the sole punishment for having committed such 'heinous crime'; boy was left with warning not to enter the village premises. Moreover, boys' involvement with the girl was taken as a small mistake often committed in young age as emphasised by majority of people in the village. 'The girl's life is ruined whereas it hardly puts any scar on boy or his family' uttered a middle-aged Chamar woman in Bibipur village. On eloping of the couple, 'it is the girl's family that suffers the most because people cast aspersions on them. She bears the moral backlash. Her kinsmen, particularly brothers, find difficult time while moving out as many people on roadside tease saying unpleasant remarks such as 'since your girl has runaway with a boy so you have no right to say anything. It is difficult to survive in such an oppressive environment and there is no place to go as we are tied to our land and village and this is our identity' as expressed by an elderly, illiterate, Brahman woman of 50 years.

There is gender bias having serious implications on the girl and her family who are held responsible for committing the so-called crime and bear the brunt. It was observed in seven cases, where girls were killed by their parents on the insistence of caste Panchayat by poisoning, whereas boys were made to run away so that their lives were saved. It was only in three cases of affluent Jat families that they did not agree with the Panchayat's decision of killing their daughters; rather, they rejected the decision and pressurised the territorial Khap to take lenient view of the entire episode. The main reason of not killing the girls was because they belonged to affluent families and marrying them in other families was not so difficult for them. On the other hand, the girls who were killed by their own parents belonged to poor families. Since poor families could not bargain with Khaps, and moreover, it was also strongly felt by the parents that no one will marry their daughters due to the stigma attached. Besides this, it was also observed that these girls belonged to higher caste and the boys they intended to marry were from Chamar caste which really led to oppressive situation. 'One can bear a girl from other castes like Brahmin, Khati as there is a common saying that *jat ke beyahi jatni kahai* (a girl from any other higher caste married to a Jat boy is accepted in the family) but surely a boy from lower caste marrying higher caste girl can just not be tolerated. How can we accept lower caste boys as our sons-in-law? It will have dangerous implications on our kinship relations. They will sit and eat with us and one fine day ask their share in property; this is just unthinkable', said Ram Singh, a 62-year-old Jat from agriculturist family. Inter-caste marriages are taken more seriously than gotra marriages and therefore not at all acceptable across caste lines. These developments have to be studied in the context of political economy of the state where the roots lie in the inter-linkage between land, property, caste, and marriage. The sanctions imposed by traditional Panchayats against individuals, families, and often caste groups or sections of its own community show that caste dynamics is taking an ugly turn. Caste Panchayats' interventions in the form of social diktats are the logical outcome of the inter-linkage of caste and gender relations with control of assets in rural India. It was also observed that whatever decision was taken by Khaps, it was conveyed through the elected Sarpanch in the meeting for more sanctity and legality.

There was entirely a different case of a married Brahmin woman and unmarried Jat man who eloped leaving their families behind. She was brought back and accepted in the family not because of liberal attitude of the family but because she was required for domestic work and to look after her small children. Now, where does the honour go! In case of a girl eloping with a boy, it is taken as a loss of family's honour and village honour and killing her is the appropriate punishment to save the lost *izzat* (honour) of the family. Since, in rural Haryana due to skewed child sex ratio, there is shortage of marriageable girls resulting into non-marriage of young men; therefore between daughter and daughter-in-law, though daughters are valued in terms of *ghar ki izzat* (family's honour), yet it is the daughter-in-law who gains importance as she is required for production and reproduction to continue the family name by producing children, particularly sons, and sustain patriarchy (Kaur 2010).

These punishments are in a way attempts to intrude into personal space of consenting individuals and dictating terms to sabotage their freedom of choice to enter into matrimony. Although society puts emphasis on education and employment of both boys and girls, yet it does not permit them to take decisions regarding marriage. The special space created as a result of exposure to outside world, rural–urban convergence, media, education, and employment opportunities does not provide enough ground to deal with emerging situations efficiently and with maturity.

In a way, serious crisis is penetrating deep inside the village social structure in Haryana, where forces of tradition and modernity are in sharp contrast defying each other. On the one hand, caste Panchayats are reluctant to have softer stand on marriages by choice. They hardly have any consensus on relaxing ban on gotras to make marriages possible. On the other hand, due to practice of hypergamy, girls are married in better status families not in terms of domination of clan or land. With fast changing rural society, education and employment, particularly in the public sector and urban set-up, are the new indicators of the status of boy and his family. Highly skewed child sex ratio in Haryana has led to acute shortage of marriageable girls leading to male marriage squeeze where Haryanvi men have no problems whatsoever in having marriage alliances with girls whose caste, culture, or even religion does not match. They bring brides from poorer states with better sex ratio such as Assam, West Bengal, Orissa, Kerala, etc. But at the same time, they have complete control over the sexuality of their own girls/women who are kept under tight control, particularly in the context of finding suitable matches for them. There were large number of cases where highly educated girls were married to constables, conductors, or peons; the criteria being public sector jobs, i.e. lifetime security of the girl (Ahlawat 2009).

Caste differentials also show that since caste Panchayats do not have any profound influence on Punjabi community, therefore, they are not much governed by their diktats. On the other hand, other caste groups in traditional framework which fall under the jajmani relationships obey the dominant caste Panchayat, i.e. the moral policing.

NEXUS BETWEEN CASTE PANCHAYAT AND ELECTED PANCHAYAT

It has been observed that the affiliation between Khap Panchayat and elected Panchayat is very strong in the sense that in every meeting along with other members of caste Panchayat, the presence of elected Sarpanch is compulsory to avoid any legal hassles. The decisions taken by them on marriage restrictions and norms have the bearing of elected Sarpanch for greater acceptability. The elected Sarpanch does not have free will of his own, rather he puts stamp on the judgement taken by caste Panchayat. Not only this, these caste Panchayats have a strong bearing while selecting candidates for Panchayati Raj Institutions (PRIs). These Panchayats enjoy not merely political support but also play dominant role in local politics so as to ensure that the authority of rural elites continues to be upheld. The patronisation of these Panchayats by the political parties seems to be the result of the hegemonisation of caste relations over the polity, whereby the political actors themselves firmly believe and support institution like Khaps and their actions too.

State government, police, bureaucrats, etc. have always remained indifferent or supported caste Panchayat, whatever decisions they may take. In the name of family honour and bhaichara, these caste Panchayats enjoy power and legitimise their existence even in changing profile of village social structure. This is how these Panchayats maintain their hegemony in the village, particularly in the absence of effective functioning of elected Panchayats. In fact, both the elected as well as the caste Panchayat mutually strengthen each other to perpetuate and control the village power structure. The hegemonic caste relations reinforce these caste Panchayats that help strengthen them to perpetuate the existing caste as well as gender inequalities in the society. The politicians have often hailed Khaps' contribution in preserving the social fabric of Haryana; titled Khaps as social organisations that are contributing significantly to maintain peace and harmony in the society.

The situation at the moment is quite grim and unpredictable as there is tussle between individuals and families and between families and Panchayats. In the process, it is the traditional Panchayat that exercises its authority in connivance with elected Panchayat. Now, it is high time that state intervenes and realises its responsibility and manages to come out of the shadow of 'vote bank politics'. It is pertinent for the state to curb extra judicial powers of Khaps. There is need to create an environment of dialogue, freedom, and gender space to protect individual interests. For this, civil society organisations, academia, activists, and media together should take the lead.

REFERENCES

Ahlawat, N. (2009). 'Missing Brides in Rural Haryana', *Social Change*, 39(1), March.

——. (2012). 'The Political Economy of Haryana's Khaps', *Economic and Political Weekly*, XLVII(47/48), December 1.

——. (2013). 'Customary Traditions, Institution of Marriage and Social Change'. Unpublished Report, Women's Studies Centre, M.D.U., Rohtak.

Chowdhry, P. (1994). *The Veiled Women: Shifting Gender Equations in Rural Haryana, 1880–1990*. Delhi: Oxford University Press.

——. (2004). 'Private Lives, State Intervention: Cases of Runaway Marriage in North India', *Modern Asian Studies*, 38(1/2).

——. (2007). *Contentious Marriages, Eloping Couples*. New Delhi: Oxford University Press

Das, V. (1976). 'Masks and Faces: An Essay in Punjabi Kinship', *Contributions to Indian Sociology*, 10 (i).

Davis, K. (1941). 'Inter-Caste Marriage in Caste Societies', *American Anthropologist*, 43(3), July–September.

Dube, L. (1997). *Women and Kinship*. Jaipur: Rawat Publications.

Dumont, L. (1970). *Homo-Hierarchicus: The Caste System and Its Implications*. Chicago: Oxford University Press.

Gupta, S.V. (1992). *Hindu Law*. Nagpur: All India Reporter.

Jayapalan, N. (2002). *Rural Sociology*. New Delhi, Atlantic Publishers and Distributors.

Joseph, E. (1911). *The Customary Law of the Rohtak District*. Lahore: Government Printing.

Kaur, R. (2004). 'Across Region Marriages: Poverty, Female Migration and Sex Ratio', *Economic and Political Weekly*, XXXIX(25).

——. (2010). 'Khap Panchayats, Sex Ratio and Female Agency', *Economic and Political Weekly*. 65(23).

Karve, I. (1965). *Kinship Organization in India*. Bombay: Asia Publication House.

Lewis, O. (1958). *Village Life in North India*. Urbana: University of Illinois.

Meillassoux, C. (1978). 'The Social Organization of the Peasantry: The Economic Basis of Kinship', in David Seddon (ed.), *Relations of Production: Marxist Approaches to Economic Anthropology*. London: Frank Cass.

Pradhan, M.C. (1966). *The Political Systems of the Jats of Northern India*. London: Oxford University Press.

Singh, K.S. (1992). *People of India: An Introduction*. Calcutta, Anthropological Survey of India.

Sudha, S. and S.I. Rajan. (1999). 'Female Demographic Disadvantage in India, 1991: Sex Selective Abortions and Female Infanticide, 1981–1991', *Development and Change*, 30(2): 585–561

CHAPTER 9

SOCIAL TRANSFORMATION OF PEASANTRY IN THE BORDER BELT OF PUNJAB: A STUDY

Jagrup S. Sekhon

The objective of this paper is to highlight the plight of the farmers living in the border belt of Punjab, particularly of those unfortunate ones who have their agriculture land across the fencing on the border and who live in abject conditions. Punjab, one of the most prominent states of India, primarily as the province that was most scared by the partition of the country leading to the creation of Pakistan and her subsequent resurgence as the leading agrarian economy has ever been in the glare of attention. The resilience of her people, though the vicissitudes of history, especially the farming community, has been exemplary.

Contiguous to Pakistan, Punjab has a long stretch of border, i.e. 553 km running across four districts, i.e. Gurdaspur, Amritsar, Tarn Taran, and Ferozpur, commencing in the North from where the west branch of Ujh river enters into Indian Punjab from the Jammu & Kashmir in Gurdaspur District and ends in South-West of Punjab where Sutlej River enters Pakistan in Ferozpur District. The border is also criss-crossed by rivers Ravi and Sutlej and many dozen of villages are located across these rivers in Gurdaspur and Ferozpur districts. As a sequel to the partition in 1947, the border was part of the Radcliff plan. It is artificially marked by stones, bars, pillars, and fence and is rigorously guarded by the Border Security Force (BSF), many times with undesirable level of man-machine interface (Bakshi 2008: 143).

The partition of the country on communal lines had an unparalleled human catastrophe of killings and uprooting of a massive number of Hindus and Sikhs from Pakistan and Muslims from India. It is estimated that there were half a million causalities and 13 million migrations (Datta 2002: 13). Since communalism was the genesis of the division of the country, it left equally deeply distracting and uneasy relationship between the two countries. Even after 64 years of partition and separation of Pakistan from India, the baggage of history weighs heavy on both the states (Kaur 2010: 4–5). Since then, both countries have looked one another as enemies and had fought many wars and had war-like situations and military stand-off on the border. There has hardly been any cordial atmosphere between the two countries. It has ever been a chronology of hostilities.

India has been vigilant enough to foil the evil designs of Pakistan and has erected a fencing to check the nefarious activities of Pakistan aimed at destabilising peace and progress within our country. The constant vigil and extra preventive measures by the Indian government to protect the border is inarguably pious in intent, but the over zeal at the border has created existential problems for the farmers in the border belt, especially for those whose agricultural land falls beyond the barbed-wire fencing, but inside the Indian Territory.

The volatility on the border has adversely affected the lives of the people. Their activities are not only restricted but are also kept under surveillance. Pakistan unleashed a series of overt and covert activities against India, trying every trick to subvert the peace and harmony in India. Infiltration of terrorists and supply of deadly weapons from across the border during terrorist violence in Punjab (1978–1993), assumed great concern in India. Consequent upon the continued belligerence of the hostile neighbour, Indian security forces have to be hypersensitive to each and every movement at and around the border. Obviously, such extra caution on the part of the security forces entail untold sufferings to those farmers living at and around the fencing. Primarily, their movements and their activities are put under restraints. Time is rationed out to these farmers to attend to their land (fields) during agricultural operations. So miserable and un-mitigating is their daily existence that they feel themselves dangling between the devil and the deep sea, held hostage by hard luck.

Many such farmers could no more suffer the perpetual harassment and humiliation and left their hearths and homes and migrated to other areas which assured them security and dignity. Others shifted their families to safer areas, but they themselves continued to stay behind to eke out their living in humiliating conditions tending to the fields as they can under given circumstances.

Yet another factor that piles up to the miseries of these luckless farmers is the fury of floods in Ravi and Sutlej rivers which criss-cross the border and visits the area unrelentingly during rainy season. The villages across these rivers remain inaccessible for days on end.

The paper is part of a research project entitled 'Problems of Border Area Farmers: An Empirical Study' sanctioned by the Indian Council of Social Science Research (ICSSR), New Delhi. The universe of the study is the border belt of Punjab. A total of 25 villages were randomly selected from the four border districts in Punjab. The study is based on field work. Two exhaustive interview schedules were prepared: one related to get comprehensive information about the village since partition of the country, and the other to know the profile and the problems of the farmers having land across the fencing on the border. This paper has been divided into four parts. Part I gives an overview of the border belt. Part II describes the available amenities in the studied border villages. Part III highlights the structural problems of the farmers having land across the fencing on the border. Finally, Part IV concludes the study.

PART I

AN OVERVIEW OF BORDER BELT

The border belt consists of the area falling in the radius of 16 km from the zero line. Earlier, the radius of border belt was 8 km from the zero line which was later on extended to 16 km by the then Akali-Bhartiya Janata Party government headed by Mr. Parkash Singh Badal in 1998. With the extension of the radius of border belt, a total of 1,838 villages, a few towns, and two district headquarters, i.e. Gurdaspur and Ferozpur became part of the border belt. These villages and towns fall in 18 development blocks of 4 border districts. Out of these 1,838 villages in the border belt, 279 are located on the zero line. These villages are very close to the international border and are located within the radius of 500 m to 3 km from the zero line. According to the official record, the number of such villages is 279 but only 212 villages exist in reality. The remaining villages have simply disappeared from the existence because of the numerous problems in the area. Such villages are called *Be-Cherag* (un-inhibited) or ghost villages. The residents of these villages fled and settled in some other villages or cities because of the vulnerability of the area due to hostility of Pakistan and proneness to the floods. However, mention to be made here is that many dozen villages still exist across these two rivers and other rivulets which criss-cross border.

An overview of the border belt shows that it has remained neglected on all counts as various studies and reports show a very low human development index (Mangat 2010: 4–5). The government institutions like schools, dispensaries, and other institutions essential for development are either non-existent or dysfunctional for various reasons, i.e. natural and human. The Green Revolution brought about an economic transformation in rural Punjab leading to the creation of infrastructure, e.g. roads, schools, markets, electricity, research, and extension services; however, the border belt remained neglected which caused further disparities in the developmental process between the two areas in rural Punjab. The people in the border belt did not get any access to modern facilities, financial assistance, etc. which further alienated them from any economic growth. Even now, after more than 63 years of independence, the farmers of the border belt face a lot many structural problems in their day-to-day life.

The overall condition of these villages Is a perfect picture of disbelief. One wonders if these areas are a part of vibrant Punjab which is proud of its agriculture community as all indicators of growth are conspicuously non-existent. Any resurgence is obviously discounted at the face of the things, whatever.

The road connectivity is in bad shape and there is large number of villages which are not connected with roads at all. It was found in almost all the villages which fall across the Satlej and Ravi rivers in Ferozpur and Gurdaspur districts. The literacy level in the border villages is dismally low. The overall rate of literacy in Punjab was 69.95 per cent, as per the 2001 Census. In Ferozpur District, it was between 49 – 57 per cent in the border blocks, while in Bhikiwind and Valtoha blocks of Tarn Taran District, it was 54.19 per cent and 41.96 per cent, respectively. It was just 54.86 per cent in Ajnala block of Amritsar District (Mangat 2010: 4)

Table 1 gives the number of villages in the border belt and number of villages on the border in four border districts of Punjab.

Table 1 District-wise Description of Border Belt

District	Total Villages	Village in Border Belt	Village on Zero Line
Gurdaspur	1,659	733	64
Amritsar	737	286	38
Tarn Taran*	579	191	116
Ferozpur	1,072	628	61
Total	**4,047**	**1,838**	**279**

Note: *Tarn Taran was made district in 2006. Earlier it was part of Amritsar.

Gurdaspur District has the largest number of villages in the border belt followed by Ferozepur, Amritsar, and Tarn Taran. But on the other hand, Tarn Taran has the maximum number of villages, i.e. 116 on the zero line followed by Gurdaspur, Ferozpur, and Amritsar. The variation in the latter case is because of zig zag boundary of the border.

PART II

INFRASTRUCTURE SETTING IN THE BORDER BELT

The countryside in Punjab witnessed enormous changes in the post-independent period with the enactment of various legislative measures. It resulted in the expansion of occupational opportunities and the administrative set-up. The new laws and administrative set-up required a rational social structure and for that education, health, and connectivity are important elements. Education and health are indicators of the quality of the population and require strong infrastructure. But in case of border belt, all these indicators are simply non-existent.

Table 2 Educational Institutions

School	Gurdaspur	Amritsar	Tarn Taran	Ferozpur	Total
No School	1	–	–	–	1
Elementary	3*	3	–	3	9
Middle	–	2	2	–	4
High	–	2	2	2	6
Higher Secondary	1	–	4 **	1	6
ITI	1	–	–	–	1
Total	**6**	**7**	**8**	**6**	**27**

** Three primary schools which caters to the needs of Wazidpur and Hasanpur.*

*** Village Khalra has two senior secondary schools.*

Table 2 shows the education scenario in the border villages. Village Kamalpur in Gurdaspur District does not have even a primary school as it is located very close to the border. The kids travel at least 4 km to attend school in Kakkar village which is situated outside the *Dhussi bandh* on Ravi River. There are three primary schools* which caters to the needs of the two villages, i.e. Wazidpur and Hasanpur. Village Bamial, which is also the block headquarter of Gurdaspur District, has one senior secondary school and an Industrial Training Institute (ITI).

The situation is not different in Amritsar District where there is no senior secondary school in the studied villages, while there are four senior secondary schools in three border villages of Tarn Taran District. It may be mentioned that village Khalra** has two senior secondary schools one for boys and other for girls. Hazara Singh Wala is the only village in Ferozpur District having a senior secondary school. Most of the students in the villages having only primary schools cover a distance of 10–15 km for their education in middle, high, and senior secondary schools. The situation is even worse in the villages which are located across Ravi in Gurdaspur District and Satlej in Ferozpur District. The students from these villages have to cover many miles to reach the schools by crossing rivers on boat.

The working conditions in the schools were found to be deplorable as there was hardly any environment of teaching and learning. There are many schools where only one or two teachers are posted and the remaining posts remain vacant as the newly appointed teachers manage their postings in the nearby towns or cities; some schools remain locked during rains or on any other adverse development on the border. We were told by our respondents that many teachers attend schools on alternate days as there are no official checks over them. There were reports of subletting the teaching in these schools. The permanent teachers live in the nearby cities or their native places and depute someone else to go to school or mark their attendance by paying them a substantial amount in return.

Although some private schools have come up in these villages, the quality of teaching is very poor. These are mere teaching shops run by untrained, unqualified, and less-paid teachers. Overall scenario of education in the border belt is dismal.

Table 3 Health Facilities

Facility	Gurdaspur	Amritsar	Tarn Taran	Ferozepur	Total
Primary Health Centre	1	—	2	1	4
Government Dispensary	1	3	4	1	9
No Facility	3	4	1	4	12
Total	**5**	**7**	**7**	**6**	**25**

Table 3 gives details of health facilities in the studied villages. The health scenario in these villages is as gloomy as it is in the case of education. The villages of Tarn Taran District are somewhat better placed for providing medical facilities than the other three districts. As there are two primary health centres in villages Rajo Ke and Naushara. Four villages have dispensaries including one established by a charitable organisation *Punjarjot*. On the other hand, the situation in the villages in other three districts leaves a lot to be desired. Although dispensaries were opened to provide medical facilities to the people, hardly any doctor or other para-medical staff are posted there to visit these dispensaries as they reside in far-flung urban areas. The pregnant and ailing women are transported to the nearby health centres on tractor trolleys or through boat. Many mishaps such as miscarriages were reported by the affected villagers. There is total deprivation of health facilities for both the people and their livestock. Untrained and unregistered medical practitioners who visit the ailing person in these villages command much respect among the villagers there. The government dispensaries particularly in remote villages are dysfunctional, hardly open, and do not get regular supply of medicines.

The situation is worst in 12 villages where no governmental medical facility is available. Most of these villages are from Gurdaspur and Ferozpur districts and fall across the Ravi and Sutlej rivers.

Table 4 Transport Facilities

Mode	Gurdaspur	Amritsar	Tarn Taran	Ferozepur	Total
Government transport	1	1	—	—	2
Private transport	2	5	7	3	17
No facility	2	1	—	3	6
Total	**5**	**7**	**7**	**6**	**25**

Table 4 illustrates the road connectivity of the studied villages. There are only two villages one each in Gurdaspur (Bamial) and Amritsar (Kakkar) districts where public transport facility is available. The residents of 17 villages have facility of private transport, i.e. mini buses, three wheelers, etc. There are six villages in three districts where no transport facility is available. The residents have to walk 3 to 6 km to catch bus to go to the tehsil or district headquarter. Most of these villages are located across Ravi and Sutlej and are close to the border. There are platoon bridges which are manned by the BSF in peace times and army in war or war-like situations. These bridges are dismantled when water rises in the rivers and during war times. The life in such villages comes to standstill in such situations.

PART III

TERRORISM AND PEASANTRY

The terrorist violence in the state (1978–1992) brought untold miseries to the people of the border belt when the Government of India decided to fence the border to check infiltration of terrorists, the supply of deadly weapons from Pakistan, and latter's involvement in terrorism in Punjab. Although the fence helped to contain terrorism in Punjab, it brought about fundamental changes in crop patterns, timings for cultivation, and other agricultural operations along with several restrictions imposed on the movement of farmers across the fence.

The central government took final decision to fence the border in 1986. There was a popular government in the state headed by Surjit Singh Barnala. He constituted a high-powered committee under the chairmanship of S. L. Kapoor, the then chief secretary, and asked him to look into the whole issue, particularly the problems likely to arise out of the fencing. The other members of the committee were three deputy commissioners of border districts, i.e. Gurdaspur, Amritsar, and Ferozpur, and various high officials of the state government. After going through the various aspects of the issue, the committee recommended the following (Randhawa 2008):

1. The fence should be just between 50 to100 yards from the international border so that a minimum number of farmers were affected.
2. Full payment of the land acquired for fencing.
3. Payment of special inconvenience bonus to the farmers for cultivating land beyond the fencing.
4. Adjustment of the timings of the opening and the closing of entry gates for the convenience of farmers.
5. Issuing of identity cards to all residents of the affected villages, in general, and farmers having land across fence, in particular.
6. Permitting the migrant labourers to work in the fields.
7. Regular supply of three-phase electricity to the villages during day time.

8. Permission to carry canal water beyond fencing wherever possible.
9. Allotment of four *Kanals* of land to each farmer whose total land falls beyond fencing, to feed the livestock.

These recommendations proved to be unrealistic because of certain reasons. Firstly, the Pakistan government raised objection to the decision of the Indian government and started creating hurdles in the execution of the fencing itself which began in mid 1987. There were reports of firing from Pakistan side on the workers who were assigned the task. The work came to a stop and most of the workers fled from the site for the safety of their lives. Secondly, by that time the state of Punjab came under president's rule, the situation in the state was deteriorating day after day due to increasing infiltration from across the border. There was complete ban on any political activity particularly of the farmers. The Government of India was determined to go ahead with the project and ordered the concerned authorities to complete the task of fencing without bothering about any hostility. The convenience and the safety of the workers were given prime consideration. Anyhow the fencing was erected at some places 2 to 3 km away from the border. The total length of the border is 553 km while the length of the fence is 462 km (Chhina 2007: 3).

This resulted into a life-long problem for more than 11,000 farmers of 212 villages belonging to four border districts. A total of more than 17,000 acres of cultivable land fell across fence which is manned by BSF in peace times and Indian Army during wars and any and every escalation of tension between the two neighbours. This development deprived the farmers of the free access to their own fields and thereby of their own convenience. The fencing left them insecure and helpless in their own country as agricultural operations across the fencing were regulated by the orders of these security forces.

IMPACT OF FENCING ON THE FARMERS

The most painful irritant that has offset their life pattern has been the denial of free access to their own lands. It has not only thrown their life out of gear but also deprived these mostly marginalised farmers of their only means of subsistence. Their working hours across the fields are limited and fixed, that too at the convenience of the security forces guarding the border. Due to the structural problems, officially the farmers can work daily in their fields from 9 a.m. to 4 p.m., but the ground reality has been far from that. The timings of the access of the farmers across the fencing are subject to many other factors.

The farmers who have the land across the fencing have to go through rigorous security checks at the gates. They must carry their identity cards. Then their body search is conducted. Their lunch boxes, fertilizer, seed bags, and farm implements are thoroughly scrutinised. Tool kits are not allowed with any farm machinery. No farmer is allowed to take labourers who do not have valid identity cards with them. Both the coming and going to the fields is recorded strictly and as per the security norms. So farmers who would like to engage more workforce in their fields for want of time or due to any other personal reasons feel handicapped. Sometimes in bad weather, be it rain, fog, or floods, the farmers cannot tend to their crops. At other times, an encounter between infiltrators or smugglers with the BSF puts additional brakes on the movement of the farmers to their fields.

Yet another predicament of the affected farmers is that they have to cover a long distance of more than 2 km on an average to reach their fields through an entry gate, since many of them do not have their land holdings right across. Such an exercise is not only time-consuming but also puts an extra burden in the form of the cost of diesel of the farm machinery and the level of productivity. There are 294 entry gates for the farmers but only 273 are operational throughout the 553 km of the fenced border. These gates are opened on alternate days only during harvesting; otherwise the gates remain closed for days together during winter and especially in rainy and foggy conditions for security reasons.

Again the cultivation of land across fence is allowed only by farm machinery. The majority of the affected farmers has small and marginal land holdings and do not own tractors. They are dependent upon farmers who have tractors and farm machinery for executing their agriculture operations. Such machinery should be already registered with the BSF and such owners should be having land across. The farmers have no choice but to toe the line as the harvesting is allowed only by the harvesting machines – monitored for time and movement by the BSF. Since marginal farmers do not and cannot have the agricultural machinery, they have to wait for their turn to get the harvesting done by some big land holder owning the machinery who in turn gets his own pound of flesh from the petty cheerless farmers, in terms of the charges for harvesting the crops and carrying the grain to this side. Meanwhile, ripe crops run the risk of accidental fire or damage by stray animals and hostile elements from the other side. Thus the petty marginal farmers, caught in vicious circle, are doubly cursed in having their holdings fenced off as also being fleeced off. In the former case, the BSF has their body, the rich farmers – their soul.

Still one more incapacitating stipulation is that the affected farmers are not allowed to grow crops that attain a height of more than three feet, since the taller crops provide an easy natural cover to the infiltrators and smugglers, waiting in the wings to sneak into India and negating the very purpose of fencing the border. Such an imperative may be perfectly in the national interest but it deprives the farmers of the opportunity to optimise the production of the crops and affects the fertility of their holdings. Diversification of crops maintains the fertility of the land. The poor farmers have been getting less and less yield with every passing year.

Additionally, the women are not allowed to work along their menfolk in these fields because of the absence of women BSF personnel to monitor and body-check the women workers. Here too, the marginal farmers have to suffer. They have to engage extra hands (men) at quite high wages, in case they need some help which their womenfolk could have done quite easily.

Misery piled on misery has led to an uncongenial agrarian environment in the border belt of Punjab, especially for farmers whose holdings are fenced off. They have lost the love of their labour. Their land at times remains unattended and untilled. In such a scenario, these farmers would prefer to rent out their holdings or sell the land outright. Here too, their choice suffers from an embargo. The poor fellow can rent out or sell the land to his neighbour only. And it is the neighbour (generally a rich landlord) who dictates and offers dirt cheap prices.

The other important issue was the market price and rent of land across the fence which is one-third of the present prices of the land at this side of the fence. There are a few or no buyers of land across fence. The formal financial institutions like banks and co-operative societies do not sanction loan on land beyond fencing. The farmers are forced to get loan from commission agents or from other informal agencies at very high rate of interest.

PART IV

SUMMING UP

These poor people are the 'dangling' farmers, who can neither own nor disown their own land. Caught between the devil and the deep sea, they lead a cursed existence. Added to their sad state of affairs is their illiteracy. They have no voice to express their grievances; it seems there is a communication gap between these farmers and those who could come to their rescue. The irony of the matter is that whole of the state and the central government, day in and day out, swear by the promises for the progress of farmers and *Aam Admi*; the farmers organisations and human rights activists cry hoarse against human rights violations; the farmers of the border belt seem to have been abandoned by the governments and punished by the nature. Recently, they organised themselves under an umbrella organisation, Border Area Sangarsh Committee, to articulate their demands for getting justice from the concerned authorities.

How and in what way this committee will change the plight of these harassed souls, is a matter of time to see.

REFERENCES

Bakshi, S. (2007) . 'Policing the Borders', *Journal of Political Science*, 4(1), April.

Chhina, M. A. S. (2007). 'Life on the Edge', *Hindustan Times* (Sunday Magazine), December 16.

Datta, V. N. (2002). 'Lord Mountbatten and the Punjab Boundary Commission Award', in S. Settar and I. B. Gupta (eds.), *Pangs of Partition*. New Delhi: Manohar.

Kaur, H. (2010). 'Study of Exclusion in the Borderbelt of Punjab', *Research Report-2,* Centre for the Study of Social Exclusion and Inclusive Policy, Amritsar: GNDU Press.

Randhawa, R. S. (2007). 'Interview with Him', July 27.

CHAPTER 10

ROLE OF MOVEMENT IN SOCIAL TRANSFORMATION: A SOCIOLOGICAL ANALYSIS OF THE DALIT CHRISTIANS AGITATION IN TAMIL NADU

Rambabu A.

Indian society has a unique system of social stratification which places the people in a hierarchical order regulated by an institutional framework namely the 'Caste System'. This system is a closed structure that restricts any movement of the persons belonging from one stratum to another as it is believed to be a divine origin, and the birth of a person into a particular caste is predestined based on his/her previous birth. It is an essential characteristic of the Hindu religion and it resulted in a number of forms of discrimination and socio-economic and political exclusion.

However, such exclusionary aspects of the casteism have been contested by people at various points of time in variety of ways. One such way is conversion to other religions as a mark of protest to the discriminatory practice of caste system. As Robinson and Khujur (2010: 5) state, 'For Dalits, religious conversion especially in the 19th century was often perceived as one of the ways of escaping from caste oppression'.[1] However, they also admit that such conversions have not guaranteed any assurance that whether their expectations were fulfilled. Similarly, David Mosse (2010) traces the complex and uneven interaction between Christianity and Dalit activism in Tamil Nadu. Many Dalits in Tamil Nadu got converted to Christianity in mass movements. Through conversion, they sought to overcome the oppression of caste and their position as the so-called untouchables.[2]

There is difference of opinions about religious conversions. While some may regard it as an act of 'liberation' others may argue that material gains too may motivate conversions. As Walter Fernandes states, 'Christians often view conversion as a purely spiritual phenomenon, while those opposed to them may view it only as a change caused by material inducements. Though spiritual motivation is important, the material factor cannot be brushed aside as irrelevant.'[3] By saying that, Fernandes also considers the 'change in religion' as a 'social movement' that paved way for a larger social transformation.

Although conversion to another religion is an individual's choice, historical evidences have shown us that it could be used as an act of attaining liberation. According to T. K. Oommen (2010: 50), 'Conversion is an individual act borne out of conviction of the converted about the goodness of the religion into which one converts.'[4] Interestingly, he further explains the causes for mass conversions that took place at various points of time. He states:

> India's caste system necessitated group conversion because the converted individual could not be located in the social structure ignoring his/her caste background resulting in the formation of new identity groups such as neo-Buddhists, Dalit Christians or Ajlaf Muslims.[5]

When Christianity began to get rooted in India, people primarily decided to embrace it as a mark of protest against casteism, seeking their right to live with equality and human dignity. Of course, it is not without any valid reason. It is a historical fact, the missionaries declared emphatically that there was no place for caste discrimination in Christianity and opposed casteism. However, when people from different castes became Christians, they carried along with them the hierarchical caste system with all its evil. In the long run, casteism got entrenched with all its evil forms and designs in the Catholic Church. As a result, the Dalits were discriminated again within the Church. Thus, a new category called 'Dalit Christians' was created.

In recognition to this, the Tamil Nadu Bishops Council (TNBC) and Tamil Nadu-Pondicherry Catholic Religious of India (TNPCRI) observe:

> Though there is no place for caste discrimination and untouchability in Christ's teaching, it is painful to see that the forms of untouchability and discriminatory practices are still prevalent in the Church.[6]

At this juncture, it is also important for us to emphasise upon the fact that how the term 'Dalit Christians' evolved and acquired significance both in the official discourses and also in the common parlance. S. M. Michael provides a detail description about the origin of the term 'Dalit Christians'. Initially, the Dalit converts to Christianity were called the

'Christians of Scheduled Caste Origin (CSCO)'. This name was commonly accepted after the First National Convention of Christian Leaders on the Plight of Christians of Scheduled Caste Origin in 1978 (NBCLC 1978) (Michael 2010: 54).[7] However, he points out that Christian circles began to use the term 'Dalit' for scheduled castes at the end of the 1970s and in the early 1980s. He further elaborates the evolution of the term 'Dalit Christian' and its acceptance by the official bodies of Christianity in the following manner:

> The concept and category of 'Dalit Christians' and the slogan 'Dalit is dignified' were formulated by the Christian Dalit Liberation Movement in 1985. National Churches and Ecumenical Councils (World Council of Churches) have become familiar with the term since 1986. Though the concept and the use of the term Dalit Christians were common among the Protestants from the end of the 1970s onwards, the Catholics began to use this term a little later. The National Convention of All India Catholic Union (AICU) in 1989, decided to refer to Scheduled Caste Christians as Dalit Christians (*ibid.*).

As the Dalits encounter the caste system even after becoming Christians, they faced a three-fold oppression. Firstly, they face discrimination from Hindus, who do not make any differentiation between the Dalit Hindus and Dalit Christians. As Kumar and Robinson (2010) point out in their article citing examples from Andhra Pradesh, caste Hindus in the countryside do not differentiate between a converted Dalit Christian and a Dalit Hindu. 'All Dalits are', they observe, 'meted out the same treatment by those considered high in the caste hierarchy.'[8]

Secondly, Dalits also face discrimination from those regarded as upper caste Christians. There are some detailed studies about how, in some places, there are separate seating arrangements for the Dalits in churches, while in others liturgical services are performed separately for those presumed 'high' or 'low' in caste. Sometimes, Dalits are asked to sit on the floor, even where raised seating is available and there are in some places, two cemeteries and two hearses for dead bodies. In some places, separate queues are formed for receiving Holy Communion (Michael 2010: 53)[9] and Mary John (2007).[10]

S. M. Michael in his article titled 'Dalit Encounter with Christianity: Change and Continuity' identifies the kinds of changes brought in the lives of converts after they embrace Christianity. He argues that due to the initiatives taken by some missionaries in admitting Dalit Christians in their schools and hostels they have attained education and were able to achieve some degree of occupational mobility. He provides examples for how some of them manage to leave behind 'menial' and 'manual' forms of labour and enter into slightly more respectable occupations (Michael 2010: 52 – 53). Thus, Michael writes, 'the Dalit Christians, who have been looked down on as "nobody" in the society, have become "somebody"' (*ibid.*). However, he also draws our attention to the fact that the structural-functional changes brought about in their lives have not resulted in an egalitarian society among the Christians.

Likewise, in the North Indian context, Schmalz (2005) records that the Dalit Christians undergo marginalisation within the Christian community. He calls the upper caste Catholics as 'Asli Catholics' (True Catholics) and the converted Chamars as 'Bhasali Catholics' (Trapped Catholics).[11] According to him, the Bhasali Catholics are trapped between Catholicism and untouchability.

We shall also take note of the fact that the Dalit Christians are not a homogenous community. The diversities among them have also been highlighted. John Webster (2010), for instance, identifies five Dalit congregations, which he has chosen for their diversity. Each belongs to a different Christian denomination. Three are from Punjab, and one each from Delhi and western Uttar Pradesh. Of these congregations, two are urban and three rural. The five congregations are Holy Trinity Church at Turkman Gate in Delhi, Our Lady of Assumption Church in Gakhlan village in Punjab, the Evangelical Church of God in Punjab's Ferozpur City, the Church of North India in Bhattian village near Ludhiana in Punjab, and the Dalit Avataris of the Rural Presbyterian Church in western and central Uttar Pradesh.[12] Webster not only analyses the diversity of forms of worship among these Dalit congregations, but also explores to draw some general conclusions about Dalit Christianity in North India from the study.

Thirdly, the Dalit Christians had to encounter the state (both at the centre and at the state levels) in order to get their political and civic rights. For instance, they are considered not eligible to the entitlements meant for the scheduled castes guaranteed by the Constitution of India. Robinson and Khujur (2010: 3) observe,

> The state also discriminates against and excludes the Dalit Christians. In independent India, they have been excluded from the list of Scheduled Castes (SCs). Thus, they have not had access to the privileges of positive discrimination that other Dalits could avail of. They were not eligible for reservations in local government structures or in education and employment.

Even more crucially, as Kumar and Robinson observe, they have been denied the protection of the Scheduled Castes and Scheduled Tribes

(Prevention of Atrocities) Act of 1989. They are, thus, vulnerable to oppression and even violence from the so-called upper castes.[13]

In some states, Dalit Christians are placed in the category of the Other Backward Classes (OBCs). As a result, they are not in a position to contest with those well-off communities that are placed in the OBC category. David Mosse, for instance, observes through his study that in Tamil Nadu the Dalit Christians are not able to compete with the dominant communities.

The above-mentioned observation acquires significance in our discussion of the Movement of the Dalit Christians which is demanding for justice. Although they have converted to Christianity to protest against the casteist oppressions they suffered in Hinduism, the historical injustice inflicted upon them needs to be redressed. Hence, it becomes important to include the Dalit Christians in the frameworks of 'Inclusive Policies'.

THE DALIT CHRISTIANS' STRUGGLES AGAINST THE CATHOLIC CHURCH

As stated earlier, the Dalit Christians do not get equal treatment within Christian Churches. Their initial struggles were mainly against the unequal treatment they had to receive from the upper caste Christians and also against the Church leadership. Mary John provides a very extensive historical account of the entrance of caste system into Christianity and gives a number of examples of conflicts between the Dalit Christians and the others within the Church hierarchical order.[14] He observes,

> The European Missionaries in India were concerned only with the conversion and did not interfere with the social order that was based on caste system. In fact they consciously decided that there is no need to change the social tradition and relationships of the converts. Even as early as 1620, discriminatory approach was adapted in teaching and training converts. Robert De Nobili, a Jesuit priest who was based in Tamil Nadu, taught and trained Brahmin converts separately, himself observing and adopting their caste practices. A complaint was sent about it to the Pope. But the Papal Bull of Pope Gregory XV, in January 1623 allowed accommodating caste practices among new converts. Thus casteism entered the Church unchallenged. With the European Missionaries leaving, the Indian priests, religious, the hierarchy and the upper caste Christians only replicated or reproduced the caste domination over Dalit Christians even more rigorously as it existed in the society outside. (Mary John 2007: 110)

It is to be noted that the Catholic Congregations justified the continuation of caste system in Christianity too. Fernandes gives an elaborate explanation about how the Portuguese Missionaries (especially the De Nobili Group), while converting the upper caste communities, were consciously allowing them to continue with their hierarchical order. He writes,

> When a few Brahmins were baptized, he allowed them to retain all their caste symbols and customs except those that went directly against Christianity. He knew that these were also symbols of hierarchy but he was convinced that since the caste system was a social hierarchy and not a religious element, it could be retained. He interpreted it according to the European Estates system and, defending the retention of its symbols, he argued that if hierarchical order could be maintained in Europe, if various classes of people could be made to kneel in different parts of the church, if Jews in Europe could be obliged to wear a yellow cap in order to show their difference from the baptized, and if such divisions could be defended in the name of Christianity, he could see no reason why the caste hierarchy and its symbols could not be retained intact in India. (Fernandes 2010: 101–102)

As mentioned earlier, the Dalit Christians realised that they are marginalised by their own religious community and do not get equal treatment in the Catholic Church activities. Hence, their first acts of protest began against the Church. The Dalit Christian Movements placed their demands before the Church leaders, seeking equality and social justice within the Church. As a result, the General Body Meeting of the TNBC and TNPCRI held at Tiruchirapalli on January 14, 1982, adopted the following declaration:

> We state categorically that caste, with its consequent effects of discrimination and 'caste mentality', has no place in Christianity. It is, in fact, a denial of Christianity because it is inhuman. It violates the God-given dignity and equality of the human person.[15]

In this context, the TNBC and the TNPCRI declared the Ten-Point Programme for the development of Dalit Catholics at Vellore on January 30, 1990. The period of 10 years from 1990 to 2000 was declared as the Decade of the Development of Dalit Catholics. Although the Ten-Point Programme was declared in 1990, no worthwhile initiative was taken to implement the programme even after 10 years.

The TNBC requested the Madras Institute of Developmental Studies (MIDS) to undertake a scientific evaluation of the implementation of the Ten-Point Programme for the period between 1990 and 2000. The evaluation report was submitted to the TNBC at Velankanni in July 2003. The TNBC constituted a review committee to study the evaluation report and make recommendations. Based on the recommendations of the review committee, the TNBC and the TNPCRI involved in a series of consultations at various levels and evolved the 'Action plan for the Integrated Development of Catholic Dalits of Tamil Nadu'. The clarion call of the Holy Father John Paul II given to the Bishops of Tamil Nadu in Vatican on November 17, 2003, also stressed the need for proactive measures of the Church towards the development of Dalit Catholics.[16]

M. Thangaraj (2003) of MIDS, who undertook the evaluative study, has provided us a detailed analysis of the Ten-Point Programme of the TNBC and TNPCRI in his report.[17] Unfortunately, as the report still remains a unpublished document for some reasons, we are not in a position to discuss the exact picture that the report highlights. However, we have reproduced the Ten-Point Programme in order to emphasise our conviction that the Catholic Church leadership never failed to recognise the prevalence of inequality within Christianity.

1. In places of worship and burial grounds, CSCO should be treated on a footing of equality and there should be no discrimination.
2. Opportunities should be created in the Dioceses to enable CSCO to join seminaries, convents, and religious congregations in numbers.
3. In order to create leadership in their ranks, CSCO should be encouraged to become members of parish councils, parish finance committees, Diocesan, pastoral councils, multi-purpose social service societies, and other Church-related organisations, and entrusted with responsible positions.
4. In matters of admission to catholic teacher training and industrial schools, preference should be given to the students belonging to the CSCO.
5. Special coaching classes should be conducted to improve the educational standards of the students who are weak in their studies to enable them to improve their performance.
6. Preference should be given to CSCO in matters of appointment in the educational institutions, social service societies, and other Church-sponsored organisations and projects.
7. In the Diocesan social service societies, developmental projects should be exclusively designed to promote the economic development of the CSCO and members of these should be chosen to involve actively in the execution of such projects and in the training programmes connected therewith.

8. To encourage higher education, particularly technical and professional education among CSCO, the Diocesan and religious congregation should jointly create a scholarship fund as a source of encouragement to deserving students.
9. An SC/ST/BC commission should be created in each Diocese immediately to monitor the programmes meant for these people.
10. In the CSCO struggle to obtain their rights and privileges from the central and state governments the TNBC commission should actively support their programme in this regard.

It is to be noted that the author admits that he could not evaluate the tenth point because it deals with the problems of the Dalit Christians with regard to their rights and privileges and the role of the central and state governments in solving them.

It is in this context, our attempt to understand the Dalit Christians' voices of resistance assumes significance. In fact, the TNBC and TNPCRI took the above-mentioned initiative mainly because of the strong protests that came from the Dalit Christians. In Tamil Nadu, the emergence of Dalit Christian Liberation Movement (DCLM) marks a new chapter in the history of such voices of resistance.

THE EMERGENCE OF DALIT CHRISTIAN LIBERATION MOVEMENT

The emergence of Dalit Movements, in general, could be traced since the 1920s when B.R. Ambedkar started his active political participation. In fact, as Mary John observes, 'The history of Dalits is being recovered and constructed since the time of Ambedkar, which is important to raise the Dalit consciousness and also to stir the conscience of the Indian Society. Today the Dalits have started to chart their own political agenda and aspirations and enter into their own party politics and forge alliance with political parties. This has given them some strength, though they have to go a long way to become a politically empowered community. Today, thanks to the reservation and other rights guaranteed by our Indian Constitution, the upward mobility of Dalits is achieved to some extent and they are able to occupy even high posts in the government and in the public sector.' (Mary John 2007: 107–108). However, Mary John also emphasises upon the fact that the Dalits in the minority communities, in general, and in Christianity, in particular, still undergo several forms of discrimination and unfortunately they go unrecognised by the mainstream society. She writes:

> The history of Dalits has gained some space in the mainstream history of India. But neither the mainstream history nor the Dalit history has paid attention to the Dalits of the minority communities. Among the Dalits of the minority communities, the worst affected today are the Dalit Christians (i.e. those converted to Christianity from the untouchable community). They are also referred to as the Christians of the Scheduled Caste Origin (CSCO) or Christians converted from Adi Dravida Community. This is a unique group facing multiple oppression and discrimination in the contemporary India and they are also referred to as the twice or thrice discriminated. The history of the Indian Church has also neglected them, or covered up their oppression within, in spite of the fact that they provided the mass movement or the mass base to the Indian Church. Dalit Christians today are stranded in the cross-roads of caste and religion. They are neither protected by the State nor taken care of by the Indian Churches of various denominations.' (*Ibid.* 108)

There have been conflicts and protests in many places in Tamil Nadu; for example, there were revolts in Uthiramerur in 1869, in Poondi in 1885, in Madurai in 1887–1896, in Konalai in 1905–1912, and in Varatharajanpet in 1944. The conflict has been between the Adi Dravida Christians (Dalit Christians) and the various upper castes Christians. There was a revolt by the Adi Dravida Christians in about 20 villages around Poondi and Koviladi in July 1907. There was some revolt in the Kumbakonam Taluk in 1931, which was a widespread revolt lasting for two years demanding end to caste discrimination. In 1953, the Adi Dravida Christians in Athipakkam and Nedungampatu had a prolonged struggle and made a successful entry into the Church. In 1979, in Kuvathoor (a place visited by Saint John De Britto in 1673), a long struggle for equality took place. There had been attacks on the Adi Dravida Christians in many of these incidents and there have also been court cases. In a few places, there has been attempt by a small number of Dalit Christians to leave Christianity (Thangaraj 2007).

The emergence of the DCLM coincided with two very important events, i.e. the celebration of the Birth Centenary of Ambedkar in 1990 and the celebration, by both the World and the Indian Catholic Church, of the Centenary (1891–1991) of the 'Rerum Novarum' (the first social teaching of the Catholic Church). At the very start, the DCLM had to take a conflict approach. Given the persistent apathy, indifference, and antagonism of the Church authorities, it was necessary and inevitable for the movement to take up struggles and militant action. The activities of the movement were stepped up throughout Tamil Nadu and Puducherry.

There were wide range of activities such as seminars, public meetings, conferences, procession rallies, hunger demonstrations, mass arrests, issue of handbills and notices, use of wall posters, etc. These created wide awareness and impact in the Church leading to some consequences and new developments (*ibid.* 131–132).

One of the important historical events of DCLM was the first state-level Social Justice Conference which was held in Valluvar Kottam,[18] Chennai, on February 14, 2001, in which the then Chief Minister of Tamil Nadu M. Karunanidhi was the chief guest, and it was presided over by the President of DCLM Mary John. Leaders of political parties, many Dalit leaders and intellectuals and Bishops participated and highlighted the problems faced by Dalit Christians. The discrimination and injustice suffered by Dalit Christians on the basis of religion was especially highlighted.

A memorandum was submitted to the chief minister appealing for the SC status for Dalit Christians from the central government, and OBC status for them in Tamil Nadu till they get the SC status. Thanks to the conference, the Dalit Christians problem received wide publicity through the televisions, radio, and newspapers (Mary John 2007: 142).

Although one decade has gone through, both the appeals that were mentioned in that memorandum have not been taken care until now. Hence, the demands of DCLM are still persisting.

Mary John also informs that from the beginning, the DCLM faced stiff resistance from the official Church in Tamil Nadu. The authorities attempted to banish the movement that was originating among the Dalit Christians. She writes,

> The priests used their Sermons in the church to speak against the DCLM. Their attempt was to create in the minds of ordinary Christians confusion between their Christian Faith and their claim for Rights in the Church. The Church is always against the autonomous movement of the Dalit Christians and their struggle or radical approach for their equal rights and human dignity. It always wanted them to depend on it. But the movement tries to bring out the truth about the sufferings of Dalit Christians so that their liberation becomes the central concern of the Church (*Ibid.* 142–143).

Thus, one could conclude that the DCLM is not only satisfied with fighting for rights with the Church, it is equally fighting the discrimination by the state and the society. Getting their equal rights in the Constitution (i.e. SC status) at par with the other Dalits is still a challenge to Dalit Christians.

NOTES

1. Robinson, R. and J. M. Khujur (eds.) (2010). *Margins of Faith: Dalit and Tribal Christianity in India*. New Delhi: Sage Publications.
2. Mosse, D. (2010). 'The Catholic Church and Dalit Christian Activism in Contemporary Tamil Nadu', in R. Robinson and J. M. Khujur (eds.), *op. cit.*
3. Fernandes, W. (2010). 'Caste and Conversion Movements', in T. K. Oommen (ed.), *Social Movements I: Issues of Identity.* New Delhi: Oxford University Press, p. 95.
4. Oommen, T. K. (2010). 'Introduction: On the Analysis of Social Movements', in T. K. Oommen (ed.), *Social Movements I: Issues of Identity*. New Delhi: Oxford University Press.
5. *Ibid.*
6. TNBC and TNCPRI. (2004). *Action Plan for the Integrated Development of Catholic Dalits in Tamilnadu.* Tiruchirapalli: Udaya Deepam.
7. Michael, S. M. (2010). 'Dalit Encounter with Christianity: Change and Continuity', in R. Robinson and J. M. Khujur (eds.), *op. cit.*
8. Kumar, A. and R. Robinson (2010). 'Legally Hindu: Dalit Lutheran Christians of Coastal Andhra Pradesh', in R. Robinson and J. M. Khujur (eds.), *op. cit.*
9. Michael, S. M. (2010). *op. cit.*
10. Mary John, M. (2007). 'The Dalit Christian Liberation Movement', in M. Thangaraj (ed.), *Dalit Movements in South India: Problems and Challenges.* Chennai: University of Madras.
11. Schmalz, M. (2005). 'Dalit Catholic Tactics of Marginality at a North Indian Mission', *History of Religions,* 44(3): 216–251.
12. Webster, J. C. B. (2010). 'Varieties of Dalit Christianity in North India', in R. Robinson and J. M. Khujur (eds.), *op. cit.*
13. Kumar and Robinson, *op. cit.*
14. The author heavily relies upon the information gathered through the interview with M. Mary John, President of Dalit Christian Liberation Movement (DCLM) in the month of November 2011. Interestingly,

Mary John (2007, *op. cit.*) gives us a comprehensive account of DCLM's origin, growth, and activities. The author also duly acknowledges his gratitude to Mary John who had readily shared some of the Unpublished Manuscripts which provide us the major source of evidence for the development of this work.

15. TNBC and TNPCRI. (2004). *op. cit.*
16. Thangaraj, M. (2003). *Evaluation of the Ten-Point Programme for the Development of Dalit Christians in Tamil Nadu.* Unpublished Report. Chennai: MIDS.
17. Thangaraj, M. (2003: 6–7).
18. Valluvar Kottam is the name of the monumental building built in the memory of the great Tamil Poet Thiru Valluvar.

REFERENCES

Fernandes, W. (2010). 'Caste and Conversion Movements', in T. K. Oommen (ed.), *Social Movements I: Issues of Identity.* New Delhi: Oxford University Press.

Kumar, A. and R. Robinson. (2010). 'Legally Hindu: Dalit Lutheran Christians of Coastal Andhra Pradesh', in R. Robinson and J. M. Khujur (eds.), *Margins of Faith: Dalit and Tribal Christianity in India.* New Delhi: Sage Publications.

Mary John, M. (2007). 'The Dalit Christian Liberation Movement', in M. Thangaraj (ed.), *Dalit Movements in South India: Problems and Challenges.* University of Madras 150th Year Special Book.

Michael, S. M. (2010). 'Dalit Encounter with Christianity: Change and Continuity', in R. Robinson and J. M. Khujur (eds.), *Margins of Faith: Dalit and Tribal Christianity in India.* New Delhi: Sage Publications.

Mosse, D. (2010). 'The Catholic Church and Dalit Christian Activism in Contemporary Tamil Nadu', in R. Robinson and J. M. Khujur (eds.), *Margins of Faith: Dalit and Tribal Christianity in India.* New Delhi: Sage Publications.

Oommen, T. K. (ed.) (2010). *Social Movements I: Issues of Identity.* New Delhi: Oxford University Press.

Robinson, R. and J. M. Khujur (eds.) (2010). *Margins of Faith: Dalit and Tribal Christianity in India.* New Delhi: Sage Publications.

Schmalz, M. (2005). 'Dalit Catholic Tactics of Marginality at a North Indian Mission', *History of Religions,* 44(3): 216–251.

Thangaraj, M. (2003). *Evaluation of the Ten-Point Programme for the Development of Dalit Christians in Tamil Nadu*. Unpublished Report, Chennai: MIDS.

——. (ed.) (2007). *Dalit Movements in South India: Problems and Challenges*. Chennai: University of Madras.

TNBC and TNCPRI. (2004). *Action Plan for the Integrated Development of Catholic Dalits in Tamilnadu*. Tiruchirapalli: Udaya Deepam.

Webster, J. C. B. (2010). 'Varieties of Dalit Christianity in North India', in R. Robinson and J. M. Khujur (eds.), *Margins of Faith: Dalit and Tribal Christianity in India*. New Delhi: Sage Publications.

CHAPTER 11

SUB-REGIONAL ASSERTIONS AND SOCIAL TRANSFORMATION IN KASHMIR

Aijaz Ashraf Wani

In present times, the world we are living in is shaped, in many ways, by pluralism. In the post-Cold War era democracy is defined maximally in terms of the existing human development, economic equality, and institutions. It is articulated that good governance means the involvement of different ethno-cultural and linguistic groups in plural societies in the process of decision making. It is considered as the only way through which we can ensure unity in diversity and eliminate real/perceived threats of hegemony and exploitation by dominant identity/identities.[1] Not surprisingly, therefore, identities based on multiple factors like religion, region, caste, language, etc. are constantly asserting themselves in order to gain recognition and, if possible, even autonomy. The concept of regional and sub-regional identity as well as regional autonomy has, therefore, captured the stage of social science. The regional autonomy aspirations and sense of regional and sub-regional identity have offered a new dimension to the assertiveness of ethnic group. A sense of regional identity means a sense of being or at with oneself; it means, at the same time, a sense of regional affinity with a community's sense of being at one with its future as history or mythology.

The post-modern thought recognises two basic human urges: urge for regional identity and urge for unity. Both would be crushed in forcible uniformed communities. The process of modernisation, democratisation, information explosion, and technological revolution has been universally acknowledged as that which sharpens the urge for regional identity. Identity has multiple natures making people live many identities at a time. This is probably because of the cross-cutting nature of social cleavages and oceanic evolution and formation of identity. Yet what is more pronounced is regional identity, even the individual's objective marker of identity acquires regional specificity. It is the performative variation in identity that distinguishes one region from other.

In the present scenario, when for varied reasons identity assertions have assumed unprecedented proportions posing serious threat to peace and stability, mainly where it was left unattended, and therefore, forcing the international community to creatively respond to the demands of identities, various new models of democracy like consociational[2] democracy have received serious consideration particularly by the countries, which besides being sharply fragmented, spread over a vast geographical area with varied sub-cultural zones each having its own distinctive historical and cultural background. Sunil Khilnani (2004) in his best seller book, 'An Idea of India', points out 'the most recent period of India's democracy has shown a tenacity of community identities, in the form of cast and religion, as groups struggle to construct majorities that can rule at the centre'.[3] This assumes importance in the face of dominant political cultures' insatiable lust to perpetuate their hegemony by means of the politics of denial resulting in the political crisis in states like Jammu & Kashmir. We need to bear in mind that identity both at state as well as at individual level has not been in any manner undermined by forces like globalisation. Rather these forces have strengthened it. Anthony Giddens while discussing the question of identity in the context of globalisation says, 'in the global age, identity becomes a fundamental issue, both on an individual and societal level'.[4]

Regional identity demands in South and South-East Asian societies have followed a uniform pattern. These regional autonomy demands, evolved over a large span of time, may be located in specific geographical and environmental spaces. They have the characteristics of a common language spoken by groups of people with a history of observing common traditions, rites, and rituals. All these components have endowed these regional and sub-regional autonomy aspirations with an aura of primordiality. The prominent aspect of these regional autonomy aspirations has been their inclusiveness in absorbing new and sometimes even foreign influences of religions and cultures, resulting in adding layer in the formation of their distinct personalities. The incorporation of shared historical and cultural values shaped these regional autonomy demands in a mould, in which the religious edges of the identity remained subdued or even dormant. It is interesting to note that the capacity of absorption and accommodation of these regional autonomy demands resulted in two diametrically opposite consequences. At one level, these demands remained humane and inclusive, incorporating and reflecting broader human and universal values.

At the other level, they acquired the traits of particularism which in the later stages of building multi-cultural and multi-ethnic nation states posed many problems.

JAMMU AND KASHMIR STATE AND THE ISSUES OF REGIONAL AND SUB-REGIONAL ASSERTIONS

The plurality of politics is the hallmark of Jammu & Kashmir state, and this polarity is essentially the result of cultural diversities that criss-cross the geographical and cultural landscape of Kashmir. The J&K state is not only a conglomerate of three distinct regions – Jammu, Kashmir, and Ladakh – but there are also regions within regions marked off from one another by geography, culture, and history. Although these regions were integrated into one single political entity in 1846, the politics of regional and sub-regionalism continues to be stubbornly informed by their respective histories and cultures – thus the resistance against hegemony and the demand for sub-regional autonomies and hill councils.

Broadly speaking Jammu & Kashmir state consists of three distinctively geographical regions: Kashmir, Jammu, and Ladakh. The three regions are not only three dissimilar geographical entities, but in regard to history and culture they are also different from one another. Throughout its history, Kashmir valley was a monolithic political entity – sometimes enjoying the status of a powerful empire and sometimes becoming a part of the great empires that emerged on its borders from time to time. However, what today constitutes the Kashmir province; never in history did it form one political entity. The petty principalities which were situated amidst hills in the immediate vicinity of the valley say Gurez, Keren, Karneh, Uri, etc. did not form a part of Kashmir Empire at any stage of its history to say least of what today constitutes Pakistan Occupied Kashmir (POK) of Jammu and Ladakh provinces. While for the most part of their history they remained independent, during the powerful rulers these smaller principalities formed tributaries of Kashmir Empire or they were occasionally brought to heels by launching a military campaign, so that according to Kalhana, they do not become powerful enough to create chaos in the valley or hob knob with the internal dissidents or foreign powers. However, in all circumstances they were allowed to stay autonomous in managing their affairs.

Culturally, Kashmir province has also been heterogeneous. Although Islam is the majority religion of Kashmir province, there are many voices within it, each of which has a dominant will to be heard and will to power.

Besides, the Kashmir also consists of 4 per cent Hindus and 2 per cent Sikhs. Linguistically too, Kashmir province is a fragmented society. Apart from the dominant Kashmiri-speaking population, there is a sizable population whose mother tongue is Pahari, Gogri, and Dardi and who live territorially separate from other groups. Their presence assumes additional significance as their habitats are situated on the borders of the state.

Similarly, the geographical area which presently comprise Jammu province does not constitute one monolithic geographical structure. There emerged a medley of small independent principalities of Jammu, Kishtwar, Doda, Rajuri, Punch, Reasi, Kathua, Samba, Chhenani, Ramban, Gol, etc. and each of them enjoyed political independence save occasionally, when either the powerful Kashmiri rulers or the powerful empires which emerged on the borders of the province and made them to accept their suzerainty. However, they were never completely integrated; even the great Mughals allowed them to stay autonomous. It was in the early 40s of the nineteenth century that Maharaja Gulab Singh of Jammu integrated, with full military might backed by the Lahor Darbar, the independent principalities of Jammu province into a single political entity. In the recent times, there has been tremendous demand for sub-regional councils in the Jammu region.

Jammu province is not only geographically heterogeneous with each unit having deep seated memories of having long independent past, but the separative sentiment has been further reinforced by cultural diversities as the province is deeply divided into a multitude of religious, cultural, and linguistic groups, each group living in its own separate habitat almost completely together. Although it is a Hindu majority region, yet it has a significant presence of Muslims. Except for Jammu-Kathua belt which is predominantly Hindu, the rest of the region has a mixed population. In fact, the Poonch-Rajouri belt has a predominant muslim population. The most diverse part of the region is the Doda belt, which though has a slender majority of Muslims but has almost an even population of Hindus.

Again, historically the province of Ladakh was also divided into small independent principalities that fragmented the province into different separate geographical zones situated far away from one another. Although occasionally the independent principalities were conquered by Kashmiris, Chinese, Tibetian, and Central Asian powers, the geographical constraints forced them to allow these principalities to remain autonomous. It was in the mid-40s of the nineteenth century that Ladakh was conquered by Zorawar Singh, the Dogra general of Maharaj Gulab Singh of Jammu Kingdom. The Ladakh province was not only fragmented into many geographical and political entities, it continues to be culturally deeply divided. While the Leh is predominantly Buddhist, Kargil is predominantly Muslim. This is besides the fact that both Leh and Kargil consist of a multitude of ethnic and linguistic groups.

Jammu & Kashmir is not only religiously diverse, with three major religions of South Asia having their followers in the state, but there are regional, cultural, tribal, caste-based, and linguistic diversities. The three major regions of the state are not only culturally and socially diverse but also in terms of their geographical terrains and their historical roots. The region is an important marker of the identity in the state and cuts across the religious continuity.[5] Muslims as well as Hindus of one region not only perceive themselves as different from their co-religionists of the regions but also emphasise their regional identity.

Secondly, these diversities in the state are so placed that a complex social and political environment is generated. There is no clear-cut context of 'majority' and 'minority'. Majority in one context becomes minority in another. For example, despite being part of the largest religious group of the state, the Kashmiri Muslims perceive themselves as a minority in the context of the larger reality of India.[6] Similarly, the Hindus of Jammu and the Buddhists of Ladakh, though constitute majority in their respective regions, viewed in the context of the Muslim majority character of the state, perceive themselves as minority. This minority sentiment of the two regions is also viewed strongly in the context of Kashmir-centric political and power context of the state.

This sense of deprivation and minority status lies deep in many other ways giving rise to sub-regional assertions and the demands of autonomous councils. For example, the Kashmiri Pandits perceive their minority status vis-à-vis the Kashmiri Muslims, while the Jammu Muslims perceive their deprivation both vis-à-vis the Hindus of Jammu as well as Muslims of Kashmir valley. The situation is no different in Ladakh region. While region as a whole views itself as marginalised with respect to Kashmir, the Muslims of Kargil perceive their marginalisation both in the immediate context of the Buddhist domination of Ladakh as well as the power centre in Kashmir.

Besides religion, the factors like region, caste, and economic backwardness are the defining characteristics of this sense of minority. Regional backwardness and deprivation remain the defining characters of discourse both in Jammu and Ladakh regions, in which Kashmir is portrayed as the centre of power, while other regions as facing 'neglect' and 'deprivation'. The regional assertions and sense of marginality is countered by sub-regional context of deprivation. That is why soon after Leh Autonomous Hill Development Council was established in 1995, the demand for similar council was forcefully raised by the Muslims of Kargil leading to the formation of Kargil Autonomous Council in 2003. The demands for similar councils are now coming from Chenab Valley, Pir Panchal, and other regions also. This sense of separate identity does not stop here. The OBCs, Gujjars, Paharis, and the people living near Line of Control (LoC) too have this sense of neglect and deprivation.

What is, however, more interesting is the overlapping context of identities. There is neither a singular nor a homogeneous character of identities. The classic example of this is provided by the Jammu region. The region is a cultural mosaic with large number of religious and social groups. Here neither Hindus nor Muslims form a homogeneous category and are differentiated on lingual and cultural basis. There are at least four broad categories of Muslims living within this region – the Dogra Muslims, Paharis, Gujjars, and Kashmiris. The Dogra Muslims belong to the Dogra belt of Jammu and have close cultural affinity with Dogra Hindus rather than Muslims of the valley. The Paharis are mainly Rajput Muslims of the hilly areas of Poonch and Rajouri belt, inhabiting another Muslim group, the Gujjars. The Muslims of Doda belt are mainly Kashmiri-speaking having close cultural affinity with the Muslims of Kashmir region. Similarly, the Hindus of Jammu region can also be classified into various groupings like Dogras, Punjabis, Paharis, Baderwahi, Kishtiwari, etc. having different cultural affinity.

All these factors combine to produce a very complex situation where the regional and sub-regional assertion discourse has assumed tremendous significance. The issues related to development, power balance, and the ideological divide have made the situation all complex.

Not surprisingly, therefore, the regional autonomy has been one of the perennial debates in J&K state in the post-independent India. The principle of regional autonomy was accepted by the popular leadership of the state both before the independence in its famous constitutional document, Naya Kashmir,[7] as well as immediately after the state acceded to the Union of India in 1947.

NOTES

1. Wani, G. (2011). *Kashmir: Identity, Autonomy and Self-Rule*. Srinagar: Apple Books, p. 145.
2. For details, see Lijphart, A. (1969). 'Consociational Democracy', *World Politics*, 21(2): 207–25. Also see his *Thinking about Democracy: Power*

Sharing and Majority Rule in Theory and Practice, Routledge, London and New York, 2008.
3. Khilnani, S. (2004). *The Idea of India*, New Delhi: Penguin Books, pp. 58–59.
4. Giddens, A. (2007). *The Tenth D. T. Lakdawala Memorial Lecture*, New Delhi: Institute of Social Science, p. 18.
5. Chowdhary, R. (ed.) (2010). *Identity Politics in Jammu and Kashmir*, New Delhi: Vitasta Publishing Pvt. Ltd., pp. 4–5.
6. *Ibid.*, p. 5.
7. The relevant clause of the document reads as: 'The political power shall be equitably distributed among the regions of the state and would be further decentralized at lower levels like district, block and panchayats. The appropriate institutions elected by the people shall be set-up at the respective levels to exercise political power that may be delegated to them. The method of elections might vary at different tiers of administration. To start with only such powers and functions shall be actually decentralized and exercisable by the respective authorities as are considered feasible and manageable. After gaining proper experience the power and functions of the lower tiers shall be expanded, subject always to the over-riding consideration of strengthening the unity and integrity of the state', Article 17 of the document.

CHAPTER 12

ELEMENTARY EDUCATION CHOICE IN A TRANSFORMING SOCIETY: A CASE OF ASSAM

Reshmi Chakraborty

Debates on school choice, competition, and factors affecting the ability of parents to choose a particular school for their child exist in the form of policies in the West and developed countries. Most advocates of choice and school autonomy support the claims that competition will enhance the efficiency and responsiveness of schools and thus increase their effectiveness. Therefore, different factions of choice proponents among educators, economists, policy makers, and government did not majorly differ on the proposal to improve the public school education system even if the chosen means and goal was either equity or privatisation, diversification of school, or based on competition. A major leap in policy reforms for choice in elementary education has been made by some of the developed nations, such as Ireland, Netherland, Australia, New Zealand, and the United States to name a few. India too has made relative progress towards education policy reforms after early 90s with the advent of policies in liberalisation, privatisation, and globalisation. Right to education as a fundamental right is one such step towards strengthening the efforts towards universalising education in India. However, the clauses which govern the right have been contested by the stakeholders. No policy has been clearly made to foster choice making in particular in India. This paper has been divided into four sections, each explaining the key vectors with regard to choice in elementary education in an urban space.

Firstly, with revitalisation in the economic structure of the society and patterns of attitudinal changes among people thereafter, the resultant social stratum began to grow with a large number of middle-class populations. Sociologists and educationists alike have raised concerns over inadequate study on this section of the society. Middle class remained hitherto unproblematised and was referred only in comparison to the lower class and marginalised/exploited section of our society. An absence of a perspective of/from the middle class demanded immediate attention. It is argued by scholars that the middle class have overcome their contentment and easy going attitude and are anxious because of the uncertainty in which their life is embedded. In reality, this can be described as a reflection of their present self and consciousness of their class.

DEFINING MIDDLE CLASS

The emergence and existence of the middle class in India can be traced back to the colonial period. What it means is that however vociferously we discuss the new middle class of contemporary time, it is essential to develop a critical outlook historically. And thus historically speaking, it has several contested geneses. In one[1] such case, it is argued that their formation is a staged act of those who derived larger advantage out of defining this social class. To quote from *The Middle Class in Colonial India, 2010*,

> '...ultimately, being middle class in India, as elsewhere, was a project of self-fashioning. In colonial India...a middle class emerged from processes by which intellectuals and activists created new and distinctive social category through a self conscious interpositions between people of rank and common people. (Joshi 2010: xix)

During earlier period, they were mostly recognised as cultural entrepreneurs who transcended the economic factors, i.e. occupation and profession and objective factors like financial assets, land, and capital which also determined their existence. They formed part of the cultural politics and created public sphere to ascertain their agency. Thus the new social by-product created by middle class was in the form of '...a new set of beliefs, values and mode of politics'. The educated groups could transform the existing traditional culture and ran the public sphere with the help of 'active press, journalism, civic and political associations and published and debated their ideas' (Joshi 2010: xviii–xix). Bourdieu as a reproductionist theorist has rendered us a methodological tool to analyse the effect of cultural capital and social capital on both families who posses it and the schools who want to perpetuate it.

It is extremely important to note that though educated, they were not among the rich and were clearly distinguished from the affluent class of the colonial period. The dilemma to define and redefine this class has been immense as it continuously seeks a new definition with the change of society or arrival of new ideologies and transformations. This phenomenon can be juxtaposed with the advent of neo-liberal policy reforms in India. Moreover, in India, the definition and position of the middle class is still ambiguous as it was because of her diversity and multiculturalism.

Having said this, it is pragmatic to bring forth the problem of research. The ambiguity and uncertainty of the class reflects in their actions, their ideas, their decisions, and their practices. Primarily, the problem is much more than the reason for existence alone, 'for the middle class it is the best of times and the worst of times', as explained by Ball (2003: 4),[2] 'a time of affluence and risk, opportunity and congestion, celebration and anxiety'. Their dynamism and prowess to challenge the existing and build a new form of social order because of their perpetual dissatisfaction with what they have in hand alarms every authority in position. To draw from the previous discussion, while new set of beliefs, values, and modes of politics were created through the public sphere, yet these practices are driven by the course of rationality and of rational being. Without contesting any further into how and why middle class came into the making, at this point it is imperative to situate what constitutes them and what guides their rational course of action in a linguistically diverse and multiethnic space.

While policies are made, amended, and restructured to suit those who are consciously or subconsciously exempting to avail the basic amenities of life, it is imperative to take a note of the middle class who are politically, socially, and economically more in control of their identity and directly or indirectly govern the course of these policies. Transgressing from super structure to the base, Ball (*ibid.*) alarms us to look into the family as the site for the rooted inequality in the society with regard to education.

THE NEO-LIBERAL RATIONALITY AND EDUCATION

Secondly, with the advent of neo-liberal policies arrives the question of choice-making ability and interest among such parents who wish to put their child in a good quality English medium school in the wake of stiff competition and demand of quality education. For middle class, education is the way to move up the social strata as they attach such achievement with prestige, remunerating profession, and other social and cultural attributes. The primordial essence of market functioning in education system begins to play an important role in governing choice. Indicators such as competition, efficiency, and consumption are the hallmark of neo-liberal philosophy. Whose, why, and how choice is exercised and governed are few questions addressed hereafter.

Theory of rational choice, rationality, competition, freedom, and market form a critical framework for the analysis of choice in education. Existence of a rational man in a market-like situation, with the freedom to choose and availability of resources will, in very likely condition, result in choosing the best possible objective condition to his benefit. If the demand and supply is of education and parents have to choose the best school for their child, a situation of this nature arrives. While the quality of public (government) school system in India is alarming with poor quality education, teacher absenteeism, school management system, accountability, it is also facing much threat from two important types of school system. One is the set of private schools run by different managements and the other being the low-cost private school either aided or unaided by the government proliferating in rural areas of the country. Withstanding the fact that urban spaces are created and negotiated in economic terms, the condition in the urban space is highly contesting in terms of educational facilities.

Choice theory as a framework for education policy emanates from the neo-liberal ideology which seeks private competition between players in the market while the market can be partially or wholly regulated by the government. The faith on the government to provide good quality, successful education is under scrutiny since long now and an alternative is sought by those who see education as an indispensable asset.

Hereby, it is imperative to unfold the process of growth and continuity of private schools in the education market which is contingent upon a large number of children from middle-class families. Nogueira (2010)[3] chalks out the inception of this growth and continuity of private institutions including schools. The market grew in magnitude with the economic re-structuralisation pregnant with seeds of uncertainties and risks especially creating a gorge in jobs to be filled with skilled manpower. The state shrunk its responsibilities leading to reforms in the public sector and allowed free choice by the users. The consequence of the revitalisation of the economy is felt in mounting individualism into the mentalities of the people and personal interests conquering collective values. The investment in education is seen to be on a rise among certain sections of the society. Krishna Kumar (1996),[4] a leading educationist of India, expresses his worry of the educational imbalance created by the proliferation of the private schools by saying that its growth increasingly drained off children of the better sections of urban society from government schools. As also, Nambissan (2010)[5] feels that the unregulated private sector sees this gradual demand of private schools as a business opportunity. The 'which' and 'why' of private schools or any school per se, is determined by the parents. There is a latent but firm mutual dialogue between these aspiring/choice-conscious middle-class families and the schools.

Schools are part of this market process trying to maintain equilibrium for parents as choice makers, between supply and demand of quality education. Elementary school choice is by no means a part of the decision of the children. It is purely through the state intervention and through mediation of the parents. The parent's choice of school is not merely an act of sending the child to learn how to read and write. It is a lot more than that. Elementary education is a public good, supposed to be of equal nature and ever available to all by the state. However, this is not the reality. Post-welfare era has seen rapid growth of neo-liberal ethos into the social, political, and economic systems of the nation. There is a compelling tendency to emulate market-like situation in every possible sphere of society. As if market is absolute, fair, and equal resource allocator and generator, the products are uniform and open to everyone. Reality is far from this, especially in the field of education.

With that they are trying to suggest the celebration of assumed superiority of the market mechanisms to ensure more than (emphasis added) economic prosperity. Market should be allowed to operate as widely as possible within the social order as it induces competition through which resources and status are allocated efficiently and fairly. Market is inherently an unequal space. It accentuates inequality as not everyone in the society can participate in the market.

According to this lobby, in educational policy making there should be a reduction of state services through privatisation via user charges, contracting out, vouchers, and others. Also, individual in a neo-liberal way are rational optimisers and are best judges of their own interests and needs with freedom that they can exercise. The new middle class suitably behaves and can be contextualised within this framework of mind. Ethics is no more a state monopoly and becomes a matter of a private individual. The market mechanism and democratic conditions, both govern witness to this sweeping change (Olssen et al. 2004: 137–139).

Choice entailed in the neo-liberal theory draws directly from an understanding of the consumer demand which is not really what is understood as social need. The demands generated are skewed and determined by the family's dispositions, purchasing power, and ability to ignore other needs for quality education for their children. Nevertheless, market breeds inequality and needs a regulation mechanism to diminish the possibility of unwarranted neglect in availing quality education. The social ends of education, justified by the neo-liberal perspective, seek to provide freedom of choice in schooling contested by the welfare state approach. The middle class does not, any more, want to remain underachievers, their values being in convergence with what neo-liberal attitude believes of what knowledge and education ought to give. Ball (2001)[6] argues that 'school choice is a critical point of cultural investment in the symbolic economy. Schooling, of certain sorts, is an effective means of storing value for future realization' (185). Choice of school for many families is a venture or strategy of adaptation to safeguard or augment their class ranking.

This is where the choice of the middle-class families comes into play. They want their children to be a certain type of finished product who can perpetuate their own cultural, political, and social values distinct from other classes for generations to follow. The idea of value retention is so strong that families cannot but choose and programme the future course of action by choosing particular type of schools for their children.

Parental choice is a debate which goes along with the neo-liberal policies of the state. The advocates of neo-liberal ideology seek 'a fully privatized system in education [word added] with vouchers' (Whitty 1997).[7] However, what matters most is to engage with the understanding that policies are part of the political reflection of the same society or more precisely of the same stratified society. Class stratification is one out of many ways of stratification that is explained in a particular society.

The idea of value retention is so strong that families cannot but choose and programme the future course of action by choosing particular schools for their children. Intermingling within a particular section of people and socialising only within the in-group is as strong as not choosing a low-quality government school for their children's education. The debate leads to indicate that middle-class families may be governed to behave as consumers of education and leave the market of education or space of education in such a position that a need may arise to look beyond the reason to establish education as a fundamental right as is the case in India.

It is articulated that schools inherently embody in their function – organisation and content; judgement regarding the nature and purpose of education; assertion about human intelligence, knowledge, and being as well as the supposition regarding the respective rights; and responsibilities of the individual and the state. Where such judgements have not been made either explicitly or tacitly, there are no schools (Kane 1992).[8]

The parents continuously seek premeditated and efficacy-maximising choices that can abridge uncertainty, by investing money in private education linking it to finer skills needed in educational and occupational contests (Aurini and Davies 2005).[9] The fear of a downfall in the inherited status forces the middle-class conscious parents to invest in private education as an act of status-consciousness, and in countries such as Canada parents have taken a step ahead to ensure their class status by providing alternative private education in the form of home schooling.

CHOICE AMONG MIDDLE CLASS

The third section of the paper draws a relational discourse between the middle-class practices and educational space and what choice does a new middle class make from the above types of schools available to them through an empirical study undertaken in an urban town in Assam.

Middle class are the aspiring class. It is fluid, ever-evolving, and ever-redefining its contours to suit academic debates. While neo-liberal framework of the neo-classical economics have discussed most about the free man and the free market ideologies, markets do not stand free. It is imperfect and seeks choice makers who risk being there to bargain their choices and possibilities. Who are they?

In the contemporary milieu, while rational being is the best man,[10] they are left with the objective realities with considerable constraints to achieve the set goal. They manage crucial tradeoffs in various spheres in their life. Educational attainment was and has been the most important credential to be achieved by the middle-class aspirant to scale up the ladder of the society in terms of affluence and success. As Daniele Checchi (2005)[11] says it is a crucial investment made by families without considering immediate tangible returns. But that is not all. Capitalising on cultural resources and freedom of expression has been a hallmark of the group behaviour since decades. The more in number they are, the more powerful will be their assertion[12] in various socio-economic and cultural processes.

The neo-liberal ethos in the contemporary milieu as it emerges has diffused into every possible socio-political institution in a developed and developing nation. The fact that there is a considerable influence of privatisation, liberalism, and neo-ideas on middle-class families, concocted with assertive/competitive individualism in a market situation only justifies its strong hold on a society (Ball 2003). While family is a primary unit of study in a social structure, their actions leading to group behaviour will indeed add rippling effect into the society.

The middle class encounters constraints of various kinds and are under continuous dilemmas. The government seeks to simulate a market-like situation as the consumers' sovereignty assumes salience in this era of rising dominance of neo-liberalism.

Assam and Its Inherent Complexities

The social canvas of the state of Assam is filled with problems of identity formation and dominion status of the various groups coexisting for long period of time now. The middle-class culture of the population in the state was brought in by the Bengali Hindus who were part of the state before the partition and outnumbered the original Assamese-speaking population. Not before the immigrant Bengali Muslims from Eastern Bengal adapted Assamese as their mother tongue in the state that Assamese became the dominant mother tongue, thereby ensuring the majority status of the Assamese and defeating the 'machinations' of the Bengali Hindu to reduce Assam into a bilingual state. Thus, Assamese were grateful to the immigrant Muslims for returning Assamese as their mother tongue. No doubt, for all practical purposes, Assam as claimed by the author is a bilingual state, with predominantly Assamese-speaking population in the Brahmaputra valley and predominantly Bengali-speaking population in the Barak valley[13] (also known as Surma Valley) (Mishra 1999; Barua 1978). In 10 years, a major shift in the linguistic population is yet to be witnessed.

The population composition of the state could thus be traced back to the historical changes during the British period. In order to reinstate the middle-class culture among the people of Assam, it may be attributed to what British did by establishing company's authority in the different government departments bringing in large Bengali-speaking areas. No doubt language problem existed; the positive fall out of this opportunity was imbibing of another culture superior than the culture of sustenance economy in the state. It was the middle-class culture. On the other hand, Assam was continuously facing influx of migrants from other states of the subcontinent as British capital penetrated the economy and started building up an infrastructure in the interests of accumulation. New skills, new ideas, and immigration labour marked the exposure of this closed society that Assam was. The tea industry which required a regular supply of labour also contributed to the diversity of the population. Thousands of labourers from Bihar, Chotanagpur, Uttar Pradesh, and Madras were annually recruited for the plantations from these provinces, most of who failed to return to their native home land and formed the biggest migrant group in Assam's population. There was no native capitalist in Assam, the artisan was independent and he supplemented his income with the products of a farm he worked on regularly. Thus another significant contribution was made to the social mosaic of Assam by the Marwari merchants. The economic and capitalist condition of the state explains the commercial monopoly of these merchants from western India. They easily tapped the means of money making in the state through money-lending, supplying provisions to the tea gardens, procuring mustard, and later jute for the market outside Assam, and meeting the demand for new household implements and articles – cheap and mass produced – that the Assamese soon came to adopt (Barua 1978: 69–70).[14]

The social mosaic of Assam is rich with its heritage, but because of the strained political relation with the centre and internal insurgencies and militancy's of the separatist groups, the society is not in complete harmony. It is largely stratified on the basis of language and religion, plains and tribes, indigenous and outsiders, and not to forget the inevitable caste-class stratification of our society. However, the trajectory of the growth of middle class in Assam according to Gohain (1973)[15] is a hundred year behind their Bengali counterpart. On a vital paper, he writes 'by a process of a simple plunder from the State treasury in the name of "development programme", the Assamese middle class has noticeably become more affluent and ambitious. But it does not hold the key to the further development of the region and the people there mainly because of its necessarily subservient relation to the Indian big capital' (*ibid.* 12).

At this juncture, scarce literature on the middle-class educational aspirations adds to our woe to understand the changing landscape of the education scenario with respect to the emerging infiltration of the global economy in the state. To note further, the percentage of educated unemployed in the state is as alarming as is the condition of school education in the state. As a considerable portion of population in an urban area belongs to the middle-class strata, here they consider to have somewhat overcome the existential dilemma of living under the fear of separation but suffer a deeper loss of privileges. The demographic and socio-economic features of Assam and its geographical location away from the larger political land only obliquely explain the story. It is important to engage further deeply to know more about the factors contributing to the middle-class educational pursuits in the state. That ethnicity and religion can play a significant role in parental reasons for school choice has been proved by studies done elsewhere in the Western countries. This research is an opportunity to bridge the ideological quest in educational demand which may subsequently allow for further implication of schooling in the region.

However, the condition of education in the state is not very promising in terms of educational development index and overall ranking of the state. The education index of Assam during the period of 2008–2009 is as given in the following figure.

Figure 1 Education Index of Assam

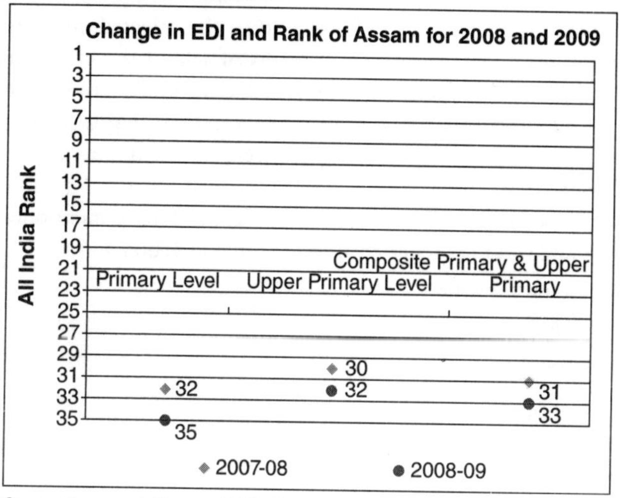

Source: Economic Survey 2009–10.

Empirical Evidences

Reminding ourselves of the public choice theory[16] as the ontological body to understand choice as a theoretical concept and exploring the field based on empirical research, let us look at the findings of the study. Before that this paper would like to bring forth the research questions addressed through the study. They are as follows:

1. Whether quality education and schooling is an important strategy to affirm middle-class status in the system of social stratification based on class?
2. How far reasons for choice by the middle-class parents are dependent on the economic and occupation status (mapping income, assets, and expenditure) of the middle-class parents?
3. In what ways quality of education in government and private schools affect parental choice in elementary level?
4. How middle-class parental choice may influence educational policy-making and govern the pattern of school education?

At the very outset, the sample population for the study was stratified on the basis of location, i.e. urban area and households with at least one child going to school between classes 1 and 8. A sample size of 51 households was used for analysis. Face-to-face/personal interview was used for the parents as the method of data collection with the help of a semi-structured interview schedule. Random sampling method was used for sampling procedure. Later within the selected strata to make the sample more heterogeneous in terms of school the child attended, and homogeneous in terms of the social class under study, snow ball sampling method was used. Filters like married couple with at least one child going to elementary school were added before a parent was interviewed.

Basic characteristic of Tinsukia town by Census 2001 is mentioned in the following table and the socio-economic profile in Tables 1–5.

Population and Sex Ratio	
Number of HH	20,672
Total population	1,01,957
% of male population	55.19
% of female population	44.81
SC population	5350
% of scheduled caste	5.25
ST population	998
% of scheduled tribe	0.98
Sex ratio	811.83
SC sex ratio	831.56
ST sex ratio	732.63
Household size	4.93

Source: Census 2001, Government of India.

The descriptive characteristics of the sample population has been analysed against various indicators, but in this paper only essential factors are highlighted.

Table 1 Ethnicity of the Sample Respondents

Ethnicity of the Respondents	**Per cent**
Assamese	23.53
Bengali	68.63
Migrant from other states	7.84
Grand total	**100.00**

Table 2 Occupation of the Sample Respondents by Gender

Occupation of the Respondents by Gender	Male	Female	Total %
Shop owner/retailer/businessman	9	–	17.65
Self employed professional	1	1	3.92
Clerical	4	–	7.84
Teacher	3	9	23.53
Senior level executive	4	–	7.84
Housewife	–	15	29.41
Others (one each) (doctor/employee in private firm, shop/ private service/student)	5	–	1.96
Grand total	**26**	**25**	**100.00**

Table 3 Monthly Household Income of the Sample Respondents (HHI)

Monthly Household Income (HHI) (In Rs)	Per cent
4,001–6,000	5.88
6,001–8,000	3.92
8,001–10,000	7.84
10,000–20,000	37.25
>20,000	45.10
Grand total	**100**

Table 4 Education Levels of the Sample Respondents

Education Level of the Respondents	Per cent
Up to matric	5.88
Matric/High School	33.33
Undergraduate	13.73
Graduate/Post Graduate	47.06
Grand total	**100.00**

Table 5 Type of Education Sample Respondents Received

Type of Education Sample Respondents Received	Per cent
Government	86.27
Private (regular)	9.80
Private (professional)	1.96
Other (government + private)	1.96
Grand total	**100.00**

FACTORS FOR SCHOOL CHOICE

To understand in real sense of the term and proposing a perspective, choice cannot be understood as *choice* or *no-choice*. It is in fact *positive-choice* and *negative-choice*. However, irrespective of the social milieu and occupation level, parents have ranked quality of school education as the most desirable choice factor for selecting a particular school for their child. Out of the total sample, 25 per cent of the parents think quality of the education disseminated in school is crucial as it is this foundation on which the child will pursue his/her future. Followed by discipline and access as choice factors which parents think are the most important reasons for which they will select a particular school, school reputation has been ranked the next most important on the priority list by 14 per cent of the total sample, followed by language of the school, and the education

Table 6 The Factors for School Choice

Factors for School Choice	Rank 1	%
Quality	13	25
Discipline	8	16
Access	8	16
Reputation	7	14
Language	4	8
Board	4	8
Affordability	3	6
Religion	0	0
Advice	0	0
others	4	8
Total	**51**	**100**

board the school follows. The remaining factors are given in the Table 6. The factors are mentioned in such a way as had been assigned rank 1 to them.

Parents were asked to rank the three most important factors on the basis of priority for school choice out of the total eight factors provided. Parents classified them in the following manner (Table 6 – 7).

Table 7 Ranking of Choice Factors

The Factors for School Choice Ranked in Order of Preference (Values in %) *N = 51											
Rank	**Affordability**	**Quality**	**Access**	**Advice**	**Reputation**	**Language**	**Religion**	**Discipline**	**Board**	**Others**	**Total %**
1	6	25	16	0	14	8	0	16	8	8	100
2	8	27	12	2	18	8	6	10	6	4	100
3	10	25	20	2	14	20	0	4	2	4	100

Table 8 Standard Deviation of Choice Factors: In Terms of Overall Ranking

	Number	**Mean score**	**ST Dev**	**Rank**
Discipline	15	1.67	0.82	1
Quality	41	2.05	0.86	2
Reputation	25	2.08	0.86	3
Access (distance)	25	2.16	0.94	4
Language	20	2.45	0.89	5
Affordability	14	2.50	1.09	6
Advice	2	2.50	0.71	7
Religion	5	2.60	0.89	8

Discipline is assigned top priority as the major determinant of school choice followed by quality, reputation, access, language, and affordability. Religion does not seem to matter in a predominantly Hindu area. Discipline comes first despite only 15 respondents thought it to be a choice factor, although it was a part of the 'others'. This implies that those who value discipline, they value it highly (Table 8). This order of preference among the parents can be attributed to their concern of an insecure and blurred future ahead. Discipline is one such factor continuously mentioned by the parents during the interviews and school-related discussion. For them discipline encompasses every such belief which will make the child learn the ethos of their middle-class behaviour. Parents want their child to learn decorum and regularity of life by conforming to the laws of the school. In a strict sense of the term, the child has to do well in studies even if (s) he is inclined to perform well in other things such as music, sports, painting, or anything else. The encouragement is only additional. While the functional perspective on education ascertains that the role of school is to produce citizen conforming to the social order and participating in the division of labour, parents involuntarily give way to this perception. As Durkheim (1956)[17] writes 'society can survive only if there exists among its members a sufficient degree of homogeneity: education perpetuates and reinforces this homogeneity by fixing in the child from the beginning, the essential similarities that collective life demands' (70). However, he also leaves space for diversity for cohesiveness through diversified and specialised education. Schools also reinforce the family socialisation of social-class position, the social class-related structure of education and their norms in education which encourages a sense of efficacy among the middle-class students is what Paulsen (1991)[18] argues. As discussed earlier, the state schools in America aspired to develop citizens with pan-American identity through schooling. Expectation from the school milieu are that classes are held regularly, teachers are engaged mostly in academic work and teaching, rare teacher-absenteeism is reported, and few holidays make school life disciplined for the child.

Table 9 Correlations between the Six Possible Choice Factors

Variables	Correlation Coefficients	Level of Significance
Affordability, quality	(–) 0.539	(0.047)**
Quality, access	(–) 0.477	(0.046)**
Quality, discipline	(–) 0.553	(0.097)*
Access, reputation	(–) 0.839	(0.076)*

The correlation coefficients between two of the eight choice variables have turned out to be negative in the all the cases. This is to be expected as the respondent assigned more importance to one choice variable compared to the other. One can expect a positive variable when two choice variables are given consecutive rankings in the majority of the cases. The statistically significant bivariate correlation coefficients are only reported. If quality matters, the respondent tends to give a low priority to affordability as the parents are willing to spend for quality education. Similarly, if reputation matters, access is low priority as the respondent seems to be willing to bear the cost. Affordability and access reflect the costs side of making the choice, whereas quality is unambiguously desirable. Since discipline ranks first, the respondents think that quality follows if discipline is ensured in the school (Table 9).

Table 10 Logistic Regression to Assess Influence of Social Milieu on Choice

Variables in the Equation	β	SE	vald	d.f.	Level of Significance	Exp(β)
Per month HH income	0.095	0.055	2.958	1	0.085	1.100
Education of parents	0.745	0.713	1.091	1	0.296	2.107
Constant	–0.991	1.034	0.917	1	0.338	0.371

The choice variable, whether the parents send their children to a government school or a private one, is binary in nature. Parents of private school goers are assumed to face unconstrained choice facilitated by levels of income and education of the parents. Again, income and education may have collinearity as higher level of education leads to higher level of income. The applied logistic regression model with income and education level as the covariates or independent variables show results as mentioned in the Table 10 above. Both the expected values of the odd ratios for income and education are greater than indicating a positive relationship. However, only income turns out to be statistically significant at 8.5 per cent level. The Exp(β) of income and education level are 1.1 and 2.1, respectively. A value of 1.1 for income measured in thousand means that if income rises by 1,000, the odds of choosing a private school goes up to 1.1, and education being a dummy variable, the odds of choosing a private school goes up by a factor of 2.1 as the education level moves from 0 (till 10+2 level) to 1 (UG and above). The overall success rate in predicting the outcome is 74.5 per cent, i.e. choice of a private school which can be considered to be reasonably good (Table 11).

Table 11 Opinion of Parents across All Socio-Economic Indicators on Government Schools

Indicator	Frequency	%
Government schools do not conduct classes properly, irregular classes, poor education.	9	17.65
Do not get child-centric attention.	5	9.80
However, free education in government school takes the load off from poor parents who seek education.	5	9.80
Government school is good and has improved.	4	7.84
Government school lacks the basic standard as compared to private.	4	7.84
In government school, all children are rural, poor quality of students.	3	5.88
Government schools are mostly vernacular and follows state board.	3	5.88
High salary negates the responsibility of the teachers in government school.	3	5.88
Parents are not caring enough.	3	5.88

FINAL REMARKS

The new middle class are the product of the unequal core of the society, of the disorder and change in the social dynamics, of revolutionary changes in the material and non-material culture, of industrialisation/globalisation/liberalisation, and they are here to stay. Nothing less than this may virtually explain the rise of the new middle class in the contemporary/modernist/democratic culture of the world. Their exigencies have been stimulated by a continuous reflection of the status gains, positions, and privileges of those better than them; their fear has emerged from experiences and empathies with the adversaries of those hierarchically lower in the social strata. They seek a soul of security and adulation and they are continuously driven by the enthusiasm and hope exhibited by the opportunities thrown open to them through neo-economic reforms, neo-culture, and neo-identity of class.

While the classical way to define middle class in the market economy is through the socio-economic scale measured in terms of their income and expenditure capacity (wealth) or education and occupation (status), other cultural traits such as their religious and language dominance, ethnicity, and historicity all have a bearing upon their middle-class status in a multicultural region. Many studies across countries have earlier tried to show the reason of school choice based on their religious and ethnic dispositions, middle-class families in the present study too have highlighted the role of their way of life as an important factor for school choice. The differentiated demands could best be understood in a specific context where schooling of their child is not merely a learning exercise in school. Ethnicity and language play an important role reflective in the indicative sample studied. That schools have their own ethnic and linguistic composition cannot be ruled out at least in the town under study, but do not offer any generalisation for lack of information from the schools about the class and cultural composition. Similar study had been undertaken in the Netherlands to ascertain the school denomination affecting choice among middle-class parents. Religion in this study did not play an important reason for selection of school for possibly two reasons. One, the sample was purely dominated by Hindu respondents, the varied preferences could not be mapped. Secondly, the next populous religion in the country is Islam and they have alternative schooling system in the form of madarssas. While Bengalis were more inclined towards maintaining their religious (Hindu) ethos by sending them to schools with such denominations, the Assamese families focused on the language aspects of their culture which should engrain in their child during schooling itself. There is apprehension of language loss and loss of lately gained dominance in the state among the Assamese. Their involvement and membership in cultural associations is much more than their Bengali counterparts. Moreover, in this particular context more than quality of education, which they feel is a natural addition in selecting a private school, what educated parents are unwilling to trade off is the 'discipline' and 'reputation' of the school which eventually they think will matter most in the future for their child.

Good quality private schools are a definite choice if the parents belong to the upper strata of the income level and have had professional education or completed basic graduation shown through studies done on white middle class in the United Kingdom and the United States. Occupation of the parents' too has some bearing upon private school choice. However, if income holds importance in parental choice, it is accentuated with higher education among the parents. The chance to choose a private school with this combination of parental attributes is around 74 per cent, a good score to predict.

Thus there are few fears. One that with the unregulated growth of the private schools in big and small cities and remote town of the country like Tinsukia, schools may compromise with the quality of education in any way because the aspirations are entangled with the constrained choice the middle-class parents have to make. It may merely turn out to be a money-making opportunity forgetting the larger agenda of education. By far, private schools share the responsibility to impart education voluntarily regulated largely by the choice of the parents than by the state. But with the new educational provision in favour of 25 per cent reservation for the economically backward people in private schools, parents expressed diverse opinion. While some parents said it is good for the poor, many disagreed to permeate the school space by 'others'. Secondly, their non-retreat to the government schools is a siphoning phenomenon, once they are aware of the availability of private schools which are better than their government counterpart is expressed by the parents in the present study as well. The government schools in the region may fall out in the race. Thirdly, with good schooling and lack of good higher education institutions and varied job opportunity in the town and the state, every parent believe that their child should learn and earn outside the state after schooling, rendering to regional brain-drain or educated unemployed which is major area of concern in economically backward states.

And there are few hopes in the middle-class parental choice practice. Firstly, the importance of their choice-making ability, their vantage point cannot remain under the veil of an isolated class culture anymore. Their ability and concern, anxiety and ambition, the way they perceive, conceive or live in absolute, relative, and relational sense in the education space cannot be undermined by the policy makers and the state. The externalities of their education strategies and aspirations have to be assessed. Secondly, their behaviour is suggestive towards their own growth, but indicative towards the need to improve the school education system of the country or a region if it has to accomplish the goal of education for all. They imply improvement in the standard of education and expect a minimum standard of quality of education prevailing with the schools. Thirdly, devolution and choice is suggested to be one of the means to provide education to the masses. In India, establishment of high quality model schools as benchmarks of excellence at the block level has already been sponsored by the government in 2008.[19] Provisioning reservation for the economically backward section of the society in all private schools is another step ahead to make education meaningful for all.

Withstanding this fact, the old contradictions need to be resolved if a society such as us seeks development with dignity for their own people. Towards the envisaged goals of the state, empowering parents with regulated choice with overall improvement in the quality of school education may resolve few contradictions in an education space and may as well resolve the dichotomies of positive choice and negative choice made by parents in school education.[20]

NOTES AND REFERENCES

1. The other cases being, are middle class a by-product of Industrial Revolution alone? Does their origin lie in the West? Are they the cultural entrepreneurs alone? Or are they the by-product of the conscious interventions in the social and public life of the nineteenth-century England or the United States (*ibid.* xxi–xxii).
2. Stephen, B. (2003). *Class Strategies and Education Market: The Middle Class and Social Advantage.* London: Routledge.
3. Nogueira, M. A. (2010). 'A Revisited Theme: Middle Classes and the School', in Apple et al. (eds.), *The Routledge International Handbook of Sociology of Education.* New York: Routledge.
4. Kumar, K. (1996). *Learning from Conflict.* New Delhi: Orient Longman.
5. Nambissan, G. B. (2010). 'The Indian Middle Classes and Educational Advantage', in Apple et al. (eds.), *The Routledge International Handbook of Sociology of Education*, New York: Routledge.
6. Stephen, B. and C. Vincent (2001). 'New Class Strategies in Education: The Strategies of the Fearful Middle Classes', in J. Demaine (ed.), *Sociology of Education Today.* New York: Palgrave.
7. Whitty, G. (1997). 'Creating Quasi-Markets in Education: A Review of Recent Research on Parental Choice and School Autonomy in Three Countries', *Review of Research in Education*, 22: 3–47.
8. Kane, J. (1992). 'Choice the Fundamentals Revisited', in Jr. P W. Cookson (ed.), *The Choice Controversy.* California: Corwin Press Inc.
9. Fuller and Robinson 1992; Goldthorpe 1996, cited in J. Aurini and S. Davies (2005). 'Choices without Markets: Homeschooling in the Context of Private Education', *British Journal of Sociology of Education*, 26(4): 461–474.
10. This is a contestable statement but will be deliberated in the third section of the paper.

11. Checchi, D. (2005). *The Economics of Education Human Capital, Family Background and Inequality*. Cambridge: Cambridge University Press.
12. However, they are not a monolithic whole.
13. Misra, U. (1999). 'Immigration and Identity Transformation in Assam', *Economic and Political Weekly*, 34(21): 1264–1271.
14. Barua, S. (1978). 'Language Problem in Assam', *Social Scientist*, 6(12): 66–74.
15. Gohain, H. (1973). 'Origins of the Assamese Middle Class', *Social Scientist*, 2(1): 11–26.
16. 'The fundamental character of the public choice theory is *homo economicus*. It is a reading of the nature of humanness as rational, in the limited sense of being aware of its preferences, consistent in those preferences, and consistent in making choices according to preferences. The limited nature of this figure makes it possible ...to make predictions as to what people will do under certain circumstances. This makes works of economics or public choice theory that propose changes for the future based on expected responses possible. Consequently, this figure has enormous importance for policy making and legislation, since policies and laws are generally based on conjecture as to how people will respond to imposed limits or removal of limits' (Devine 2004: 15).[20] Devine, N. (2004). *Education and Public Choice: A Critical Account of the Invisible Hand in Education*, Westport: Praeger Publishers.
17. Durkheim, E. (1956). *Education and Society*. New York: The Free Press.
18. Paulsen, R. (1991). 'Education, Social Class, and Participation in Collective Action', *Sociology of Education*, 64(2): 96–110.
19. MoF, GoI, Economic Survey 2009–10, New Delhi: Oxford University Press, 2010.
20. Right to Education Act, 2002.

CHAPTER 13

CHANGING HEALTH INFRASTRUCTURE AND SOCIAL TRANSFORMATION IN HIMACHAL PRADESH

Seema Chauhan

There has been considerable development and growth of health infrastructure in the modernising India in comparison to what it had been immediately after independence in 1947, especially in the case of rural and the hilly areas of the country. Himachal Pradesh which emerged as a full-fledged state in 1971, almost 23 years after India's independence had only 728 health institutions including 53 hospitals comprising of both allopathic and ayurveda, 77 primary health centres, 194 allopathic dispensaries, and 404 ayurvedic dispensaries by the year 1979. There were a total of 5,524 beds for the treatment of indoor patient, with 535 doctors, 419 *vaids*, and 1,602 nurses and *dais* (GOHP 1985: 55). However, the number of health institutions and facilities has increased over the years to 89 hospitals, 441 primary health centres, 66 community health centres or referral hospitals, 39 dispensaries, all based on the modern allopathic medicine system. In addition, the state now has 23 ayurvedic hospitals, 1,112 health centre or dispensaries, and 1 nature cure centre. In addition, there are 3 unani dispensaries and 14 homeopathy hospitals. The potential indoor patient intake is about 10,087 in the allopathic hospitals and 724 in the ayurvedic hospitals in terms of available bed facilities (GOHP 2004: 106).

A comparative analysis of the health infrastructure scenario, as depicted above, in terms of quantitative change in physical facilities, directly linked with heath care services indicates considerable change over a period of 20 to 25 years. The official version of the health scenario, as has also been claimed in the case of Himachal Pradesh, is characterised by appropriateness in terms of adequacy in meeting health needs; comprehensiveness that covers the preventive, curative, and promotional dimensions of health; and adequacy indicating the balance between need for services and the provision of services in the similar proportions. In addition, the claim is also made that the health infrastructure ensures availability of services, accessibility to services, affordability, and feasibility. The National Rural Health Mission (NRHM) launched in 2005 also aimed at strengthening the rural health through ensuring the above-stated dimensions to provide quality health services at the village level. However, in qualitative terms the change belies all the claims of the state as instead of decreasing the per capita institutional burden of population, the existing scenario with regard to 1979 and 2004 indicate the per capita institutional population burden has increased from 2020 to 3403 persons per institution, respectively. Given the paradox of quantitative rise in the number of infrastructural facilities, but instead of decline the rising burden of population on the existing infrastructure, a question arises, can this ensure qualitative transformation in the health of population, especially the one living in the rural and the semi-urban areas? In the backdrop of the paradoxical situation, this paper aims at the nature and type of transformation in health sphere that has taken place in Himachal Pradesh, in general its rural and urban areas by undertaking analysis of data from NFHS surveys (NFHS-I in 1992, NFHS-II in 1998–1999, and NFHS-III in 2005–2006). Since the three rounds of NFHS survey did not have uniform contents of investigations, it is not possible to have comparative analysis of data on all the parameters of reproductive morbidity during the three rounds of surveys. In order to fill the gaps, in addition, the paper also takes into consideration an empirical study undertaken by the author herself in a semi-urban setting, predominantly rural in setting known as Junga, also an erstwhile princely hill state situated in the peripheral Shimla, the capital of Himachal Pradesh. The place is also of significance as it has a Himachal Police training school, state's forensic laboratory catering even to neighbouring states in north India, a Primary Health Centre, and other facilities for school education. Since the present study concerns with reproductive morbidity the parameters taken for analysis pertain to women's reproductive health. More specifically, the focus is laid on the analysis of one of the most critical issues of reproductive morbidity. The rationale of taking up this dimension emerges from the basic contradiction which exists between the quantitative growth and development of infrastructure and increasing per capita burden on health institutions on the one hand, and the objective of the state to ensure quality health services for better mother and child health and the socio-cultural inhibitions inhibiting the availing of the existing services on the other.

WOMEN AND HEALTH IN HIMACHAL PRADESH: REFLECTIONS FROM NFHS-I (1992), NFHS-II (1998–1999) AND NFHS-III (2005–2006)

Women's health constitutes a nation-states' most precious asset having considerable determining effects on socio-economic development of society, its identity in the international development context, and the foundations of its future growth and progress. The Indian state, ever since its independence, has made continuous endeavours to make health the top most priority in order to achieve the dream objective 'Health for All', though limited by budgetary allocations. This dualism between according priority and sanctioning lower budgetary allocations is quite intriguing. However, whatever may be the nature and type of state, health remains constitutional obligation of the state towards its citizens. Moreover, health is the basic right of every citizen of a society. Although health for all remains elusive at the national level but some states, despite their socio-economic development limitations, have been able to achieve higher levels in terms of development and growth of health infrastructure as well as making health accessible for most people, if not in absolute terms but to a minimum expected level. The case of Kerala and Himachal Pradesh is often mentioned in this regard. The fact also remains modernisation of health infrastructure is also necessary for enhancing the levels of productivity and inducing motivation among the people to adopt family welfare measures and reduce the family size (Goel 2005: 10–11).

The perusal of three National Family Health Surveys of Himachal Pradesh are quite revealing in terms of changing profile of women and child health. The basic demographic parameters indicate the state doing better than the nation as a whole. While state has a density of population around 93 in 1991 which further rose to 109 in 2001, due of course to increase in population, the all India scenario suggests 273 (1991) which has surely gone up in 2001. The state has better sex ratio 976 against 927 at all India level. However, the 2001 figures show some decline from 976 to 968 which can also be due to recording errors. Even in the context of literacy it is quite high 63.9 against 52.2 for India (1991), often correlated with health. The crude birth rates have been declining constantly (37.3 in 1971, 31.5 in 1981, 27.9 in 1991, 20.7 in 2002, and 17.7 in 2008) (H&FW, GOHP, 2010). Similarly, there has been considerable decline in the death rates prevalent in the state since 1971. From 15.6 in 1971, the death rates came down to 11.1 in 1981, then to 8.9 in 1991, 7.1 in 2001 but increased marginally to 7.4 in 2008 (H&FW, GOHP, 2010: 51).

In the same way, one finds considerable improvement in the case of child health indicated by their fluctuating declining mortality rates (118 in 1971 to 71 in 1981, 75 in 1991, 54 in 2001, and 44 in 2004) (H&FW, GOHP, 2010: 51). In comparison to the rates prevalent in these respects at all India level, Himachal Pradesh has achieved considerable success and therefore forges ahead of many states in the country. The demographic parameters indicating change appears to be the result of growth and development of health infrastructure in the state, implementation of the National Health Policy 1983 and 2000 as well as the rising literacy levels which have a definite positive function in improving the basic health parameters.

The other important area of health is the prevalence of morbidity among the people in the state in general and gynaecological morbidity among women in particular. The morbidity data (NFHS-I 1991: 126) pertaining to general morbidity indicate blindness (partial or complete), tuberculosis, leprosy, physical impairment, and malaria are some of the most prevalent health problems. There are 2.5 and 4.6 males and 1.3 and 3.1 females per 1,000 population who suffer from partial and complete blindness, respectively, in the urban Himachal Pradesh. In comparison to them, there are 10.5 and 5.5 males and 9.5 and 3.7 females per 1,000 of their respective population in rural areas suffering from partial and complete blindness, respectively. In the case of tuberculosis, the urban and rural data reveal 0.8 males and 0.9 females in relation to their counterparts numbering 3.3 males and 1.9 females per 1,000 of their respective gender population, respectively. The cases of leprosy are missing in the urban areas whereas in the rural Himachal the male number 1.1 and female 0.2 per 1,000 of their respective gender population, respectively. Generally, the physical impairment of limbs begins with aging process. This is quite understandable from the age-specific data indicating the number of such persons is found in the higher age groups. The impairment in the case of female in the urban areas is higher (9.8) in comparison to males (7.6) per 1,000 persons. In the rural setting the number of persons with this problem is much lower in comparison to urban setting. The male female data indicate 6.3 and 4.4 per 1,000 persons, respectively. Although malaria is now eradicated, the data indicate 5.5 male and 4.5 females in urban and 13.9 male and 10.4 female per 1,000 persons in rural areas suffered from this problem.

The reproductive morbidity, a commonly known concept among the medical fraternity, implies departure from state of physical as well as mental well-being interfering with reproductive functions among women. Under such a condition, a female is neither able to have fulfilment of her sexual desires nor able to conceive a child. Such a condition is caused by multiplicity of factors, including biological, physiological, bio-social, economic, and individual related. Among the multiplicity of factors, much also depends upon the nutritional status of women which is a function of their socio-economic status also. In a society characterised by social and economic inequalities, the differential nutritional status is determined largely the differential ability of the people to afford nutritious food. The nutritional status of women when correlated with their standard of living (in NFHS-II 1998–1999: 146) revealed that women with high standard of living index have lesser percentage of women in the category of less height than the desired height whereas women with low standard of living index had higher number of women with less height. When the Body Mass Index was compared with the standard of living index, the findings showed that the women with low standard of living index had higher percentage (43.3 per cent) with Body Mass Index below the standards. However, women with higher standard of living index had relatively very small number (22.1 per cent). The function of such surveys is to ensure that those who are detected with some deficiency their cases be followed up for betterment. This does not seem to be the case in India. The 2005–2006 NFHS survey reveal that instead of improvement in the situation it further worsened with the increase in the number of those having height and body mass index lower than the prescribed standards. What holds for future in this context, especially when the cost of health care, nutrition, and other valuables for living are on the rise, is a difficult question to answer. The same may also be true in the case of health deficiencies related with reproductive health of women.

Among the indicators having determining influence on health, in general, and reproductive health, in particular, anaemia is highly critical. There are several reasons accounting for this. It is a known fact that during pregnancy the demand for iron increases in women. Consequently, majority of pregnant women are anaemic during the course of their pregnancy. The demand for the total iron requirement during the normal course of pregnancy is about 1,000 mg. Foetus and placenta is believed to account for 300 mg of iron. About 200 mg is lost through normal routes of excretion. It is stated that the loss of iron is an obligatory loss even when the mother is severely iron deficient. Therefore, in each pregnant woman, these conditions cause an additional demand for 500 mg of iron (Cunningham et al. 2001 in Reddy 2004a: 8). Second, empirical reality indicates 'currently in India, the iron deficiency anaemia has almost assumed endemic proportion at the level of intergenerational prevalence. The sinister cycle of anaemic mother begetting – anaemic offspring – growing to become anaemic mother goes on. This is an already established fact constituting a non-obstetric maternal risk factor during the pregnancy in India' (Reddy 2004a: 28). But the matter does not end here as a large number of studies (Whitefield 1988; Raman 1989; Bhatt 1992; Sharma 2003 cited in Reddy 2004b: 29) also warn against the serious complications caused by iron-deficient anaemia among the pregnant women. These are antepartum haemorrhage, preterm delivery, postpartum haemorrhage, maternal mortality, mild to moderately increased cardiac output (hyper-dynamic circulation), progressing cardiac failure, thrombo-phlebitis and thrombo-embolic phenomenon, puerperal infections, and stillbirths.

Consequent upon the prevalent conditions, one of the problems faced by the women in particular is anaemia, which is also related to reproductive health. The anaemia poses high risk to expectant mothers, especially in the process of pregnancy as well as delivery. It primarily means low level of haemoglobin in the blood. But certain levels of haemoglobin are necessary in human body for transporting oxygen from lungs to other tissues and organs of the body. Its cause is nutritional deficiency of iron, folate, vitamin B12 or some other nutrients. According to some estimates, iron-deficient anaemia is the most widespread form of malnutrition in the world which had affected more than two billion people (Stolzfus and Dreyfuss 1998 cited in NFHS-II 1998–1999: 147). In India, anaemia affects an estimated 50 per cent of the population (Sheshadri 1998 cited in NFHS-II 1998–1999: 147).

Analysis of anaemia based on NFHS-II (1998–1999: 149) reveal three distinct categories of anaemia suffered by women in India and Himachal Pradesh, i.e. mild, moderate, and severe. This is observed that across different age groups for women in the 15 to 49 years of age, 40.6 to 43.2 per cent women suffer from one or the other type of anaemia. In the 15 to 19 years of age, there are 43.2 per cent women with mild (30.4 per cent), moderate (12.2 per cent), and severe (0.6 per cent). Their number is highest in the lowest age group, but in highest age group the women are having mild anaemia. However, in the next higher age group (20 to 24 years) one finds the number of women sliding down to 40.4 per cent, then to 40.3 in the next higher age category (25–29 years), to 40.1 in the 30 to 34 years, and to 40.6 per cent in the 35 to 39 years age. However, the pattern of anaemia is almost similar in all the age groups, i.e. highest number of those who have mild followed by those having moderate and finally smallest number with mild anaemia. Although the number of women with anaemia in Himachal Pradesh is much lower than women in India, at same time the very fact that more than 40 per cent women suffer from this is a challenge.

The data does not indicate the patterns as uniform but suggest wide variations in relation to different variables. The rural–urban differences indicate more rural women (40.7) suffering from anaemia than the urban women (38.5). Although the gap is not wide, yet it is suggestive of the fact that rural masses do suffer from a obvious lag of quality health services. The variations between the currently married and not currently married is rather more than what has been witnessed in the case of rural–urban differences. In comparison the currently married have 40.2 per cent anaemic whereas the not currently married number more (45.4 per cent) are anaemic. Why is the difference in this context found to be more than in the context of rural–urban? The simple reason accounting for this is that the women who have been married for long do not proper diet and therefore more vulnerable to suffer anaemia. The educational qualifications do not show any significant variation. While illiterate women constitute 40.9 per cent anaemic, the high school complete and above are 39.9 per cent. One of the reasons here being that education can make people aware but the health conditions, especially involving iron and folate deficiency is more because of low nutrition. The religion-wise distribution also indicate marginal variation between Hindu, Sikh, and Muslim women as they all constitute 39.9 per cent, 40.6 per cent, and 40.3 per cent, respectively. It is only among the Buddhist and the Neo-Buddhists that 67.8 per cent of their women suffer from anaemia. The caste-wise data also indicate variations. While the scheduled castes and others account for 37.1 per cent and 38.4 per cent, the other backward class women form 51.1 per cent anaemic. One can understand such differences by way of correlation between the standard of living index and the prevalence of anaemia among different classes. The women in the lower standard of living have surprisingly lesser number of anaemic (34.4 per cent) whereas those falling in the medium and high have higher numbers, i.e. 41.4 per cent and 40.5 per cent, respectively. In the beginning of discussion pertaining to anaemia, it was stated that due to physiological reasons the pregnant women tend to be more anaemic than the others. The data here, however, reveal to the contrary. While among the pregnant women there are only 31.8 per cent suffering from anaemic conditions, and 39.5 per cent anaemic were neither pregnant nor breast feeding, the highest number of anaemic (47.6 per cent) is found among those who are lactating but not pregnant. It implies that lactation process also causes deficiency among women, especially those whose nutritional intake is deficient. The lesser number of pregnant women falling in the anaemic category is because they are given iron and folic acid supplement during their three mandatory check-ups.

Once a problem is detected it is expected that the system would initiate corrective measures so that the problem remains under control, if not eradicated. The problem of anaemia is an all India phenomenon and its intensity is high in comparison to Himachal Pradesh. In comparison to even economically developed states, this tiny hill state is better placed. Ironically, even after its detection the intensity of the problem instead of decreasing has gone up by the time NFHS-III (2005–2006) report was published. The overall anaemia among women in Himachal increased from about 41 per cent in 1998–1999 and other states increased to 43.3 per cent (*ibid.*: 313). Given the fact that the situation has not improved despite the best efforts of the state since 1951, its fall out on general reproductive and maternal health is likely to be negative in future too.

This is common place knowledge that the government has initiated a number of schemes for the delivery of reproductive and other health services for the people, particularly in the rural areas through the network of Primary Health Centres (PHCs), Rural Dispensaries (RDs), and Sub-Centres (SCs). In the urban areas too reproductive health services are available mainly through government run health institutions of varying levels. The NFHS-II (1998–1999: 169) data pertaining to health problems during pregnancy points out 3.8 per cent women (2.3 urban and 3.9 rural) suffer from night blindness, 20.6 per cent (18.8 urban and 20.7 rural) have blurred vision, 6.8 per cent (2.8 urban and 7.2 rural) experience convulsions not from fever, 20.6 per cent (23.7 urban and 20.3 rural) suffer the agony of swelling of the legs, body, or the face, 45.5 per cent (42.4 urban and 45.3 rural) excessive fatigue, 2.8 per cent (2.8 urban and 0.9 rural) have vaginal bleeding. Although the data for NFHS-III is not available, the indications otherwise suggest that maternal health being conditioned by multiplicity of other factors than the maternal health care services, the situation has not improved much over the years.

THE EMPIRICAL REALITIES OF WOMEN AND HEALTH

The study based on a small sample of 150 women in the reproductive age group of 15 to 49 years is quite revealing *vis-à-vis* what the state claims with regard to the provision of quality health services and what exists in actual reality in the far-off areas as women experience in the rural areas. The health services are marred by shortage of doctors, nurses, pharmacists, and other para-medical staff. Because of which the state is unable to meet the health needs of the people in totality. Second, the women due to lack of awareness, low socio-economic conditions, cultural barriers, and unhygienic practices suffer from reproductive morbidity which adversely affect their health.

Third, the socio-cultural beliefs, the fear of a disease being exposed to the public, and prevailing traditional health practices further prevent them to avail health care despite the existence of PHC, CHC, and private nursing home/hospital.

The study reveals that despite the rising age at marriage at the macro level, there are women in the younger age group who got married before even completing 18 years, the legally permissible age. Because of marriage at a tender age with little exposure to varying parameters of health care, the possibility of their falling prey to gynaecological morbidity becomes very high. More than half of the women in the field were found to suffer from one or the other problem of gynaecological morbidity, including broadly reproductive tract infections (RTIs), sexually transmitted diseases (STDs), and coital-related problems, such as excessive bleeding, excessive pain, and urinary complaints after coitus. Although it was difficult to determine whether the problems reported by women were real or psychologically felt, especially in view of their socialisation in which fears, doubts, and inhibitions were build into their minds during the period these women were growing. Interestingly, the less investigated areas, such as the role of religious faith, religiosity, mythical beliefs related to food intake, conception of reproductive health problems related to one's luck, or divinity all such notions continue to prevail even among the educated. All these factors are found to have a direct impact on the reproductive health and fertility behaviour among the rural women. Coupled with these problems is the lack of knowledge among the poor women about the health services which also create hurdles in their accessibility to and utilisation of health services.

It is quite alarming to find that women in the rural areas in general do not take reproductive health problems in a serious manner, partly because of their lack of knowledge and partly due to inhibitions. During the field work, the women would not come out with their problem for the fear of it becoming public. It was after considerable assurance that they agreed to talk about it, especially when they were told that through them their husbands can also be in problem. While the narration was made the mother-in-law or other elder woman would often interrupt by saying '*Chalo bahut ho gya*' (It is enough). Even during the NFHS-II (1998–1999: 173) it was found that 64.1 per cent women did not even think it was necessary to go to a doctor for ante-natal check-ups during pregnancy even though they suffered from pregnancy-related morbidity. Among the other reasons preventing them were high costs, distance, family did not allow, and lack of knowledge. The physical difficulties and attitudinal irresponsible behaviour is also a hindrance in the way of achieving health for all.

The reproductive morbidity begins right from the age at puberty (12 to 14 years) when the girl child experiences the most traumatic experience, especially when she has not been guided by her mother or elder sister in the family. The agony of pain during the cycle, irregularity especially among those who are anxiety-prone, excessive blood flow, and inhibitions to consult a doctor complicate the simple natural physiological process. Among the women, with whom long interactive sessions were held during the field work, 54 per cent of them have painful menstrual cycles, 40 per cent back pain, and 14 per cent lower abdominal pain. Among those suffering from such pricks of the menstrual cycle only 33 per cent go to a doctor or health facility for resolution of their ailments. Among other reproductive health-related issues, 70 per cent of them reported of vaginal discharge with 60 per cent out of them referred to whitish discharge, 10 per cent yellowish, 18 per cent watery substance, and others reported of thick and curd-like discharge. Along with this problem, itching often occurs and excessive itching to get respite results in small but highly irritating bounds. A small number of women talked of urine dribbles during laughing or coughing.

Apart from the said, the problems related to contraceptive morbidity are also many which occur in the process of intra-uterine devices such as copper T, or use of contraceptive pills leading to nausea and sometimes vomiting, etc. and the unforeseen consequences of female sterilisation. While women, irrespective of their personal knowledge or no knowledge but only on the basis of what they hear from others, expressed fears about the post-sterilisation consequences, such as becoming fat, loss of interest in relationships with husband, and pains in the joints. Such responses point out the fact that reproductive-related education is not imparted to the patients visiting gynaecologist with reproductive health-related problems. There is need to sensitise women about their reproductive health and de-sensitise them about the socio-cultural inhibitions and pressures of social fears.

CONCLUDING OBSERVATIONS

The foregoing brief discussion on the relationship between health infrastructure and reproductive morbidity suggests a long way to go in the achievement of the best reproductive health among women, especially the one living in the rural areas and belonging to poor sections of the society. What is highly intriguing is the fact that the two basics to reproductive health, namely, nutritional status and haemoglobin levels, being affecting almost 40 per cent of the women, become the stumbling block in the way of their good health. The efforts in this direction are not of much help to people because of the structural inequalities which continue to characterise the society and are further deepening. The much-needed transformation remains elusive. Whatever is visible in the name of change refers to the success stories highlighted through media by the state.

REFERENCES

Bhatt, R. (1992). 'Obstetric Management of Anaemia in Pregnancy', in *Proceedings of the Symposium on Anaemias, XXXV All India Obstetric and Gynaecological Congress.* Chennai: Post Congress Volume, Obstetric and Gynaecological Society of Southern India.

Cunningham, F. G. et al. (2001). *Williams Obstetrics.* 21st Edition. New York: McGraw-Hill.

Government of Himachal Pradesh (GOHP). (1985). *Statistical Outline of Himachal Pradesh.* Shimla: Directorate of Economics Statistics, p. 55.

Government of Himachal Pradesh. (2004). *Statistical Outline of Himachal Pradesh.* Shimla: Directorate of Economics Statistics, p. 106.

National Family Health Survey (NFHS)-I. (1992). Himachal Pradesh, Mumbai, IIPS-ORC Macro.

National Family Health Survey-II. (1999–1998). Himachal Pradesh, Mumbai, IIPS-ORC Macro.

National Family Health Survey-III. (2005–2006). India, Mumbai, IIPS-ORC Macro.

Raman, L. (1989). 'Anaemia in Pregnancy', in M. K. Krishna Menon, P. K. Devi, and K. Bhaskar Rao (eds.), *Postgraduate Obstetrics and Gynaecology.* 4th Edition. Hyderabad: Orient Longman.

Reddy, R. a(2004 a). *Prevalence of Iron Deficiency Anaemia and Malnutrition in India.* Bangalore: Institute for Social and Economic Change.

Reddy, R. B. (2004 b). *Prevalence of Iron Deficiency Anaemia and Malnutrition in India.* Social and Economic Change Monographs 3.

Sharma, J. B. (2003). 'Nutritional Anaemia during Pregnancy in Non-Industrialized Countries', in John Studd (ed.), *Progress in Obstetrics and Gynaecology.* Vol. 15. London: Churchill Livingstone.

Whitefield, C. R. (1988). 'Blood Disorders in Pregnancy', in C. R. Whitefield (ed.), *Dewhurst's Textbook of Obstetrics and Gynaecology for Postgraduates.* Singapore: PG Publishing Pvt. Ltd.

CHAPTER 14

LOCATING 'SOCIAL' IN CORPORATE SOCIAL RESPONSIBILITY

Ketaki Dwivedi

INTRODUCTION

In business, one phrase – corporate social responsibility – has become synonymous with companies' attempts to appeal to an increasingly demanding world of customers and shareholders. Like flypaper, corporate social responsibility (CSR) has attracted dozens of other pieces of jargon, such as 'ethical trade', 'stakeholder dialogue', and 'engagement', and embraced many fine concepts, such as transparency and accountability. Within a decade, a whole new corporate language, championed by multinational corporations, has evolved around the notion of more ethical business practice. A new industry has grown up to help companies present, implement, and monitor what they are doing in the name of CSR. But behind the fine words, is there substance? Does the new language and the emergence of some specialist consultancy firms reflect real change in business practice? Is there more to CSR than grand allusions to 'global citizenship' and 'interdependence'? Most importantly, has CSR delivered tangible, sustainable benefits to marginal communities in developing countries, where governments are increasingly desperate for the investment multinational corporations provide? The paper here tries to examine these very social issues that have been deliberately and successfully masked/omitted so far by the definitional boundary in favour of corporate strategies.

Some organisational and academic definitions widely accepted for the term 'CSR' are the following:

1. CSR is the continuing commitment by business to behave ethically and contribute to economic development while improving the quality of life of the workforce and their families as well as the local community and society at large (World Business Council for Sustainable Development 2000).

2. CSR is a concept whereby companies integrate social and environmental concerns in their business operations in their interaction with their stakeholders on voluntary basis (European Commission, EC Green Paper 2001).
3. CSR is voluntary initiatives that enterprises undertake over and above their legal obligations (ILO World Commission on the Social Dimension of Globalisation).
4. Corporate social responsibility is a business process wherein the institution and the individuals within are sensitive and careful about the direct and indirect effect of their work on internal and external communities, nature, and the outside world (IndianNGOs.com 2003).
5. The firm's consideration of and response to issues beyond the narrow economic, technical and legal requirements of the firm (Davis 1973: 312).[1]
6. A commitment to improve community well-being through discretionary business practices and contribution of corporate resource (Kotler and Lee 2005: 3).[2]

The concept of CSR thus refers to the general belief that modern businesses have responsibilities to society that extend beyond their obligations to the stockholders or investors in the firm. Societal stakeholders that business would also have some responsibility towards include consumers, employees, the community at large, government, and the natural environment. Further, according to these definitions, CSR emphasises upon entirely voluntary, corporate-led initiative to promote self-regulation as a substitute for regulation at either national or international level. At the heart of CSR is the idea that companies, on their own, can be trusted to fill this regulatory gap and address any problems their operations may cause. CSR is about companies defining what responsible behaviour is and promising to act accordingly, identifying where they are falling short of the standards they set, and deciding for themselves when they have gone far enough in changing their practice. The voluntary approach is widely endorsed by European governments. Business groups and international institutions, such as the Organisation for Economic Cooperation and Development (OECD) also support self-regulation. In India, the Ministry of Corporate Affairs on conclusion of 'India Corporate Week – 2009' announced Corporate Social Responsibility Voluntary Guidelines 2009 which advocated value-based and ethical business practices, cordial labour relations, customer satisfaction and loyalty, generating benefits to the community and the environment, activities for social and inclusive development, and respect for human rights being the major stakeholder.

THE 'SOCIAL' DIMENSIONS OF CSR

The dominance of the economic paradigm in the social sphere is reflected in the consolidation of the market system in the global economy through the emergence and deployment of a particular kind of corporate rationality. Inevitably, corporate rationality overrules, co-opts, or marginalises interests that could threaten corporate advantage and the polity-economy nexus. The practice of CSR emerged out of a strategic management process or to put it more clearly, as *corporate strategic response* to deal with the legitimation crisis due to many cases of notorious corporate crimes, misconduct, and scandalous events since the 1980s. CSR, while managing the image of corporations, counters any real or potential criticism of the social impacts of profit-driven businesses on the lives and values of people. In the course, it takes upon a projected role of responsibility through a guided philanthropy that is quickly publicised to the public that count. The target public of CSR is evident in the fact that CSR is now an industry in its own right, and a flourishing profession as well. Consultancies have sprung up to advise companies on how to do CSR, and how to let it be known that they are doing it. Most multinationals now have a senior executive, often with a staff at his disposal, explicitly charged with developing and coordinating the CSR function. In some cases, these executives have been recruited from Non-Governmental Organisations (NGOs). Further, there are executive-education programmes in CSR, business-school chairs in CSR, CSR professional organisations, CSR websites, CSR newsletters, and much, much more (*The Good Company* 2005).[3]

Consequently, social dimensions of publics/community are not in the range of CSR's vision. Thus, it has been suggested 'when commercial interests and broader social welfare collide, profit comes first'. Companies' performance on social aspects like human rights, labour standards and working conditions, corruption, exploitation of natural resources, marketing practices, and local community impacts, among others, increasingly calls into question corporate integrity and stakeholder and ecological responsibility. The omissions in the 'social' aspect of the CSR discourse include, most centrally, any recognition of the impacts of economic globalisation and ecological degradation on Third World and its people.

The limited vision of 'social', is also designed to serve elite publics of the First World. As Waddock (2007) says, it is the *paradox*, the *dark underbelly* of corporate citizenship, that the more successful a corporation is, the more likely it is to have negative impacts on the societies and communities in which it is embedded.[4] Further, it can be pointed out that these impacts are also gender-, class- and community-specific. Following are four cases that emphasise the neglect, subjugation, and ultimately the annihilation of 'social' by the corporates that have been lauded for their responsible behaviour.

CASE 1: SUBJUGATION OF 'SOCIAL'

As early as 1991, Enron made a controversial deal with the Indian government to build a power plant in Dabhol, India.[5] The deal initially was lauded by the business press, but rumours emerged from the beginning that the contract was corrupt and full of political improprieties. Human Rights Watch reported that Enron misled the public from the start when the firm boasted it had received no complaints during the legally required solicitation of citizen comments about the proposed project. Yet, by 1995, thousands of people protested the Dabhol project on grounds of its negative social, economic, and environmental impacts. By early 1997, demonstrators condemned the displacement of more than 2,000 people, and the misappropriation of Indian land grew in size, frequency, and violence, as well. Both Amnesty International and Human Rights Watch reported that Enron colluded with local police, who followed, arrested, beat, and detained peaceful protestors, holding them without trial. Protesters and activists have been subjected to harassment, arbitrary arrest, preventive detention under the ordinary criminal law, and ill treatment. Amnesty International (1997) cites a report by the People's Union for Civil Liberties fact-finding team that investigated the arrest of 26 women and 13 men on June 3, 1997, which concluded: 'the police targeted mainly women, some of whom were minors, and the arrests were made violently, in violation of the legal, constitutional and humanitarian principles'. In fact, stories of women being dragged from their homes and beaten with batons were common. In January 1999, Human Rights Watch starkly concluded, 'Human Rights Watch believes that the Dabhol Enron's abuses of human rights, coupled with its documented ecological abuses (e.g. destruction of indigenous mango and cashew plantations and fisheries, and contamination of rivers and seawater) and disregard for mandated consultation processes and political processes represented "business as usual" for the company. Unfortunately, it was only when Enron's American-based scandals became exposed that policy makers, the media, and the general public grew enraged.'[6]

Framing Enron activities and its relations with stakeholders illustrates the interdependency among social, political, economic, and environmental dimensions and the evolution of CSR. The Enron scandal in Dabhol is not merely ecological/social. In today's global economy, profitability cannot be separated from issues related to political equity, social dignity, and environmental viability, and responsibility cannot be limited to whether or not a corporation violated the letter of the law in a particular country, or even a simple calculation of whether or not it did harm economically. A new generation of CSR has to begin to recognise the futility of compartmentalising ethics from profitability, as well as local from global (or global from local) business practices and requirements.

CASE 2: DISRUPTION OF 'SOCIAL'

Yet another instance of corporate rampage on the ecology and the cultural uprooting of tribals from their ancestral land is that of Vedanta Aluminium Limited (VAL) and its refinery project at Lanjigarh, a small village inhabited by Dongria Kondh tribe and, subsequently, at Jharsuguda, Orissa. VAL tried with all its might to influence the political circles and higher executives, who in the beginning gave the environmental clearance for the expansion of the project, despite this fraud, VAL also concealed the involvement of the forest land in the project.[7] The paradox is that in January 2009, VAL was awarded the ISO 9001:2008, ISO 14001:2004, and OHSAS 18001–2007 certificates for adopting global standards in quality, environment, and occupational health and safety systems by British Standard Institute (BSI). It was then the Civil Society Organisations registered litigation against the plant and exposed the VAL's designs.

The VAL represents a company that has strived to make huge profits on the expense of local tribal people and local ecology. This case also shows the large-scale mismanagement of resources and corruption in the higher echelons of the ministry. But the case also depicts the large-scale community resistance, civil society awareness and upheaval, and socially responsible investors. It also becomes evident here that companies with poor reputations in the area of human rights often try to gain a good environmental reputation to offset their human rights record through cultivated image management. From a post-colonial perspective, managing the image of corporate reputations through philanthropic aspects of CSR is much like the way in which the empires of the colonial era talked about their 'benevolent' acts in building institutions such as courts, railways, and universities in the colonised world.

CASE 3: DISPOSSESSING 'SOCIAL'

It is noteworthy that corporations, most prominent in donating large sums to social and environmental causes in the name of CSR, often continue to be involved in activities that jeopardise the lives of people elsewhere.

Srivastava (2006) underscores this point by mentioning that Coca-Cola was one of the major sponsors of the World Water Forum held in Mexico in 2006, although 'Coca-Cola's abuses in India are being challenged vigorously by communities all across India.' According to Srivastava, the company's water extraction has led to 'sharp drops in groundwater levels, resulting in severe water shortages' as well as pollution of the scarce remaining groundwater and the soil because of the discharge of wastewater into farmlands. There have, in fact, been protests in India against transnational beverage companies, including both Coca-Cola and Pepsi. A journal published by the Centre for Science and Environment in India, *Down to Earth*, also documented in 2003, and again in 2006, how the soft drinks manufactured by the two Cola giants had levels of pesticide in them that were much higher than what is considered safe for humans. The sum of all pesticides in the PepsiCo brands added up to 0.0180 mg/L, 36 times higher than the European Union's limit (EEC) for total pesticides.[8] Coca-Cola brands had 0.0150 mg/L of all pesticides, 30 times more than the same EEC limit (Centre for Science and Environment 2006).[9]

A well-documented dossier of seven case studies put together by the Corporate Responsibility Coalition (2005), highlighted the ways in which the transnational companies provides a haven to siphon off much-needed tax revenues from cash-strapped developing countries; regularly undermines human rights protection by financing projects which pose a threat to the implementation of human rights laws in developing countries, in breach of their own codes of conduct; and often fail to assess adequately the environmental impacts of projects and yet continues to reap the reputational benefits of participation in voluntary CSR initiatives. Therefore, the capitalist firm with claims of responsible business practices is not a moral entity but rather a political one, it consciously invests in perpetuating unequal relations of power, both internally and externally for its own convenience.

CASE 4: ANNIHILATION OF THE 'SOCIAL'

Although the insidious corporate-state nexus is evident in both developed and developing nations, the implications and repercussions of such a nexus are often experienced differently by the publics/citizens of the First World and the Third World. In most cases, the worst impacts are reserved for Third World publics – whether it is the thousands of slum dwellers who died in one of the world's worst industrial disasters at the Union Carbide Plant in Bhopal, India, or trade in toxic waste. This is the area that illuminates the nexus among First World states and transnational corporations, on the one hand, which have increasing amounts of wastes to be disposed of, and Third World states, on the other hand, that seemingly have the facilities to treat the wastes. In February 2006, the French Navy's decommissioned aircraft carrier *Le Clemenceau*, was destined for Alang in India, Asia's largest maritime graveyard very much against Basel Convention.[10] However, it was ordered back to France after protests and a court challenge by environmentalists who argued that Alang had no facilities to deal with the asbestos-riddled ship. For Alang workers, however, the ship-breaking contract represented a chance of at least short-term economic security.[11] The whole event serves as a classic example of how the public of the Third World bear the social, political, economic, and ecological brunt of the projects managed by corporations with the blessings of obsequious states.

BRINGING BACK THE 'SOCIAL'

Mainstream research on business focuses on directions and flows of foreign direct investment, joint ventures, offshore production and outsourcing, exports, or cross-cultural issues, with very little attention paid to the social and cultural transformations produced by international business activity. The bland and impersonal econometric models need to be illuminated by rich ethnographic accounts of social dislocations, cultural transformations, and political and economic marginalisation wrought by foreign investment and transnational corporate activity along with accounts of local and global resistance movements that inevitably accompany any exercise of power in the political economy. Investigation needs to be done at multiple levels of analysis: the organisational level, the institutional level, and the societal level. A critical research agenda for CSR involves exploring relationships between corporations and other actors using partnerships, industries, and coalitions as units of analysis through critical discourse analysis of the power dynamics that underlie interactions between corporations and their stakeholders.

NEED FOR REGULATION

It can be concluded that safeguarding the social and environmental rights of poor people, as they come into contact with multinational corporations, cannot be left solely to the discretion of those corporations and legally binding and internationally agreed regulations for business are needed to protect the rights of poor communities. Time and again, flaws in self-regulation appear in the gap between the claims of company CSR policies and the reality of social groups, communities, and civil societies affected by corporate actions. There should be important distinction between this burgeoning industry and the delivery of tangible benefits to communities in developing countries, whose lives are damaged by the activities of multinational corporations. The World Bank, itself a CSR player, notes, 'Despite widespread rhetoric, impact is still patchy; in practice, many companies' implementation (of CSR strategies) is shallow and fragmented.[12]

Multinational companies that operate in developing countries often fail to live up to their own standards because, where national laws are weak, they may be able to engage in unacceptable conduct with impunity. A transparent and rigorous system of evaluating, monitoring, and verifying company performance against an agreed set of international standards, with a clear system of penalties when standards are breached, is urgently needed. This must be accompanied by a strengthening of national laws and regulations, and a complementary system that provides those who suffer as a result of current corporate practice with the resources to gain redress. This requires new legislation to make companies legally accountable for international human rights and environmental standards wherever they operate and whatever they do. Standards must be made to apply across all of a corporation's operations, regardless of an operation's location or an employee's position.

SOCIAL MOVEMENTS AND CIVIL SOCIETY

The history of social movements and civil societies show that they play an important role of challenging beliefs, norms, and values of existing institutions and effectively de-institutionalise established norms and institutionalise new beliefs, norms, and values through collective action. The new social movements and civil societies also represent alternate forms of social organisation of resistance to corporate power to the traditional forms of resistance such as unions, political parties, and governments, which can be 'compromised'. However, it cannot be assumed that NGOs automatically hold the moral high ground when it comes to social and environmental issues. NGOs and civil society actors might not be profit-driven, but their power and legitimacy to represent marginalised groups must also be scrutinised along with their motives and intentions.

Social theorists, management scholars, community groups, activist groups, and NGOs have proposed a range of interventions at multiple levels that may redress some of the social ills caused by economic activity and corporate behaviour as well as actively promote positive social outcomes. Both specific policy interventions and alternate theorisations of the nature of the firm and the nature of the political economy have been proposed. Social movements like the World Social Forum and other coalitions for social and environmental welfare have called for wide-ranging institutional reform in order to address global poverty, labour conditions, climate change, environmental destruction, and biodiversity conservation. At the corporate level, these groups have called for more corporate accountability and democratic control over powerful transnational corporations.

CONCLUSION

While there are many problems with CSR – and in particular with its voluntary nature – there have also been some notable achievements. CSR has led to developments in company reporting, and in the elaboration of good principles and good practice in company behaviour like Tata Group of Companies, Birla Group Companies, and Azim Premji Foundation (in 2001, earmarking Wipro shares worth $125 million). Further, world's leading philanthropists – Warren Buffet and Bill Gates – visited India in March 2011 in a bid to persuade billionaires to pledge at least half their fortunes under the 'Giving Pledge' programme.

In a bid to bridge the gap between CSR initiatives on the part of India, the Ministry of Corporate Affairs (MCA) decided to mandate corporations to set aside a part of their earnings towards CSR under the Companies Bill 2009. However, fierce opposition by firms against mandatory CSR has led the MCA to reconsider the provision. However, companies cannot hold upregulation indefinitely. If the public pressure and political will is there, government can hold companies to account for their behaviour, and protect the rights of vulnerable communities and individuals.

NOTES AND REFERENCES

1. Davis, K. (1973). 'The Case For and Against Business Assumptions of Social Responsibilities', *Academy of Management Journal*, 16: 312–322.
2. Kotler, P. and N. Lee (2005). *Corporate Social Responsibility – Doing the Most Good for Your Company and Your Cause*. New Jersey: John Wiley & Sons Inc.
3. The Good Company. (2005). 'Companies Today are Exhorted to be "Socially Responsible". What, Exactly, Does This Mean?' *The Economist*, January 20.

4. Waddock, S. (2007). 'Corporate Citizenship: The Dark-Side Paradoxes of Success', in S. May, et al. (eds.), *The Debate Over Corporate Social Responsibility*. New York: Oxford University Press.
5. From 1992 to 1998, Enron owned 80 per cent of the Dabhol Power Company. General Electric and Bechtel each held a 10 per cent share.
6. Stohl, M. et al. (2007). 'A New Generation of Global Corporate Social Responsibility', in S. May, et al. (eds.), *The Debate Over Corporate Social Responsibility*. New York: Oxford University Press.
7. *The Hindu*. (2004). 'It Is 'No' to Vedanta's Mine Project in Orissa', *The Hindu*, August 24.
8. Srivastava, A. 'Coca-Cola and Water'. *India Resource Center*, http://www.indiaresource.org/campaigns/coke/2006/cokewwf.html.
9. Centre for Science and Environment. (2006). 'CSE Releases New Study on Pesticides in Soft Drinks'. http://www.cseindia.org/misc/cola-indepth/cola2006/cola-index.htm.
10. While the Basel Convention, an international treaty, prevents rich countries from transporting hazardous waste and chemicals to developing countries without prior information, the shipping firms and those in the market for dismantling old ships get around the treaty quite easily. The ships are registered in developing countries under shell companies carrying what are called 'flags of convenience' which permit them to bypass the treaty.
11. 'Banned in Bangladesh, Toxic Ship Heads to India, Nitin Sethi, *TNN* June 1, 2011.
12. 'Christian Aid, Behind the Mask', 2005 Report, www.christianaid.org.uk.

CHAPTER 15

STATE INTERVENTION IN SOCIAL TRANSFORMATION: A SOCIOLOGICAL STUDY OF CHILD LABOUR

Km Sohini

Historically, childhood has been viewed as lovable, a stage of protection with care and warmth, besides training for physical and mental growth. Ostensibly, the child is a 'national asset' for nation and capital building. Ironically, in underdeveloped countries like India most children can hardly dream of childhood let alone realise the promises of adulthood. The reasons are in-built and multivariate (Sahoo 1990). In India, during ancient time, exploitation of child labour did exist within the Hindu caste framework where the children from the lower caste were forced to do manual labour, but the scope of child labour has increased in number, more confined to certain caste or region and today it has emerged as a very complicated developing issue, affecting human society all over the country. India and other developed and developing countries are plagued by the problem of child employment in organised and unorganised sector. It is a matter of grave concern that children are not receiving the education and leisure which is important for their growing years because they are sucked into commercial and laborious activities which is meant for adults.

The issue of child labour in India attracted public attention and debate for the first time in 1985; however, it became the focus of major concern in the aftermath of globalisation in 1991, where by India ushered in a new era of liberalisation and privatisation. With the signing of the agreement at Marrakesh, trade issues have focused on labour costs and the rights of labour. The international community has clearly expressed, through various conventions and declarations, its belief that child labour needs to be eliminated; apart from International Labour Organisation (ILO), other international agencies, and the United Nations (UN) system as a whole pledged their full support to eliminate child labour and signed a joint declaration in New Delhi in August 1998. The Government of India and the United States Department of Labour (USDoL) launched a major project in October 2002 to eliminate child labour, especially in hazardous industries in certain states and districts (Agarawal 2004).

According to the 2001 Census, there were 12.7 million economically active children in the age group of 10–15 years. The number was 11.3 million during 1991 (population Census 1991), thus showing an increase in the number of child labourers. As per the census data, the trends on the magnitude of child labour are not uniform across the country. There is a broad decline in the incidence of child labour in the southern and western Indian states and Union Territories (UTs) between 1991 and 2001 (Ravi 2001). However, there has been an increasing trend in the eastern and north Indian states and UTs. There is an increase in the absolute magnitude of child labour between 1991 and 2001 in states of Uttar Pradesh, Bihar, Rajasthan, Punjab, and Haryana. As far as the per cent share of child labour across the states is concerned Uttar Pradesh accounts for a larger share of about 15 per cent of all child work-forces in India followed by Andhra Pradesh (NSSO 2000). In 2000, the International Labour Organisation estimated, 246 million child workers aged between 5 and 17 were involved in child labour, of which 171 million were involved in work, that by its nature is hazardous to their safety, physical or mental health and moral development. Moreover, some 8.4 million children were engaged in the so-called unconditional worst forms of child labour, which include forced and bonded labour. In 1996, at least 120 million children between the ages of 5 and 12 worked full time in the paid jobs; mostly in underdeveloped regions. This figure would at least double if we took into account children working part time. This statistics raises concern of both developed and developing countries and command theoretical as well as policy-oriented analysis. A central question for the national government and international organisation is therefore, how to intervene in order to reduce the extent of the phenomenon. It is clear that any government intervention aimed at reducing or eliminating child labour will affect the current and future welfare of children and is likely to have relevant spillovers on others. It is therefore important to understand the determinants of child labour and design policy interventions upon careful analysis and research (Belletlini and Ceroni 2005).

The conspicuous structural variations in terms of organisation of production and recent trends towards capitalist development in both industry and agriculture have paved the way for the perpetuation and use of child labour-force. The state always claims that child labour is a harsh reality resulting from poverty, as a result of which many families are forced to send their children to work to ensure survival. Undoubtedly, this is partly correct but the main reason is the vested interests of the state. For instance, Sivakasi match-stick manufacturers are able to compete with multinational like WIMCO, primarily because of cheap labour provided by children. Adults are deliberately not employed by them. Similarly domestic and multinational companies producing bulbs, tubes, bangles, etc. largely employ child labour and profits are estimated to be 25 per cent higher because of the cheap availability of labour. The fact of 44 million child labourers in a country of high adult unemployment cannot be a harsh reality attributable only to poverty. The argument that since poverty cannot be abolished overnight, child labour needs to be regularised in certain sectors is not valid. Similarly, agriculture, a dominant sector of the Indian economy, which alone contributes nearly one-half of the national income and provides raw material for a large section of the industry, also increasingly coming under the sway of capitalism, is widespread in the form of bonded child labour in its various guises mostly pledged by indebted parents. In short, the policies pursued by the government are reflected in the fact that among Third World countries child labour is highest in India (Sahoo 1990).

In spite of having numerous constitutional and legislative measures, guaranteeing welfare measures, banning or prohibiting their employment in hazardous occupations has not been realised. Ironically, total laxity prevails in enforcement of these provisions with not even a single evidence of conviction during the last more than 65 years of independence. For instance, Article 24 of the Indian Constitution provides that 'No child below the age of fourteen years shall be employed to work in any factory or mine or engaged in any other hazardous employment'. Likewise Article 45 (directive principle of state policy) states that 'the state shall endeavour to provide within a period of ten years from the commencement of this constitution for free and compulsory education for all children until they complete the age of fourteen years'. Similarly, many acts were periodically enacted with a view to providing legal protection to children in various occupations. To begin with the Indian Factories Act, 1948, and its several amendments and many other acts like the Mines Act, 1935; Employment of Children Act, 1938; Plantation Labour Act, 1951; etc. hardly provide any protection to the children by limiting their working hours, wages, and safety in hazardous occupation. On the contrary as cheap source of labour, their exploitation continued unabated.

One wonders why the government has not so far been able to retaliate. Another aspect of these ineffective protective legislations is that they apply only to less than 20 per cent of the child labourers. Nothing is done about the remaining 80 per cent working in the agricultural sector. Nearly, 40 million child labourers do not come under the purview of the legislation. This is primarily because of the indebtedness of their parents. Paradoxically, in fact, prohibition of child labour makes it harder to protect children from exploitation and diverse forces of oppression. If a phenomenon is not allowed to exist in law, little can be done to improve it. Thus child workers are automatically excluded from organisations such as trade union which could fight to improve their working condition, hours of work, and levels of wage. In effect, their defencelessness is increased. All this shows that the 'political will' is strongly biased in favour of the proprietary classes (Sahoo 1990). In the second half of the twentieth century, an international consensus developed on the elimination of the practice based upon the desire to protect children and favour their mental and cognitive development (Dessy and Pallage 2005). Year 1979 has been celebrated as the International Year of Child and year 1990 has been celebrated as a girl child labour year, its aim was to do welfare of every child in the world. Soviet Union also declared the Child Right Act in which it was said that it is a debt of child on humanity to provide them basic needs and facilities of life to them, but these government declarations for the child welfare are only written in files (Sohini 2008).

Although the government has accordingly being taking proactive steps by framing schemes and policies, amending the Acts and provisions, and initiating a series of strategies, both at centre and state level. This was done to eliminate the practice of child labour but has not been successful, because to perform any work in society, proper administrative system is necessary but it is possible only when there are experienced and examined employees in an administration and along with this they should also be honest towards their work. So many social welfare programmes are going on in our country but they are not implemented in proper way because of maladministration and corrupt officers and employees as a result of which people are unable to use these government policies of future construction (Sohini 2008).

OBJECTIVES

- To explore and highlight the causes of child labour
- To study and analyse the existing strategies and practices adopted by the state to eliminate child labour in Uttar Pradesh
- To identify and understand the role of NGO's and their strategies and practices for elimination of child labour
- To know and theorise some new strategies for elimination of child labour in global context

METHODOLOGY

Field study was conducted employing both primary and secondary methods of data analysis. The secondary data involve policy documents on child labour of government statistics like National Sample Survey Organisation (NSSO) report, report of working group on child labour for the Twelfth Five Year Plan, and population Census of India. The primary data were collected from child labourers, their respective families as well as the concerned departments of the state government and other civil bodies. Further, study has been done by using exploratory research design by making use of both qualitative and quantitative methods of data collection and employed both primary and secondary data based on interviews. Sampling was done at three levels – first and foremost is the effected children and their parents/guardians. Secondly, representatives of civil society organisation and third was the concern authorities in state government.

Tools and techniques of data collection are the following:

- Structured interview with interview schedule.
- Focus group discussions with civil society organisations, governmental authorities, and other concerned people.
- Key person's interviews/case studies with check list and interview guidelines.

RESULTS AND SUGGESTIONS

The study was conducted in Jhansi District of Uttar Pradesh. In the following paragraphs, some of the major findings are discussed. These are; (1) Agricultural labours – people who are landless labour, their children are also working with them and in this way they are helping their parents and their family in livelihood. (2) Household labours – a large number of children are working in the houses of officers, politicians and high class businessmen, and these children are prone to more and more work and social harassment. (3) Employed labours – in many parts of Jhansi District and cities there are bidi, agarbatti, electroplating, polish-working, dying, and stone-breaking factories where the children work under physical, cognitive, emotional, social, and moral hazards. By interviewing the respondents, I concluded that male child labour (76 per cent) in Jhansi is more than female child labour (24 Per cent). The caste composition of the sample indicates that most of the child labour is drawn from backward classes constituting 40 per cent of the total respondents. The child labour from general category included only 12 per cent of the sample. On educational status-wise distribution of respondents, it appears that 56 per cent of them are uneducated, 36 per cent are educated up to primary level, and 8 per cent up to secondary level; large number of children, i.e. 44 per cent are working due to pressure of their parents, 34 per cent desire to earn money, and 22 per cent by their own wish. There are some common causes and circumstances which are forcing these children to work in their tender age like insufficient income of their parents, big families, illiteracy, ignorance of their parents, poverty, and above all error in implementation approaches, nexus of politicians, administrative loop holes, police, and owners of the factories. A large number of them not even have families or not even count themselves for support in these circumstances; the alternative to work may be idleness, destitution, and crime. All this is wrong, but the worse thing is that whatever the child earns for himself to fulfil his needs, someone else takes most part of this earning.

The only way to ensure compliance with the act is to make punishment for violations more stringent and incorporate a provision for surprise checks and establish separate vigilance cells. With regards to the workers interest, it should be mandatory for all the employers to take steps for the intellectual, vocational, and educational well-being and upliftment of child worker. The political will and commitment of individual government to address child labour, in cooperation with employers and workers organisations, other nongovernmental organisation, and relevant parties in societies such as universities and media is the starting point of all International programme on the elimination of child labour (IPEC). A phased and multi-sectoral strategy should be applied consisting of following steps:

- Facilitating income-generating activities.
- Convergence with the other ministries.
- Campaigning for enrolment and elimination of school dropouts.
- Taking action to foster a well-functioning labour market.
- Strengthening existing education system, organisation, and setting up institutional mechanism.
- Monitoring the progress and grassroots level implementation of programmes, projects, and schemes.
- Conditional cash transfer, payment to poor households made on condition that child attend school and health clinics.
- Carrying out situational checks of the officers who are appointed for the implementation of these policies related to child labour.

REFERENCES

Agarawal, S. C. (2004). 'Child Labour and Household Characteristics in Selected States: Estimates from N.S.S. 55th Report', *Economic and Political Weekly*, 39(2): 173–185.

Belletlini, G. and C. B. Ceroni (2005). 'Child Labour and Resistance to Change', *Economic New Series*, Blackwell Publications, 72(287): 397–411.

Census of India, 2001, Economically Active Children, Government of India.

Dessy, S. E. and S. Pallage (2005) 'A Theory of Worst Form of Child Labour', *The Economic Journal*, Blackwell Publications, 115(500): 68–87.

Government of India Planning Commission, Report of the Working Group on Child Labour for 11th Five Year Plan.

India, 2001, Government of India: Ministry of Home Affairs and Census Commissioner.

NSSO, 2000, *Theories and Concepts*.

Ravi, A. (2001). 'Combating Child Labour with Labels: Case of Rugmark', *Economic Political Weekly*, 36(13): 1141–1147.

Sahoo, U. C. (1990). 'Child Labour and Legislations', *Economic and Political Weekly*, 25(46): 2529–2530.

Sohini, 2008, A Study of Socio-Economic Condition of Child Labour in Jhansi with Special Reference to Sainyergate. M.Phil. Thesis.

CHAPTER 16

SOCIAL TRANSFORMATION AND THE STATE INTERVENTION FOR HUMAN RIGHTS

Swati Singh

Over the past few decades in India, there has been an increasing global discourse on human rights. This paper seeks to foreground a grassroots perspective of certain issues which had been central to sociological enquiry (like caste and tribe) and which itself have been transformed under the hegemonic discourses of human rights and become contested issues in international debates.

THE MEANING AND RELEVANCE OF HUMAN RIGHTS

Human rights are the 'protean forms of social action, assembled by convention, under a portal named "human rights"'. It is unfortunate that dominant approaches to human rights fail to register this reality yet. Human rights are essentially ethical imperatives that deal with certain human freedoms that are inexcusable for a humane and just society. Any society or civilisation that calls itself 'progressive' or 'developing' has to provide to its people certain opportunities and resources not only material but also non-material, i.e. not only economic and social but also political and cultural rights. Some thinkers and theorists dismiss the use of human rights as 'ideal' and unrealisable. But in spite of the marketisation of human rights, what Upendra Baxi calls 'politics of human rights', there is still a 'politics for human rights' that listens to the voices, suffering, and anxiety of people and communities for a secure and just life. No society can call itself civilised if its fabric is not based on notions of justice, equality, and fairness. Human rights are a means to forge ahead in the realisation of these principles, to not alienate people in the meta-narratives of nation, market, globalisation, etc.

Thus as 'rights culture' as one can call it, is becoming more complex by each passing day. Some use the language of these very rights to flagrantly violate what they pretend to protect, the interests and rights of individuals, for the interests of global capital and aggression of nation states in the name of national interest. But as Upendra Baxi points out, this complexity is some form, an accomplishment if the many ways of rights talk and related social action tend to create 'something like a cooperative or altruistic individualism'. He argues that 'the authorship of human rights rests with local communities in their struggle against illegitimate power formations and politics of cruelty', to connect the macro with the micro narratives of struggle and to include that 'violence of the oppressed can be rights generative'. Thus as global capital seeks to mute the voices of suffering, it is important to understand the 'materiality of globalisation' signified by 'techno scientific mode of production' as the only legitimate way for gaining 'progress and development'. As sociologists, it is important for us to understand and discern the changing nature of reality, due to various changes in institutions or social processes over the years. One has to see how social movements are the sources of tension and change that a sociologist should analyse. They may identify previously undiagnosed characteristics of and possibilities within a given institutional order. Human rights help us to interrogate if a society is just, equal, and fair.

Thus one can see how human rights which had been framed and brought into existence for protecting the individual from any form of oppression has itself got caught in certain institutional and structural arrangements of capital, which mostly speak for the interests of capital first before communities. Yet, it does stand for causes that are of concern to communities, but these causes and their understandings have to emanate from within people, their community and culture. It has to be rooted in people's everyday messy existence and reality distinct from the legal or developmental understandings.

TRIBES AND CASTE: CONTESTED MEANINGS

Human rights act as a pressure group to influence the activities of the state and to force it for action when there is negligence or non-fulfilment of rights. In India, we can see the exploitation and suppression of Dalits or the tribals who have been the most oppressed and marginalised of the lot who have suffered over the decades. In spite of the provision in the constitution for their protection and welfare, they have not been able to enjoy all the benefits promised. But after these issues of their deprivation were pressed for greater visibility at the international forums by civil society groups and human rights organisations, the government was forced to take note of these and act on them. Human rights are certain inalienable rights, which at least help these groups by providing platform to register their protest. Although sovereignty of nation states rests on the idea of non-interference in its internal matters by other states, in reality, if we take globalisation with its open borders and transnational classes and institutions, it helps in creating a space for these organisations as an opposing force to the government. One cannot ignore the dependence of a nation state in terms of aid and trade relations with other countries. Thus sovereignty is, as it is, not absolute, and human rights organisations do impact sovereignty. In reality, the government is also caught up in a political economy with its own logic and exploitative features. One would begin by looking at the caste issue first.

The beginnings of the world-level Dalit organising can be traced to the period of the emergency, when in August 1975 Dalits in the United States, under the leadership of Laxmi Berwa, organised a demonstration against the visit of Indira Gandhi. Berwa, a physician practising in Washington, DC, had mobilised under the banner of VISION, 'Volunteers in Service to India's Oppressed and Neglected'. Berwa's organising had also illustrated one of the first examples of unity between Dalits and Black Americans (African Americans), for he was offered the chance to present his case on radio stations controlled by African Americans in Washington, DC. For perhaps the first time, in the very backyard of the Indian Embassy, stories of atrocities on Dalits and the continuing burden of casteism could be heard by Americans, whose image of India had been only that of the 'Land of Gandhi'. About the same time, a small businessman in Toronto, Yogesh Warhade founded the Ambedkar Mission and began efforts to take the cause of Dalits to the forums of the United Nations. In England, T. Hirekar began to work along similar lines, and Buddhist groups began to organise. Gradually, a world-wide Dalit movement began to take shape (Omvedt 1994).

Pressure groups belonging to the Dalit Diaspora in North America and Europe such as 'Volunteers in the Service to India's Oppressed and Neglected' (VISION) and the 'Ambedkar Centre for Justice and Peace' (ACJP), based in Washington, DC, and Toronto, respectively, began to lobby other NGO's as well as UN organisations to make them recognise caste-based discrimination as descent-based discrimination at par with racial discrimination and to view caste-based discrimination as a human rights offence. During the late 1990s, Convention on All Forms of Racial Disclimination (CERD) reported critically on the efforts by the Government of India to minimise caste discrimination. 'The situation of the Scheduled Castes and Scheduled Tribes falls within the scope of the convention' (the International Convention on the Elimination of All Forms of Racial Discrimination [ICERD]). In 1997, the international human rights NGO, Human Rights Watch decided to engage with the Dalit issue. Funded by the Ford Foundation, in 1999, it published the report 'Broken People: Caste Violence against India's "Untouchables"'. In 1998, Human Rights Watch organised a meeting of a number of regional Indian Dalit organisations to advise on and engage with the report. This helped to initiate the Indian umbrella organisation National Campaign on Dalit Human Rights (NCDHR), also in 1998, which quickly became the focal point for most of the new Dalit political activities. NCDHR was started by organisations from 14 Indian states, but their coverage on ground was less. NCDHR achieved national recognition when, in 1999, it released its own 'Black Paper: Broken Promises and Dalits Betrayed' and presented 2.5 million signatures demanding the end of caste discrimination in Asia, and proper implementation of Indian anti-caste discrimination legislation, to the Indian prime minister. Outside India, a 'Dalit World Convention' was held in Kuala Lumpur, Malaysia, in 1998. This led to the establishment of an international Dalit and NGO network. Also in 2000, Human Rights Watch awarded the leader of NCDHR, Martin Macwan, the Robert F. Kennedy Human Rights Award. However, its highest point was when in 2001 World Conference Against Racial Discrimination, Xenophobia and Related Intolerance (WCAR) in Durban, the Dalit caucus and its international supporters managed to place caste discrimination in the spotlight of the international media and on the agenda of the social movements and NGOs present in Durban.

The international Dalit support movement had been organised around the International Dalit Support Network (IDSN) since 2000. IDSN comprised the main national Dalit coordination organisations in South Asia (NCDHR from India), Dalit solidarity networks from 6 European countries and the United States, and 11 'international associates' (mainly human rights-related organisations and international church organisations). Its main objective was to lobby national governments and international organisations for Dalit rights. IDSN members routinely took part in, and often organised, the international Dalit conferences, and there was a close interrelationship between conference declarations and IDSN activities. The 2003 International Dalit Conference in Vancouver fleshed out the argument for diversifying ownership of capital as well as diversifying access to jobs, with reference to the United States experience. It also widened the target of the IDSN advocacy to international organisations other than the United Nations (UN): the international financial institutions, development aid agencies, private corporations, universities, and the 'world community'. The international organisations were given responsibility for ensuring that Dalits receive their 'rightful and proportionate share in India's national institutions, wealth and capital'; international financial institutions (the World Bank and the International Monetary Fund (IMF)) should ensure that Dalits receive their 'rightful share' of their lending; and donors should focus on Dalit development and empowerment initiatives. IDSN also lobbied with EU parliament and other European Union (EU) institutions, the UK government. The 2004 conference in Kathmandu funded by the World Bank, drafted 'Ambedkar principles' requesting foreign private companies and development agencies working in South Asia to implement job quotas for Dalits in their operations there, as part of their corporate social responsibility (CSR) codes, and the companies reacted positively rather than suffer bad publicity. In 2005, the UN Commission on Human Rights, by consensus, appointed two special rapporteurs to conduct a three-year study of caste discrimination and anti-discriminatory policies. The Dalit issue firmly came on the international public agenda. It came with the award of the 2006 Alternative Nobel Prize to Ruth Manorama, an activist for the rights of Dalit women and for Dalit rights in general (Lerche 2008: 246–252).

Indian government officials and political parties discussed not only the move towards internationalisation of the caste discrimination issue, but also the economic, social, and cultural realities of caste discrimination and the failure to eradicate it. The internationalisation of strategy had effectively raised the profile of the struggle against caste discrimination within India itself. The Dalit question became a party political issue. The main opposition party in India at that time, which had lost its party base after the emergence of BSP in North India, Congress in 2002, organised the Bhopal Conference entitled 'Charting a New Course for Dalits for the 21st Century'. It included 250 leading academics, writers, and social activists supportive of the Dalit cause, as the conference document states, the internationalisation of the Dalit question formed part of the political background for the organising of the conference. The resulting Bhopal declaration was important in two ways:

1. It marked the re-engagement of the national Congress with the Dalit political agenda.
2. The focus of the Dalit efforts changed to the issue of which pro-Dalit policies to propagate.

Many issues raised by the Bhopal declaration were classical Dalit policy points. What was new was an additional focus on capital and the private sector with demands that Dalits receive a share in capital and in government contracts and that a minimum job quota for Dalits be introduced in the private sectors. Until then, this had not been an issue among Dalit grassroots activists, and not even been on the agenda of the union for Dalit employees. The new policy proposals drew on the US experience of 'diversity' policies, including supplier diversification. If similar policies were implemented in India, it could lead to the creation of a strong Dalit entrepreneurial class, as well as to more private sector employment for Dalits. In India, Dalit advocacy also pressed on. A national seminar in Bangalore in 2003, with US expertise in attendance, was followed by a workshop sponsored by the Government of India's ministry responsible for SC/ST policies, the Ministry of Social Justice and Empowerment. A proposal was drafted for a new private sector affirmative action bill, explicitly making reference to the US experience. The World Social Forum in Mumbai in January 2004 provided another major platform for the Dalit movement, both during and before the event, in the national election of April to May 2004. In its Common Minimum Programme, the winning United Progressive Alliance (UPA), led by the Congress, included action points; reservations in the private sector was one of the eight points listed under the heading 'SC/ST'. The official dialogue was led by an All Ministry group. In March 2006, the All Ministry Group recommended to the cabinet that the government should go ahead with private sector reservation legislation. However, the private sector produced a counter-plan in August 2006, rejecting job quotas, and proposing instead a voluntary agreement centred around a code of conduct according to which preferential treatment would be given only to SC/ST candidates – a principal used in, for example, UK equal opportunities programmes. A typical recent policy demand is that of the Dalit 'National Summit on Reservation in Private Sector', which combined support for private sector job reservations with demand for reservations within capital markets, quotas in agricultural products purchases, and reservations in religious trusts, all policy-making bodies, NGOs, co-operative societies, private housing, and other areas. In July 2006, Prime Minister Manmohan Singh suggested a proportion of government purchases should be made from SC/ST entrepreneurs. This was approved by the cabinet Committee of Ministers for Dalit Affairs in October 2006, but is yet to be made into government policy. As part of its counter-proposal to a job quota arrangement, the private sector also countered this proposal with a suggestion that they would mentor at least 100 SC/ST entrepreneurs during the first year of reaching agreement with the government. In 2006–2007, the private sector began implementing aspects of its proposals. Meanwhile in Uttar Pradesh, the BSP government agreed a scheme for private sector reservations, where government subsidies are offered to enterprises in exchange for a commitment to a voluntary reservation scheme, reserving 10 per cent of jobs to SC/STs, 10 per cent to other so-called backward castes, and 10 per cent to economically weaker sections of 'upper castes'. At least one other state government claims to be considering similar scheme. It is difficult to see how Congress could gather support without some concessions in these areas (*ibid.* 2008).

The official position thus stated that caste is not race and that caste is an internal matter of India and any problem arising out of this should not be taken to any international forum. We have enough number of internal mechanisms and these internal instruments or also internal forums should be approached for redressal of grievances, if there are any.

Even in 2010, India has opposed the inclusion of caste in UN. According to a senior official,

> Inclusion of caste in the definition of racial discrimination is completely unacceptable. We reject the notion that caste falls under the rubric of racial discrimination...descent was used by an Indian delegate in 1965 in a completely different context. It referred to nationality of origin or the nationality of parents. It was not at all the intention to include caste... in the definition. It would be legally, politically and historically incorrect to do that...besides how can anyone seriously suggest that India's fight against caste- based discrimination will be helped by international attention on the issue? Are we a closed country where debates do not take place and correctives not applied? It will just muddy the waters instead of helping us remove this evil. Imagine the reaction when UN bodies begin accusing India of being intolerant to the weaker castes. Progressive people who are working to this end will become sidelined if there is uproar against foreign advice. (*The Hindu* 2010)

As we can see from above, the Dalit advocacy network's efforts to turn caste as a race issue to make it a human rights offence did not consider the way in the Indian context how caste has evolved over the years. The constitutional safeguards and other movements that have achieved greater results than any international forum could ever do.

Tribes in India being the original inhabitants have always lived an independent social, cultural, and economic life. Since the pre-independence times, their distinct lifestyles have been preserved but they have also been exploited and marginalised by outsiders for the rich resources of the lands they have called their territory and way of life for centuries. Being invisible as citizens, and without recognition from the larger civilisation, they have been forcibly displaced, exploited, so much so, to remain at the bottom of the rung of the larger society. With the advent of independence, the land which has been naturally theirs was passed on to the government, which then termed them as 'encroachers'. Also the aggressive neo-liberal policies which demand extraction of mineral resources from the territory which these tribes happen to inhabit have led to their complete marginalisation and brutal exploitation, to the extent of repressing their resistance by the deployment of security forces for the smooth operation of mining for the greater world market and profits of multinational companies. It is the most flagrant violation of complete denial of citizenship rights along with human rights.

Years of neglect by the successive state and central governments of these resource-rich areas and its populace has led to abject poverty, dispossession, and deprivation and thus increased disillusionment with the Indian state among the tribals. Improper implementation of land rights and their manipulation has led to complete helplessness of the people of these areas. This space has been usurped by the Maoists for political mobilisation, as supporting them has become the only form of resistance against a neo-liberal state more influenced by the investors with interests in resources and land of these areas. There have been protests by international NGOs like Amnesty International against these moves by Vedanta. But there are safeguards for tribal rights under the Indian Constitution. The proper implementation of these rights by the Indian state and civil society can provide a possible solution. According to Xaxa, the rights and privileges associated with a community which can identify and relate itself with a special territory are denied to the tribal communities in India (Xaxa 1999). This is leading to their exploitation and loss of control over resources in their territory. The Constitution of India's thrust towards tribals was of integration rather than assimilation but they have been assimilated in language and religion but not in economic and social development. International Labour Organisation (ILO) declared 1993 as the international year of the indigenous people, and adopted in 1989, a new convention later accepted by UNO in order to protect the indigenous tribal and semi-tribal population in all independent countries. This has sharpened the tribal consciousness as it entails certain rights and privileges; also the non-recognition of their rights under Indian situation only leads to greater crystallisation of this Adivasis identity. This is also a reflection of the yearning to establish a special relation with the territory they inhabit. But in social and cultural life, the above is not a part of consciousness of tribals at large; it is more of a middle-class consciousness (Xaxa 2005). Thus the neo-liberal policies of the government which increasingly displace tribals from their territory and non-recognition and non-implementation of their rights guaranteed under the constitution have led to a civil war-like situation. The International Non-Governmental Organisations (INGOs) help only to the extent of highlighting certain issues which have not been taken care by the Indian government but do not highlight the imperialist workings of the world capitalistic order. The issue can be resolved by the Indian government and civil society at large.

In the end, as one can see from above, in the two cases, even when the issues of caste and tribes were contested in the international forums, their comprehensive solution lies with the state. As the NGOs fight for human rights and highlight their violations, they do not do it at an international level and the complicity of the geopolitics associated with it. The international experts speaking against these are not accountable to the people, but the government is. Thus the NGOs fighting for human rights act as pressure groups, but the jurisdiction of the state remains intact. The human rights violations and their fundamental resolution rests on the state. For these reasons, it becomes important to understand the nature of the state and its transformation in a globalising international context with the transformation of capitalism. How this transformation impacts the vision of nationalism, civil society, and media? In the next section, we try to analyse this change to unfold the transformation of Indian state over the years.

As one can observe the liberal thinkers had faith in the state, as they assumed it to be the sovereign or have complete power inside its territory but as seen above this power has seriously been curtailed, and the hegemony of the capitalist development dominates the interests of the state. In such a situation what happens to the marginalised and oppressed in society, as during the time of independence when India was attaining independence from the colonial government it had on its way to become a sovereign power, envisaged an idea of India as a nation. On becoming a free state with complete jurisdiction, it would become a particular kind of state. These ideas were incorporated and put together in the constitution as the idea of a nation, with a certain form of nationalism.

Nationalism and secularism in India has been exclusionary to some extent. With globalisation, its inherent unequal practices and tendencies are further intensifying the marginalisation of the excluded groups of tribals, minorities, and Dalits, and the old practices and ideas that kept them separate from completely enjoying their citizenship status need to be recognised by making a special place for them in these particular ideas of nationalism and secularism and granting them full citizenship benefits and status, as equal members of one nation. Any ascriptive identity should not become a source of disadvantage. Groups historically discriminated against should be treated fairly as equal citizens of a nation. Before a nation acts as sovereign with jurisdiction in its affairs in the international context, it first needs to fulfil its role of a sovereign within its own boundaries. Only when the rights of all citizens irrespective of caste, class, community, creed, sex, etc. as provided in the Constitution are realised, the state acts as a true sovereign, otherwise the sovereignty of the state would be illegitimate as espoused by the liberal thinkers. It is based on a social contract (the ideas incorporated in the constitution) and when it is not followed, the contract is broken. When the state does not treat its own citizens as equal, it compromises its sovereignty or jurisdiction. The idea of nationalism has to be inclusive and incorporate the welfare and rights of all as equals. Secularism's meaning has to be clearly spelt out and practised accordingly to make sure that state fulfils the meaning of true sovereignty, which as Foucault (1991) describes, is the obedience of law. When law is not followed or manipulated, where lawyers become the voices of the development forces and use law for the ends of these forces. It is in the realisation of justice and true essence of law where the real sovereignty lies. Nationalism and secularism have to follow this for being a true sovereign. To make the state realise people's needs as the final objectives to be achieved, a robust civil society and media are indispensable. In this context, the role of civil society and media, as watchdogs and institutions that hold power accountable, become important. They help in moulding public discourse and putting pressure on state, when it fails to fulfil its duty, or acts authoritarian.

The 'regulative idea' is pursued by the civil society, which is intrinsic and fundamental to the constitution and entrenchment of a vibrant functioning democracy. Civil society organisations should not be either state-controlled or should not be purely commercial profit-making entity. But there are grey areas. Thus taking from what Oommen (1997) mentioned about civil society in India, the fight for rights of Dalits or tribals has been of identity assertions of a group. It has been absent as seen earlier in the Gujarat riots, the active intervention of which could have averted this inter-community rioting. Civil society in India lacked the rigour; it should have had for sustaining a liberal democracy, in striving for the rights of these excluded and marginalised groups. The role of media in supporting these civil society initiatives is indispensable. Thus one can see the importance of media for upholding the vision of a nation by shaping the public discourse and how its changing priorities distort the public discourse, in turn, affecting the form of nationalism and secularism (as the two are interrelated).

One can observe the transformation of media and its priorities in a changing 'globalising India' where the terms of debate whether in the tribal, Gujarat or Dalit issue, is set more by the advertisement concerns and commercialisation dictates. Instead of raising critical questions and becoming a true representative of voices of citizens to hold government accountable, it only represents what 'sells' and helps a particular media house to earn profits and stay afloat in a competitive environment. Thus injuring the healthy functioning of a genuine efficient democracy, in which citizens demand and realise their rights. It has almost lost its role as an honest mediator to be trusted by the citizens and becomes a soft target (to be manipulated) for fulfilling the agendas of the corporate and ruling classes. Thus, unless the civil society and media guard democracy efficiently, by fighting for human rights issues which are moulded by people's and communities lives and existence, in accordance with the law of the land, with justice as its objectives, the public discourse on nationalism and secularism are not possible, leaving glaring inconsistencies in the healthy functioning of a democracy. True sovereignty lies in constitutional independence and when it is not followed it betrays the idea of sovereignty. As one has argued, unless the priorities of a nation are not clear in a national context, it cannot articulate its concerns and deal with other states confidently and forcefully in an international context. The functioning of a democracy with people's and communities concerns as ends is imperative.

CONCLUSION

One has tried to analyse here the transformation of the state. One of the reasons that have been analysed here is how state sovereignty is being impacted in myriad ways. When human rights organisations fight for basic human rights as mentioned in UDHR, they act as not only representatives of the voices of people, but they also reflect broader interests of the world capitalistic order. They become the 'humanising face' of the world capitalistic system, which has inherent inequalities, is exploitative, and has exclusionary structures and institutions (Chimni 2009). These human rights organisations are themselves caught in 'politics of human rights', where the suffering of victims due to institutional lapses are not taken into account and capital appropriates the 'production of human rights goods and services' serving 'investors, consumers and producers'. The meaning of human rights needs to be understood from anthropological insights and also according to the manner that this is reflected in international law. Even when these NGOs genuinely fight for human rights, they never question the imperialistic, oppressive capitalistic trade practices and policies in the international system. This leads to a lot of human rights violation in the first place. The Gulf War of Iraq is perhaps the most obvious example.

The international institutions are not accountable to the people of the Third World but their decisions affect livelihoods in Third World countries in myriad ways. Joseph Stiglitz in his book *Globalization and Its Discontents* mentions why globalisation in not working for millions across the world. According to him, it is due to the mismanagement of globalisation by international economic institutions that serve the interests of more advanced industrialised countries and particular interests within those countries, also they approach problems with a particular vision of the economy and society (Stiglitz 2002: 215). He further observes,

> The most fundamental change that is required to make globalization work in the way it should is a change in governance...there can be democratic accountability only if those to whom these public institutions are supposed to be accountable are well informed about what they are doing including what choices they confronted and how these decisions were made. (Stiglitz 2002: 226–229)

He further observes how globalisation and the present international order affect democracy:

> Globalization, as it has been advocated, often seems to replace the old dictatorships of national elites with new dictatorships of international finance. Countries are effectively told that if they don't follow certain conditions, the capital markets or the IMF will refuse to lend them money. They are basically forced to give up part of their sovereignty, to let capricious capital markets, including the speculators whose only concerns are short term rather than long term growth of the country and the improvement of living standards, "discipline" them, telling them what they should and should not do. (Stiglitz 2002: 247)

The above observation aptly captures the consequences of a world system, which is unequal, undemocratic, and oppressive, creating systemic disorders and impacting sovereignty of nation states in this world order. Also the lack of resources that these nation states have to consequently face further erodes the sovereignty within their own boundaries by not being able to realise equal rights of all citizens states, resort to violence to curb dissent against the authoritarian decision making, due to lack of enough resources to fulfil all promises.

As seen above and earlier, Indian nationalism failed to be inclusive and failed to uphold the concept of secularism. This made the state less conscious of its responsibility towards certain citizens, whose identity has been historically a source of disadvantage to them. In addition to this, the new liberalisation era, with primacy on markets and development, follows the logic of capital, profit, and consumption. The state veered towards the interest of transnational capitalist class, institutions, and groups. It exchanges its share of power with the above for greater development in an international context, where 'development' is synonymous with power and strength within the global comity of nations. Usually these disadvantaged groups bear the consequences of the ill effects of this form of development, with the liberalised state giving greater space and influence to markets. Even civil society and media are being dominated by the hegemonic structures of the capitalist classes, thus impacting their role in shaping a public discourse. As mentioned earlier, when the media ceases to speak for the people the state does not listen to its own citizens, it compromises on its sovereignty. Real sovereignty rests on the 'general will' which is contained in the laws and the nature of the constitution. A full realisation of this leads to an active democracy, which strives for the fulfilment of the ideas present in the Constitution. Only when the states are strong enough and have enough clarity about their priorities, they can fight for those issues that emanate from disorders in the world system that weakens or cripples their efforts to be a true sovereign so that these issues rest with communities and citizens following the law of the land. As states can effectively debate and present their problems in an international context, they highlight the problems created by dependencies in a world system, which is overlooked by human rights organisations and donor countries, where world imperialistic orders are not held accountable and questioned, which actually impact the sovereignty of the states and shrink the welfare role of the state where the resolution of the human rights issues substantially lies.

Thus in the end, one would argue the following. To actually realise human rights, the understanding of which should stem from the ethnographic accounts of everyday lives of citizens and communities, the state needs to be sovereign. The following steps are needed:

1. An efficient strong government, based on justice and law of the land, where citizen's objectives are the ends.
2. A clear articulation of the form of nationalism and secularism, which is moulded into a proper vision and public discourse by a vigilant civil society and media (free from the interests of capitalist class) pressing the state for an inclusive nationalism and secularism and justice for all.
3. The above would help define better the particular needs and specific problems of individual communities and citizens. Thus states would be their representatives to solve these by welfare policies aimed at the

marginalised and oppressed people. This way the state can keep its sovereignty intact. This would also help the state to highlight its particular problem which is a result of the imperialist world order. This would demand accountability at the international level, to safeguard the sovereignty of the states at the international and national level. It is only when human rights organisations fight for the above as well that the real resolution of the human rights issues would take place. Otherwise they just remain as pressure groups and nothing more.

4. Thus one can see, how human rights which had been framed and brought into existence for protecting the individual from any form of oppression has itself got caught in certain institutional and structural arrangements of capital, which mostly speak for the interests of capital first before communities. Yet it does stand for causes that are of concern to communities, but these causes and their understanding has to emanate from within people their community and culture. It has to be rooted in people's everyday messy existence and reality distinct from the legal or developmental understandings.

REFERENCES

Chimni, B.S. (2009), 'The Changing World Order, the Structural Role of Humanitarian NGOs, and the Protection of Displaced Persons and Migrants' from www.icvach/doc00000936.html

Foucault, Michel (1991), 'What is Enlightenment?' in Paul Rabinow (ed.), *The Foucault Reader: An Introduction to Foucault's Thought*, Harmondsworth: Penguin Books.

http://www.ambedkar.org/gail/theUN.htm

http://www.ambedkar.org/news/durbanconference.htm

http://www.idsn.org/international-advocacy/un/durban-review-conf?

India rejects bid to include caste in the UN Conference, *The Hindu*, March 31, 2010.

Larche, Jens (2008), 'Transnational Advocacy Networks and Affirmative Action for Dalits in India', *Development and Change*, 39(2): 239–261.

Omvedt, Gail (1994), *Dalits and the Democratic Revolution: Dr. Ambedkar and the Dalit Movement in Colonial India*, New Delhi: Sage Publications.

Oommen, T.K. (1997), *Citizenship, Nationality and Ethnicity: Reconcilling Competing Identities*, Cambridge, U.K.: Polity Press.

Stiglitz, Joseph (2002), *Globlization and its Discontents*, New Delhi: Penguin Books.

The Hindu, February 9, 2010.

Xaxa, Virginius (1999), 'Tribes as Indigenous People of India', *Economic and Political Weekly*, December 18, pp. 3589-3595.

Xaxa, Virginius (2005), 'Politics of Language, Religion and Identity: Tribes in India', *Economic and Political Weekly*, March 26, pp. 1363-1369.

CHAPTER 17

UNDERSTANDING GENDER IN SOCIAL TRANSFORMATION

Pradeep Kumar Parida

Understanding gender relations is particularly important in times of disaster, not only because women are disproportionately affected, but also because emergency interventions can seriously compromise the long-term future for women by creating further imbalance in their relations with men at a time of stress. It is women who are concerned with the basic necessities of human existence: the provision and preparation of food, the collection of water, the management of the home, and keeping both family and homestead clean and in good health. Women are emotional managers too – providing security for their children and support to their men. When disaster strikes, women need support in maintaining their reproductive role, but too often, they have been marginalised and undermined. Moreover, gender relations place women in central roles in disaster, in part because women are particularly subject to environmental risks. Economic, caste/ethnic, and age stratification make some women needier than others before, during, and after disasters, both among and within cultures. The vulnerability of the single mother, widow, or frail elderly woman is especially evident, reinforcing for disaster managers and the observing public, the familiar notion of women as economic and emotional dependents – prototypic disaster victims. As a group, women-maintained households are economically and politically disadvantaged and have acute needs and reduced resources when disaster strikes their homes. The less economic and cultural power women enjoy before an event, the greater their suffering in the aftermath.

Taking the above backgrounds into consideration, this paper identifies several questions such as how gendered vulnerability is socially produced and maintained? How do gender relations shape disaster practice in organisations and households? How is gender relations affected, if at all, through the social experience of disaster? The paper is qualitative in nature.

Thus, the present paper highlights women's lower status and lack of economic power in so-called 'normal' times has serious ramification in a disaster situation. Moreover, the paper also illustrates women's subordinate position in many ways such as women's lack of decision-making power in evacuation, the denial of leadership positions to women in emergency management, women's subjection to domestic violence, and the devaluation of women's work throughout the disaster process. The hardships which women suffer, both as members of a community in crisis and as women within that community, are also addressed. The paper concludes that disasters, like non-disaster periods, are a time and place where gender inequality is maintained and reproduced. In disaster situation, women face difficulties because of their subordinate position. Also, there is a sad contradiction between the generous assistance offered to women survivors and the predatory approach to those who have lost the protection of male relatives.

Gender relations as well as natural disasters are socially constructed under different geographic, cultural, politico-economic, and social conditions and have complex social consequences for women and men. For the purposes of discussion, however, this report foregrounds common patterns rather than differences, negative impacts rather than opportunities created by disasters, and gender and disaster issues primarily impacting women.

NEGLECTED GENDER IN DISASTER RESEARCH

If addressed at all, gender has been integrated into disaster research and practice as a demographic variable or personality trait and not as the basis for a complex and dynamic set of social relations. Gender is also seen as an aspect of women's lives more than men's and as derivative of social class, i.e. women are disaster victims because they are poor. Notwithstanding significant progress integrating gender analytically and in the field (e.g. Oxfam's approach to gender and emergencies), neither governmental agencies nor Non Governmental Organisations (NGOs) have as yet fully integrated gender relations as a factor in disaster vulnerability and response, nor have they engaged women as equal partners in disaster mitigation and community-based planning.

Arising in opposition to the dominant technocratic emergency management approach, vulnerability theory and feminist theory suggest an alternative approach linking social justice and gender equality to disaster mitigation through sustainable development. International researchers, based primarily in developing societies and drawing on case studies, survivor narratives, and accounts from field workers, are now analysing the gendered political economy of disasters. Gender is less evidently a part of current disaster planning and policy, though women and children were identified as 'keys to prevention' during the International Decade for Natural Disaster Reduction and women organised conferences on these issues in Central America and the Caribbean (1993), Australia (1995), Pakistan (Duryog Nivaran, 1996), Brussels (1996), Washington, DC (InterAction 1998), British Columbia (1998), Miami (June 2000), and Bangladesh (June 2000). Seeing disasters 'through women's eyes' raises new issues for planners, identifies critical system gaps, and brings gender centrally into development and disaster work. Questions for researchers and policy makers include the following:

- ❖ Can or should a cross-cultural research agenda on gender and natural disasters be developed?
- ❖ What effective models exist for effectively integrating gender analysis in disaster planning at the grassroots and institutional levels?
- ❖ How can gendered perspectives and empirical knowledge about gender and disaster best be transferred to practitioners (policy makers, planners, field workers, community responders)?

GENDER POWERFULLY SHAPES HUMAN RESPONSES TO DISASTER, BOTH DIRECTLY AND INDIRECTLY

Women are especially hard-hit by the social impacts of environmental disasters. While natural disasters often impact human communities very broadly, residents are not equally at risk of loss and harm nor equally able to recover. Poor households are well-known to be especially vulnerable but gender-specific effects are also suggested, for example, by such indicators as the following:

- ❖ Post-disaster mortality, injury, and illness rates which are often (but not universally) higher for girls and women;
- ❖ Economic losses which disproportionately impact economically insecure women (e.g. agricultural losses of women farmers, the destruction of women's home-based businesses, limited access to post-disaster economic aid);
- ❖ Work load changes which suggest that disasters increase women's responsibilities in the domestic sphere, paid workplace, and community through the disaster cycle of preparation, relief, reconstruction, and mitigation;

- Post-disaster stress symptoms which are often (but not universally) reported more frequently by women; and
- Increased rates of sexual and domestic violence against girls and women in disaster contexts.

Additionally, a wide range of gender differences have been documented regarding emergency communication; household disaster decisions about preparedness, evacuation, mitigation, and use of relief assets; voluntary relief and recovery work (e.g. search and rescue, emotional and material care of survivors); access to evacuation shelter and relief goods; employment in disaster planning, relief and recovery programmes; and other areas relevant to disaster practitioners.

Disaster practitioners and planners knowledgeable about these and other gender patterns in disasters can target scarce resources more effectively. Questions for researchers and policy makers include the following:

- What social indicators best predict the relative impact of natural disasters on women and men, girls and boys? Are sex-specific data on these points available to institutional and community planners?
- In diverse environmental, politico-economic, social, and cultural contexts, how do gender relations differently shape the impacts of natural disasters and the (often) varying responses of women and men to them? What cross-hazard and cross-cultural patterns can be identified?

GENDER INEQUALITY AND WOMEN'S DISASTER

Far from unmediated 'natural' events arising from human settlement in an inherently uncertain environment, natural disasters are social processes precipitated by environmental events but grounded in social relations and historical development patterns. Gender inequality is a significant contributing factor in the social construction of risk.

Women's subordination is a root cause of disaster vulnerability. Women's economic insecurity (e.g. high poverty rates, contingent labour, homework, lack of credit and savings) increases their need for post-disaster financial assistance. Ideological constraints on female mobility may limit access to life-saving information, shelter, or relief goods. Male dominance in disaster decision-making undermines women's greater willingness to mitigate the effects of known hazards (e.g. moving livestock, tools, or household goods to safer locations, making evacuation plans), may misdirect disaster relief from family needs to personal interests, and often leads to gender-biased relief and reconstruction programmes (e.g. targeting funds to male heads of household, limiting women's paid disaster recovery work). Sexual and domestic violence magnifies the demands women face during crisis but is not integrated into post-disaster housing policies or disaster public health initiatives. Extensive care giving responsibilities throughout the disaster cycle substantially increase women's emotional and material work load and when caregivers put the well-being of others first, may endanger women's lives. Heterosexist practices and kinship relations place women outside the norm (e.g. widows, single women, lesbians, single mothers) at greater risk when relief programmes are designed to reach women through male-headed households (Blaikie 1994).

Women are also at greater risk due to power relations intersecting with gender (e.g. social inequalities based on race/ethnicity, social class, age) and to global patterns of development. Economic globalisation increases women's economic insecurity (e.g. through contingent labour, job loss in restructuring industries, increased informal sector work) and expands their unpaid work (e.g. through structural adjustment cutbacks in social services disproportionately used by women). Urban migration and hyper urbanisation brings women to unsafe living conditions and informal sector work in huge urban centres, where they are increasingly exposed to urban environmental pollution and disasters such as mudslides and earthquakes. Environmental degradation clearly endangers women as the primary users and managers of natural resources (e.g. drought effects on women farmers, deforestation effects on fuel wood gathering).

Demographic trends also increase women's relative risk. Increased longevity results in an older and more feminised population more likely to be living with significant physical and/or mental limitations. The global rise in women heading households overloads women during crises, generally increases their economic insecurity, and may exclude single mothers and their children when disaster relief is geared to male-headed households. Changing household structure also puts more women at risk. Rising rates of women living alone increases social isolation and hence reduces access to disaster warnings or recovery information; at the same time, more older and frail women will reside in group homes or nursing homes where they may have acute needs for assistance during natural disasters.

Gender relations also increase men's vulnerability, for example, through risky but 'heroic' search and rescue activities, self-destructive 'coping strategies' involving interpersonal violence and substance abuse, and masculinity norms which may limit their ability to ask for needed help.

Understanding the root causes of gendered vulnerability is essential if relief and reconstruction programmes are to reduce rather than reconstruct people's risk in future natural events. Questions for researchers and policy makers include the following:

- How and to what extent do gender relations, development patterns, or demographic shifts affect women's and men's exposure to disaster impacts and losses and their relative ability to recover?
- How can these large patterns be assessed in specific contexts? What sex-specific data are available to institutional and community planners (e.g. on economic insecurity as a factor in disaster vulnerability, or gender patterns in post-disaster economic recovery)?
- To what degree have gender patterns increasing disaster vulnerability been included in the design and implementation of emergency response, relief, and reconstruction policies? With what effects?

GENDER AND DISASTER EFFECTS

Taking gender relations into account suggests that those most likely to be hard-hit and needing long-term assistance recovering from environmental disasters include the following:

- destitute, low-income, and economically insecure women; women who are contingent workers or unemployed; home workers and others in the informal sector; small-scale farmers; women in care giving jobs and professions;
- women in subordinated racial/ethnic/cultural groups; recent immigrants and undocumented women; women migrant workers;
- women heading households, those in large complex households, and women caring for many dependents;
- frail senior women, undernourished women, and those with chronic health problems or disabling physical and mental conditions, and women whose mobility is restricted due to pregnancy or childbearing;
- widows and single women; socially isolated women; rural women;
- women subject to domestic and sexual violence, and those insecurely housed in shelters; and

- functionally illiterate women; women not fluent in majority languages.

Highly vulnerable girls and women may not be socially visible or included in disaster plans but they have urgent needs, for example, for safe and accessible evacuation space and temporary housing; equitable access to food, clothing, and other relief goods; transportation assistance and emergency communication in community languages; child care and other services supporting women's long-term care of surviving dependents; reproductive health care and gender-sensitive mental health services during evacuation, relocation, and resettlement; provision for mitigating violence against women in disaster contexts; and long-term economic recovery assistance and access to paid disaster relief and recovery work.

Disaster interventions must be informed by knowledge about context-specific patterns of preparedness, impact, response, and recovery. Questions for researchers and policy-makers include the following:

- In case studies of disaster events, what social indicators best predict the vulnerabilities of which women and men? Are sex-specific data on these patterns available to institutional and community planners?
- What models exist for the successful integration of gender analysis into pre-disaster vulnerability assessments, and for collaboration between disaster planners and women's organisations knowledgeable about local power structures and highly vulnerable girls and women?
- What are the specific short-term needs of highly vulnerable girls and women in specific contexts? What are women's long-term interests in reconstruction?

GENDER AND VULNERABILITY

Media images of weeping women passively awaiting rescue by strong-armed men influence, reflect and reinforce deeply imbedded notions of gender which shape responses to disaster by organisations, political leaders, and local residents. In fact, gender relations and the gendered division of labour situate women at the centre, not the margins, of disasters as active responders as well as likely victims.

Women's disaster work includes the following:

- mitigating the effects of hazards on residences and possessions;

- organising the activities of family, kin, neighbours, and community members to prepare for an anticipated disaster (e.g. cyclone, flood);
- securing relief (food, water, clothing, medical care, emergency shelter and temporary accommodation, economic aid, rebuilding materials, information) from emergency authorities and in other ways;
- meeting the immediate survival needs of family members;
- providing comprehensive and long-term care for children, ill and disabled family members, and seniors;
- managing temporary household evacuation and temporary or permanent relocation; and
- making or managing household repairs and reconstructing residences.

Women's post disaster work includes the following:

- mitigating the effects of hazards on land, livestock, tools, and other economic resources;
- provisioning households for crisis (e.g. planting drought-resistant crops; organising emergency food supplies);
- preparing, cleaning up, and repairing job sites and home-based work spaces;
- responding to disaster survivors through skilled jobs and professions in the human and social services (e.g. child care providers, crisis workers and counsellors, teachers, social workers);
- waged disaster relief positions (e.g. food-for-work programs, emergency relief jobs, 'front-line' medical responders); and
- responding to changed economic conditions (e.g. through migration, retraining, new jobs).

Women's community disaster work includes the following:

- identifying and assisting highly vulnerable girls and women (e.g. single mothers, isolated rural women, foreign domestic workers, women and children in battered women's shelters);

- voluntary neighbourhood/community emergency preparedness, evacuation, search and rescue, emergency relief, and recovery work;
- formal and informal political leadership through crisis and reconstruction, e.g. making women's needs known, organising politically against gender or racial bias in the relief process.

Women's local community knowledge, strong social networks, key roles in families, and active work roles make them resourceful social actors in crisis, yet they are rarely recognised as 'frontline' responders. Questions for researchers and policy makers include the following:

- What models can be documented of the effective integration of community-based women's groups and organisations into disaster planning, response, and mitigation projects?
- What are women's short- and long-term needs as primary household preparers, long-term caregivers, employees, and volunteers in disasters?
- What organisational or other barriers limit response to these needs, under what circumstances, and with what effects?
- How have women historically and in specific contexts organised politically across class and cultures around disaster issues?
- Are women (which women?) at the table in the development of disaster-resistant communities?

GENDER ISSUES MUST BE EFFECTIVELY INTEGRATED

These observations suggest the need to fully incorporate gender analysis into disaster planning and practice by:

- materially supporting a comprehensive gendered research agenda to identify in specific contexts the immediate needs and long-term interests of disaster-vulnerable women;
- generating sex-disaggregated data for community vulnerability and capacity assessments;
- supporting action research projects, programme evaluations, and case studies designed and conducted with at-risk women in vulnerable communities;
- engaging women from vulnerable social groups as full and equal partners in community-based disaster planning and 'non-structural' mitigation initiatives;

- developing gender and disaster materials for use in cross-training representatives from women's organisations and disaster organisations;
- increasing awareness about gender bias in disaster practice, e.g. through training, planning guidelines, recruitment, and retention of gender-aware staff, and mechanisms for professional accountability to gender issues; and
- supporting regular gender audits to identify factors increasing and decreasing gender bias in the culture, policy, and practice of institutions and organisations with disaster-response missions.

REFERENCES

Blaikie, P., et al. (eds.) (1994). *At Risk: Natural Hazards, People's Vulnerability, and Disasters.* London: Routledge.

Byrne, B. and S. Baden (1995). *Gender, Emergencies and Humanitarian Assistance. Bridge Briefing on Development and Gender.* Oxford: European Commission.

Department of Humanitarian Affairs News. (1997). *Focus: Women in Emergencies (22)*. Geneva: UNDHA.

Downs, R. E. et al. (eds.) (1991). *The Political Economy of African Famine.* Philadelphia: Gordon and Breach Science Publishers.

Dufka, C. (1988). 'The Mexico City Earthquake Disaster', *Social Casework: The Journal of Contemporary Social Work*, 69: 162–170.

Eade, D. and S. Williams (eds.) (1995). *The Oxfam Handbook of Development and Relief*, Vols. 1–3. Oxford: Oxfam.

Enarson, E. (1998). 'Through Women's Eyes: A Gendered Research Agenda for Disaster Social Science', *Disasters*, 22(2): 157–173.

Enarson, E. (1999). Violence against Women in Disasters: A Study of Domestic Violence Programs in the United States and Canada. *Violence Against Women*, 5(7): 742–768.

Enarson, E. and B. H. Morrow (1997). 'A Gendered Perspective: The Voices of Women', in Walter Gillis Peacock, Betty Hearn Morrow, and Hugh Gladwin (eds.), *Hurricane Andrew: Race, Gender and the Sociology of Disaster*. London: Routledge, pp. 116–140.

Enarson, E. and B. H. Morrow (eds.) (1998). *The Gendered Terrain of Disaster: Through Women's Eyes*. Westport, CT: Greenwood/Praeger.

Enarson, E. and M. Fordham (1999). 'Lines That Divide, Ties That Bind: Race, Class, and Gender in Women's Flood Recovery in the US and UK', *Paper Presented to the European Sociological Association Meetings*, Amsterdam.

Fernando, P. and V. Fernando (eds.) (1997). *South Asian Women: Facing Disasters, Securing Life*. Colombo, Sri Lanka: Duryog Nivaran, ITDG.

Fothergill, A. (1996). 'Gender, Risk, and Disaster', *International Journal of Mass Emergencies and Disasters*, 14(1): 33–56.

——. (1999). 'Women's Roles in a Disaster', *Applied Behavioral Science Review*, 7(2): 125–143.

Fordham, M. (1998). 'Making Women Visible in Disasters: Problematising the Private Domain', *Disasters*, 22(2): 126–143.

——. (1999). 'The Intersection of Gender and Social Class in Disaster: Balancing Resilience and Vulnerability', *International Journal of Mass Emergencies and Disasters*, 17(1): 15–37.

Gibbs, S. (1990). *Women's Role in the Red Cross/Red Crescent. HDI Studies on Development* #1. Geneva: Henry Dunant Institute.

Guha-Sapir, D. (1997). 'Women in the Front Line', *UNESCO Courier* (October): 27–29.

Hossain, H., et al. (eds.) (1992). *From Crisis to Development: Coping with Disasters in Bangladesh*. Dhaka: University Press Limited, pp. 55–80.

Ikeda, K. (1995). 'Gender Differences in Human Loss and Vulnerability in Natural Disasters: A Case Study from Bangladesh', *Indian Journal of Gender Studies*, 2(2): 171–193.

International Decade for Natural Disaster Reduction. (1995). 'Women and Children: Key to Prevention', *STOP Disasters* (24).

Khnondker, H. (1996). 'Women and Floods in Bangladesh', *International Journal of Mass Emergencies and Disasters*, 14(3): 281–292.

Krishnaraj, M. (1997). 'Gender Issues in Disaster Management: The Latur Earthquake', *Gender, Technology and Development*, 1(3): 395–411.

League of Red Cross and Red Crescent Societies. (1991). *Working with Women in Emergency Relief and Rehabilitation Programmes.* Field Studies Paper #2. Geneva, Switzerland.

Lentin, R. (ed.) (1997). *Gender and Catastrophe*. Zed: London.

Morris, P. (1998). *Weaving Gender in Disaster and Refugee Assistance*. New York: Commission on the Advancement of Women.

Morrow, B. H. and E. Enarson. (1996). 'Hurricane Andrew through Women's Eyes: Issues and Recommendations', *International Journal of Mass Emergencies and Disasters*, 14(1): 5–22.

Morrow, B. H. and B. Phillips (eds.) (1999). 'Special Issue on Women and Disasters', *International Journal of Mass Emergencies and Disasters*, 17(1).

Reardon, G. (1993). *Women and the Environment*. Oxford: Oxfam.

Rivers, J. (1982). 'Women and Children Last: An Essay on Sex Discrimination in Disasters', *Disasters*, 6(4): 256–267.

Shaw, R. (1992). '"Nature", "Culture", and "Disasters"', in E. Croll and D. Parkin (eds.), *Bush Base: Forest Farm: Culture, Environment, and Development*. Routledge: New York, pp. 200–217.Walker, B. (ed.) (1994). *Women and Emergencies*. Oxford: Oxfam.

Vaughan, M. (1987). *The Story of an African Famine: Gender and Famine in Twentieth-Century Malawi*. Cambridge: Cambridge University Press.

Wiest, R., J. Mocellin, and D. Thandiwe Motsisi (1994). *The Needs of Women in Disasters and Emergencies*. Report prepared for the Disaster Management Training Programme of the United Nations Development Programme and the Office of the United Nations Disaster Relief Coordinator. Winnipeg, Manitoba: The University of Manitoba Disaster Research Institute.

CHAPTER 18

ROLE OF CIVIL SOCIETY IN SOCIAL TRANSFORMATION

Ajai Kumar

Corruption in India is a manifestation of unhealthy state of its political system. A lot of degeneration has taken place in our polity since independence. Those who were young at the time of independence had expected a very great deal from the transfer of power in 1947. Many of them became bitterly disappointed when they saw that no miracle accompanied the change from colonial to a national state. They watched with dismay as the apparatus of the government became corrupt and inefficient (Beteille 2000). Politicians who led the freedom movement were men of high principles and moral values. A new kind of political culture has evolved in post-independence period in which people are joining politics for sheer greed for power and wealth. The values in public life have become a thing of the past. The common man is at the receiving end and is bearing the full brunt of the corrupt system. There is crisis of values and crisis of governance. The agony of the *aam adami* has become unbearable. People are losing faith in the system and there is desperation among different sections of the society.

The traditional moral order is giving way. The restructuring of the society is not taking place along ordered lines, and the future shape of the society has become unpredictable. In the prevailing confusion and turmoil and in the face of weakening sense of social responsibility, people are mercilessly exploiting one another without any qualms of conscience, giving the country the unenviable reputation of being among the most corrupt countries in the world (D' Souza 1998).

There has been disenchantment not only with administration, but, if anything, even with politics. The state legislatures and to some extent even parliament has lost much of the dignity with which they were invested 50 years ago. Not only the legislative skills are absent among many if not most legislators, but also some among them are of doubtful virtue while others have criminal records. It is not that there were no corrupt or uninformed legislators in the past, but on the whole they remained quiet. Today, the corrupt and the uninformed are also the most vociferous (Beteille 2001). A number of politicians are facing the corruption charges and a few are behind the bars after much public pressure. The moral base of society is weakening and it seems that the political system has deviated from the core Gandhian values. Unfortunately, much of the discussion of Gandhiji's ideas is marked by hypocrisy and insincerity. It is quite common today to swear by the ideas put forward by him without any serious attempt to pursue them (Deva 1998). It is painful to observe that the farmers who toil hard in the fields to feed the country are committing suicide. People are dying out of hunger and disease whereas the corrupt politicians are amassing huge wealth for their comfortable and luxurious living.

In this scenario, the emergence and crystallisation of civil society in India to take up the just cause of the suffering masses assumes much significance. Disenchantment with the state forms the backdrop to the revival of interest in civil society (Gupta 1997). In a democratic set-up, when the political system becomes corrupt and inefficient and elected representatives become insensitive to the miseries of common man, the civil society led by conscious, knowledgeable, and honest citizens of the society becomes an effective and powerful way to highlight the problems and aspirations of the people. Corruption has become a vicious cycle. Politicians spent huge amount of money to contest the election and once elected they start amassing wealth and property. Their close associates also indulge in corruption to satisfy their selfish interests. There are honest politicians indeed but they seem to have become helpless and ineffective in the present situation. They need to be assertive in performing their role.

Civil society as a space of creativity, public deliberation, self-cultivation, socio-political, and socio-spiritual struggles calls for continued self-development on part of actors and institutions. Some of the challenges of self-development in the sphere of civil society are development of the capacity of listening, overcoming the logic of power and domination, creating a condition for critical reflection, and establishing relations of non-duality, non-domination, and non-violence not only between self and other but also as a foundation of social order (Giri 2008). Civil society's ordering of politics and governance is the take-off point for humane governance. Such a re-entry is what contemporary social movements strive for. Human rights movements, ecology movements, women's movements, and the peace movements are all about restoring the first principles of the 'good' and 'good life' in the conduct of human affairs (Kothari 1988). Civil society is seen as an instrument of democratisation, a symbol of perestroika that can energise the struggles for individual liberty and assist in the gradual transition to more open and democratic polity (Mahajan 1999).

In Gandhiji's civil society, the self would always look the other in the eye as its second self, and offer dialogue and non-violent conversation without fear of the possible consequences. For him the national freedom movement of swaraj meant essentially the self-reform and self-rule of civil society, and Ram Rajya was to bring the rule of salvation in the society, a 'kingdom of Heaven' in politics viewed as self-management of the institutions of civil society rather than of the state (Uberoi 1999) .

The strength of civil society in India would rest in its commitment to the just cause of the common man and its adherence to the Gandhian values of truth, honesty, and non-violence. There need to be an unceasing struggle to constitute a society free from corruption and exploitation and which ensures individual freedom, equality, justice, pluralism, and tolerance. The civil society activist and Gandhian Anna Hazare has recently brought the issue of corruption in sharp focus. His country-wide non-violent movement has instilled confidence in the common man to fight corruption to its logical end. Now it is for the state to take effective measures to eradicate corruption from all spheres of public life. State and civil society in India cannot be conceived as antagonistic to each other rather they are and ought to be complementary to each other to constitute a good society.

REFERENCES

Beteille, A. (2000). 'Civil Society and Its Institution', in *Antinomies of Society: Essays on Ideologies and Institutions*. Delhi: Oxford University Press.

Beteille, A. (2001).'Civil Society and the Good Society', *Sociological Bulletin*, 50(2).

Deva, I. (1998). 'The Future of Independent India: What Can Sociologists Do?' *Sociological Bulletin*, 47(1).

D'Souza, V. S. (1998). 'Beyond Fifty Years of India's Independence: Challenges to Scientific Sociology', *Sociological Bulletin*, 47(1).

Giri, A. K. (2008). 'Civil Society and the Calling of Self-Development', *Sociological Bulletin*, 57(2): 267.

Gupta, D. (1997). 'Civil Society in the Indian Context', *Contemporary Sociology*, 26(3).

Kothari, R. (1988). *The State against Democracy: In Search of Humane Governance*. Delhi: Ajanta Publications.

Mahajan, G. (1999). 'Civil Society and Its Avatars: What Happened to Freedom and Democracy?' *EPW*, 34(20): 1188–1196.

Uberoi, J. P. S. (1999). 'On Civil Society', *Sociological Bulletin*, 48(1 & 2).

INDEX